The MiFID II Framework

Mario Comana · Daniele Previtali ·
Luca Bellardini

The MiFID II Framework

How the New Standards Are Reshaping the Investment Industry

Springer

Mario Comana
Department of Business and Management
LUISS Guido Carli University
Rome, Italy

Daniele Previtali
Department of Business and Management
LUISS Guido Carli University
Rome, Italy

Luca Bellardini
Department of Management and Law
University of Rome "Tor Vergata"
Rome, Italy

ISBN 978-3-030-12503-5 ISBN 978-3-030-12504-2 (eBook)
https://doi.org/10.1007/978-3-030-12504-2

Library of Congress Control Number: 2019930264

This Springer imprint is published by the registered company Springer Nature Switzerland AG
The registered company address is: Gewerbestrasse 11, 6330 Cham, Switzerland

Contents

Chapter 1
Introduction

If you destroy a free market you create a black market [...] If you make ten thousand regulations you destroy all respect for the law.

(Winston Churchill at the House of Commons, 3 February 1949)

Almost every time a financial crisis occurs, we witness a profound revision of that-time legislation. Over the last years, a number of analysts and institutions have sought to explain the crisis, its origin, its development, and its consequences. They have highlighted several shortcomings: inter alia, various distortions of the regulatory framework have been considered as co-responsible for the problem. It happened after the depression ignited by the 1929 crash, as well as following the Latin American crises of late Seventies. Nowadays, in the aftermath of the *Global Financial Crisis* (GFC) peaked in 2008, that story is repeating one more time.

It is difficult to attribute the reasons for complex phenomena such as financial crises to a well-identified single cause, whether it be of an economic or legal nature. More often, a whole range of circumstances contribute to the inception and development of the problem, and deserve to be analysed through a holistic approach. In the most recent episodes we observed a sort of accumulation phase of imbalances that eventually exploded, triggered by a single event. This is the case of the GFC, commonly associated with the securitisation of subprime mortgages and their "silent" dissemination in investment portfolios worldwide.

Of course, this was neither the only cause of the crisis, nor the most important one. We would rather look at the technical causes of the crisis as the outcome of several tensions, gradually accrued over time. Fiscal and monetary policy accounted for it, along with the attempt to prevent even the softest recession. The goal of a number of political actions, mainly but not exclusively in the United States, seemed to be in pursuit of a never-ending economic growth. Financial markets were key in the process, and several players had their own share of fault. Bankers, traders, brokers, investors, managers at financial institutions were incredibly prone to widen

M. Comana et al., *The MiFID II Framework*,
https://doi.org/10.1007/978-3-030-12504-2_1

their activity, enlarging the size of their business (and bonuses, too). This was instrumental to achieving both their personal objectives and the political ones: in fact, a very dangerous alignment of interests took place.

And what about supervisors? We do not think they were part of an obscure conspiracy; yet, it is evident that the they have not been able to stop the process before it went too far, A large number of gaps had clearly opened in the regulatory framework, allowing the "avalanche" to be triggered. As we may see, it was the combination of several critical elements to yield a general imbalance which, having reached the breaking point, ultimately sparked the collapse. Moreover, while it cannot be thought that a single cause led to the crisis, we can even less believe that the inadequacy of the regulatory framework can be the basis for all such connected events. Much more likely, a series of legislative imperfections—more or less serious—allowed the accumulation of such imbalances. Might a better regulatory setting have limited—not avoided, perhaps—the outbreak and the propagation of the GFC? Probably yes. However, what went wrong can be known just after the flaws of the current regulatory framework have slowly arisen.

Nevertheless, the occurrence of a crisis is a good opportunity to start revising the regulatory framework, just as a car needs to stop at a service station from time to time for periodic inspection, and a house needs extraordinary maintenance. This type of intervention is more often of a preventive nature, while the rethinking of regulatory structures following crises often appears to be late, albeit its aim is to avoid a repetition of past mistakes and foreclose regulatory loopholes. Needless to say, this is a dutiful effort, of course, but doomed not to work, sooner or later. Crises, not only financial ones, often have common features and similar path of development; yet, they appear in different guises.

Responses have been numerous and apparently robust: they ranged from the thorough revision of the Basel Accords to the *European Markets Infrastructure Regulation* (EMIR, No. 648/2012) and, coming to the main topic of this book, the launch of the 'Package' made of the second *Markets in Financial Instruments Directive* (MiFID II, No. 2014/65/EU) and the *Markets in Financial Instruments Regulation* (MiFIR, No. 600/2014). However, we would be wrong in attributing all this legislative overhaul to the outbreak of the crisis. MiFID I was released in 2004 and came into force in 2008. Of course, in light of such timing, no co-responsibility can be attributed to it. On the other hand, it is also reasonable to think that, a decade after the first regulatory system was introduced at EU level, a profound revision had to be envisaged. The 2009 G20 summit, held in Pittsburgh, had already generated a number of comments and observations on the effectiveness of existing financial discipline, which were then taken into account in the design of MiFID II interventions.

Said Directive brings together the same objectives as its predecessor—namely, market stability and investor protection—while seeking to increase its effectiveness. While keeping its objectives straight, the emphasis shifts onto enforcement. The novelties are numerous and will be analysed in detail in the book. We just want to recall that MiFID I was inclined—above all—to increase the degree of competition in financial markets, foresee the requirements for the granting of the European 'passport', and enhance investor protection. Conversely, MiFID II basically aims at making the markets more efficient, resilient and transparent, and furtherly improving the relationship between intermediaries and their clients, by keeping the latter in even higher regard. The two MiFID waves should not be intended as separate, but rather two stages of a single journey. The stream of events occurred during the decade between them was of global proportions, and its intensity has few parallels in contemporaneous history. Thus, we can consider the MiFID II/MiFIR package as a tough yet necessary "stress test" of pre-existing discipline.

In this book, we also covered the way in which the Directive has been implemented, and the Regulation applied, across the leading European economies. A potential drawback of an intervention aimed at maximum harmonisation—as the Package undoubtedly is—lies in the fact that each country retains a significant degree of domestic autonomy in transposing EU rules into its domestic legislation. This is a serious concern, for it results in something more akin to a "patchwork" rather than a proper "framework", as it should be. This contributes to maintaining—and, perhaps, increasing—the segmentation between national financial markets (which is at odds with the goal of integrated financial markets in the EU). However, there is no viable alternative to this: on the one hand, the Member States are not expected to drop the remainder of their sovereignty in law-making; on the other, any piece of EU legislation deserves to be adapted to different contexts. In fact, the 'one size fits all' approach—entailing the application of exactly the same rules in each EU country—would face problems of application for several reasons:

(a) it would not comply with each country's pre-existing legislation;
(b) it would not be able to gather the peculiarities of each financial and social context;
(c) it could introduce some negative aspects in countries where a given aspect has been regulated in a more detailed manner. Upon its passage, MiFID I attempted to level the playing field, though results may have been disappointing. The Package still contains an effort to smooth cross-country discretionary implementations; yet, we cannot reasonably deem such discrepancies to have been fully overcome.

The aim of this book is to provide, by proposing a detailed discussion of the new regulatory framework brought by the Package and its implementation, useful thoughts to shape a broad vision on how European financial markets could evolve and the financial intermediaries might interpret the new role the Package assigns to them. The approach to the analysis is manifold:

- describing the content of the new Package rules, which came into force on 3 January 2018, and discussing how they address the concerns raised by the GFC (also, compared to pre-existing legislation) as well as the theoretical implications from a EU-wide perspective;
- comparing different implementation processes and results in different domestic frameworks (among the leading EU countries, *plus* the UK), each one endowed with its own features in terms of structure of financial markets, as well as the intermediaries' conduct and performance;

- investigating the likely impact of the Package upon its various recipients, with a focus on the banking industry; in particular, this will take into account not only 'direct' effects, such as additional compliance costs, but also 'indirect' ones, such as the potential reshaping of business models.

In the light of this, the book is divided into three main parts:

- Chapters 2 and 3 provide an overview of the framework designed by the Package, which is a pillar of the EU 'single rulebook' as far as the regulation of financial markets is concerned;
- Chapters 4–6 go into detail in respect of the relevant content addressed by the Package;
- Chapters 7 and 8 are specifically devoted to analysing how the Package has been implemented across the largest countries in the Eurozone, *plus* the UK, and explaining what might be the expected impact in terms of banking business.

Chapter 2 provides an overview of the most salient changes occurred in the wake of the GFC in terms of new markets and instruments arising, the intermediaries' business models being disrupted, and negative spill-overs affecting the whole of the economy. This is done by making reference to the Recitals of both the Directive and the Regulation, by highlighting the development of OTC transactions and the subsequent increase in the overall level of risk, as well as the growing dualism between multilateral, "formal" trading venues, on the one hand, and bilateral, mostly unregulated ones, on the other.

Chapter 3 deals with the relevant changes in the regulatory framework and highlights how MiFID II differs from MiFID I, with regard to trading venues, instruments and entities affected by the new legislation, as well as the changes to the supervisory architecture. This is done by highlighting the legislative path undertaken and explaining the three-pillar content addressed by the Package (product governance, product intervention, rules governing the interaction between intermediaries and the clients), how they deal with specific issues, and how their enforcement is put into practice. In particular, this last point is treated by explaining the rationale behind including certain rules into the Directive rather than the Regulation, and vice versa. Moreover, we focus on the provisions entailing a close cooperation between different supervisory authorities. Finally, we discuss corporate governance and risk management issues, as well as those dealing with investor protection and transparency to clients, which are highly significant in order to ensure an efficient implementation of the principles inspiring the Package.

Then, we go on investigating how exchanges work: trading venues, algorithmic and high-frequency transactions. So, in Chap. 4 we discuss the functioning of exchanges, in terms of the features of different types of trading venues (inter alia, the role of newly-introduced OTFs is debated), the technology behind transactions (which is increasingly shifting towards algorithmic and high-frequency solutions, often seen as a potential threat to systemic stability) and some regulatory tasks (e.g., the platforms being required to 'self-assess' themselves by means of a stress test).

Also, we devoted a specific part to market platforms whereby stocks of small and medium-sized enterprises (SMEs), so-called 'SME growth markets', are traded.

Chapter 5 is aimed at discussing the wide regulatory framework, introduced by means of the Package, regarding *pre-* and post-trade transparency obligations, aimed at reducing information asymmetries and contributing to the overall 'market infrastructure'. In particular, we devoted a special attention to waivers and deferrals, which are critical in order to assess the likely impact of these new rules. As far as derivatives are concerned, we underline how the Package is consistent with another seminal piece of legislation—namely, EMIR—enacted in the wake of the GFC.

The last part of the book, as we have ideally divided it, is completed by the analysis of the investor-protective framework of the Package, through a number of regulatory provisions from client categorisation to best execution. In doing so, we analysed the major changes occurred in investor protection—which is one of the broader aims of the whole of MiFID legislation—such as the *know your merchandise* rule. In fact, although the traditional breakdown of clients into 'retail', 'professional' and 'eligible counterparties' has clearly been preserved, some relevant provisions about product governance and product intervention (i.e., in a sense, the core of the Package rules) have been newly introduced. This is expected to dramatically reshape the relationships between intermediaries and their clients, carrying investor protection at the highest level in European history, in a context where other exogenous factors are negatively impacting the profitability of the industry of investment services.

Then, we propose a cross-country view of the implementation of the Directive. We compared the latter, along with the enactment of MiFIR, across the largest EU economies (namely Germany, France, Spain, Italy, and the UK). This is done by underlining the connection between the different characteristics of financial markets and the response to the crisis and macroeconomic shocks in general, on the one hand, and the stances held in respect of Package-related issues, on the other.

At this point in the story, we discuss the effectiveness of the Package vis-à-vis MiFID I. While the latter was widely welcomed as a modernizing novelty, nowadays the financial community tend to worry about the 'legislative flood' witnessed during the last decade, whose capacity to fulfil its goals is widely questioned.

Moreover, we analysed some of the greatest concerns for the financial intermediaries affected by the Package: from the rising of additional compliance costs to the consequences of a widened cost disclosure to clients, from the change in distribution channels up to the duty of separating the research-related revenues from others: all issues that could likely reshape the business models of many entities. We focused mainly on technological disruption, compliance and disclosure costs, and the changes in distribution channels and business strategies.

Chapter 2
Why the Package? Financial Markets Before and After the Crisis

Abstract The chapter provides an overview of the salient features of the *Global Financial Crisis* (GFC), which may be seen as a fundamental cut-off point in the legislation of markets, both in the USA and the European Union. The trouble interrupted a trend of apparent long-term growth, rapidly spreading negative spill-overs onto the so-called "real" economy. When the GFC broke out, new instruments and activities had arisen; new subjects had entered the investment industry; and regulators were desperately trying to keep on track with technology-driven financial innovation. Supervisors have powerfully intervened to halt the crisis: in particular, they have addressed some structural issues in finance (lack of transparency, insufficient protection afforded to investors, etc.). As a result, the business models of several intermediaries have been disrupted. The chapter discusses the main macro-financial characteristics of the years usually labelled as *Great Moderation* (GM): 'easy credit' practices, liquidity created by means of assets furtherly revealed to be illiquid, and a loose monetary policy fuelling the other two phenomena. Then, it analyses the propagation of the GFC, with a focus on credit institutions and the threats (e.g., shadow banking) that traditional players have been facing over recent years.

2.1 A Brief Overview of Financial History Before the Global Financial Crisis

Throughout the eight decades before the GFC, many economists have repeatedly acknowledged that modern-day economic science is the result of the debate which followed the Great Depression, stemmed from the 1929 Wall Street crash (so-called *Black Tuesday*). Once the Second World War had marked a discontinuity in the prolonged, worldwide recession, the Bretton Woods Agreement—reached in the summer of 1944—showed that the shift in paradigm was a matter of fact, not merely an academic speculation. From the deep crisis of the Thirties, the global economy had come out with lower reliance upon the self-regulating virtues of markets, a renewed belief in the interventionist role of both governments and

M. Comana et al., *The MiFID II Framework*,
https://doi.org/10.1007/978-3-030-12504-2_2

central banks, and an urgent need to endow the international monetary systems with a 'safety net' given by the interconnection between currency issuers and their mutual foreign-currency reserves.

This was granted under the aegis of a dollar-centric scheme in place of the old, inadequate 'gold standard', which had so restrained monetary policy from effectively counteracting the recessionary phase by stimulating demand (Keynes 1936). At that time, many believed that the new era of open markets at a global realm, coupled with the larger role attributed to national authorities, would have yielded a steady, sustainable growth, also avoiding future crises. Taken as a whole, the sixty years afterwards have apparently proven this conviction to be well-grounded. The new doubts on the efficiency of the international financial system, cast in the wake of the oil shocks occurred in the Seventies, were contrasted by a furtherly loosening monetary stance—enshrined in the 1971 Smithsonian Agreement—and, most importantly, by the tide of financial deregulation in the Eighties, which spurred a new era of optimism and growth. The sudden 1987 Wall Street crash (so-called *Black Monday*) did not ring any alarm onto policymakers and supervisors, albeit some started questioning the role of technology as a crash amplifier (Mitchell Waldrop 1987) and, even before the GFC fully deployed its effects, some posited that the systematic underestimation of risks inherent to financial exchanges paved the way for such a 'black swan' event (Bogle 2008), though with the clear benefit of hindsight.

The confidence towards the wealth-creating attitude of financial markets was undoubtedly strengthened by the period of remarkable stability—termed *Great Moderation* (GM)—comprised between the end of the Eighties and the beginning of the new century. Despite the overlap of the post 9/11 crisis and the burst of the *dot-com* bubble, it peaked right before the first GFC symptoms were detected. During such period, financial activities were boosted by a sustainable growth rate in output, whereas interest rates and prices kept at substantially low levels. An early proof of the fact that 'moderation' was a worldwide reality, rather than just a market-friendly slogan by Alan Greenspan's Federal Reserve, is given by the fact that early upward trends in Eurozone prices—immediately following the introduction of the euro—did not translate into any substantial inflation rise, but were instead absorbed relatively soon, notwithstanding an increase in inflation uncertainty and a break in the classical association between the two variables (Caporale and Kontonikas 2009). The reason behind such observed path can be easily explained in terms of agents' expectations: after an initial 'crowding out' effect deriving from the introduction of the new single currency framework, investors started perceiving that the European Central Bank's (ECB) policies were as reliable, for financial stability purposes, as the *Bundesbank*'s ones had previously been (González-Cabanillas and Ruscher 2008). In summary, the implementation of the Economic and Monetary Union (EMU) can be reasonably regarded as an element contributing to the GM worldwide. Hence, neither the United States, nor the EU, nor any other large economy, was truly prepared to what was about to come.

The literature on the GFC causes is understandably huge. However, before focussing on issues closely linked to the functioning of financial markets and the intermediaries' risk-taking behaviour, we should take into account the 'big picture' of those *macro* trends which explain the widening phenomenon of globalisation. First, technological progress should be consistently taken into account. However, as far as monetary flows are concerned, it deploys its effects in a twofold direction: on the one hand, in a direct manner, it enhances financial transactions—which becomes speedier and more efficient, with a reduction in counterparty risk—and, thus, has a positive impact on the frequency, the number and the volume of transactions; on the other, it also plays an indirect role by enlarging the opportunities that subjects in *surplus* match with those in *deficit*, something which is commonly deemed to be the raison d'être of markets and intermediaries. Via the payment system, this yields positive spill-overs onto so-called 'real' markets, i.e. those for goods and non-financial services. Such mechanism works particularly well in underdeveloped and developing countries, which can benefit from a 'catch-up effect' due to their poor starting conditions.

Drawing from the wealth-creating upheaval associated with globalisation, Jagannathan et al. (2013) build up a very interesting theory on how demographic trends—directly stemming from technological progress—greatly contributed to the GFC. The authors maintain that, thanks to such development, a significant stock of human capital was formed in emerging countries, with the new labour supply eventually flooding advanced economies. According to the authors, this phenomenon might have resembled what the discovery of America meant to major European countries, suddenly dealing with the availability of large resources. Moreover, since most of international currency reserves are either denominated in dollars or pegged to the USD, the growing American current account deficit—determined by the export-oriented growth in developing economies—came in association with a 'liquidity flood' which soon revealed to be fiscally unsustainable, at least in the long term, for it magnified the debt burden as a proportion of GDP.

The surge in foreign workforce yielded a shock that was hard to absorb: first, these people could not channel savings towards their domestic financial system, still suffering from underdevelopment; second—as widely acknowledged by the extant literature—central banks in developed countries either failed to use their powers, as exchange rates did not adjust along with capital flows, or even burdened the macroeconomic environment with wrong-headed policies, such as the interest rate rise pursued between 2004 and 2006 (Turner 2017). The comprehensive result was what Ben Bernanke first labelled as the *Global Savings Glut*, which in the USA ultimately created the perverse incentives lying at the basis of the GFC.

In fact, this overwhelming amount of savings was mainly addressed to risk-free securities (e.g., US sovereign bonds), making interest rates decrease and, thus, fuelling the GM landscape where such incentives arose and propagated. However, the consequences would have been not so heinous had the 'gluttony' been directed at Government issuances only, without pouring into the private sector. In the end, unfortunately, this was the case: given the contemporaneous surge in housing and the upward pressure in markets for residential mortgages, so that a real 'bubble' was eventually created, many financial institutions centred their business around the securitisation of 'subprime' debt, i.e. the one owed by subjects of poor creditworthiness. Such borrowings were supported by a very favourable environment, dominated by large Government-sponsored enterprises whose main objective was issuing high-seniority guarantees to residential mortgages: namely, the so-called *Fannie Mae* and *Freddie Mac*. Moreover, 'cheapness' was not circumscribed to the 'easy credit' for real-estate investments but affected consumption goods as well. As a result of these forces, notwithstanding the huge amount of savings available to be invested, the savings rate fell below 2% for the first time since the Great Depression (Jagannathan et al. 2013).

While this occurred in the USA, China experienced opposite movements, thanks to the tide of liberalising, market-oriented reforms, implemented in a period between the end of the Seventies and the two following decades. Along with substantive migrations from rural to urban areas, the savings rate in the latter ones surged from 73 to 83% between 1995 and 2007; besides, the percentage of consumer loans over total credit extended by commercial banks decreased in favour of durable goods, whereas the vast majority of such loans was oriented towards residential housing. As a result, the Chinese annual flow of savings grew from less than one third to 130% of American ones between 2000 and 2007, something which can be regarded as another confirmation that globalisation spurs convergence rather than widening pre-existing divides. In this case, however, the overall effect did not yield positive spill-overs onto macroeconomic dynamics in the West. While immigrant workforce positively contributed to the expansion of retail financial services, as the living standards of once-indigent households significantly soared (not only in recipient countries but even in their fatherlands, via remittances), a sharp wealth decline affected those American families whose workforce was neglected in favour of 'close substitute' foreign one. Therefore, it is a matter of fact that the comprehensively good performance of the US economy in terms of output over the 2000–2007 horizon—even more evident if we rule out the short recessionary phase at the beginning of the Millennium—actually conceals a dismal reality of impoverishing middle and working classes, which had always been central to the expansion of American credit markets. Nowadays, we are fully aware of even the political long-term consequences of these trends (Fukuyama 2016), ended up with a de facto redistribution of income from citizen workers to foreign ones in the USA, driven by the latter ones' higher propensity to saving.

Counterfactual history might tell us what would have happened had the deterioration in US households' wages translated into shrinking financial activities. However, such a plain consequence never materialised. While the stock market stayed substantially flat, the credit boom did not recede: driven by the growing easiness of getting financed, consumption kept soaring in excess of disposable income. Right before the GFC broke out, the ratio between mortgage debt and wages—which is a proxy of households' leverage—had approximately doubled since the Eighties; moreover, it showed that the aggregate amount of financial obligations owed by American households significantly exceeded their total income. As already anticipated, the most striking evidence of this trend is given by house prices: in 2007, they peaked both in absolute terms and as a growth rate from the previous year (15%, compared to a value around 5% at the end of the Nineties).

Conversely, the percentage of home equity dropped from 52% over the 1980–2000 horizon to 29% between 2000 and 2007. The S&P/Case-Shiller index—based on price differences between repeated property transfers of ownership involving non-related people—gained more than 80% between 2000 and 2007 (first quarter data). Besides, despite such individual behaviours had been captured by US official statistics, empirical figures allowed for very little awareness on financial institutions' mounting risk exposures (Palumbo and Parker 2009).

Jagannathan et al. (2013) link these macroeconomic conditions to what they call 'permanent income hypothesis': namely, American households might have wrongly believed that house prices would have continued soaring, also thanks to a very favourable monetary policy environment (on which we shall come back soon). Confident in a steady asset revaluation over time, and notwithstanding the personal income drop, many people thought that their personal wealth would have expanded, or at least kept stable. In 2007, however, such skyrocketing trend backfired, as property values had become largely unaffordable. A suddenly narrowing demand prompted a large reduction in prices; in turn, this yielded an increase in the borrowers' probability of default: in fact, if the present value of outstanding debt is higher than the current value of the underlying asset, the avoidance of mortgage payback becomes the economically optimising choice.

2.2 What Went Wrong: The Dissemination of Risks

During the housing boom, the subprime mortgage exposures had fuelled the market of securitisation, creating that huge amount of risk exposures that, once the bubble burst, would have pushed several large conglomerates on the brink of collapse. The widely acknowledged mechanism has been channelled through the so called 'shadow banking system' which still keeps great relevance over financial activities worldwide. As already anticipated, in the US, it was propped up by the housing boom and the generalised surge in the demand for low-risk investments, which was so contrasting with 'easy credit' policies. In fact, asset-backed securities (ABS) originated by the transfer of banks' "dubious" financial claims onto special-purpose vehicles (SPVs), which then 'securitised' them by issuing debt securities, were generally welcome by credit rating agencies (CRAs). These institutions had no problem in basing their assessment upon the ostensible solvency of originator banks. Actually, even *senior* tranches incorporated default risks much higher than what CRAs deemed to be. In fact, ABS markets provide additional evidence on the trade-off between efficiency and instability as the two effects of progress in the financial industry.

Up until 1990, ABS had been strongly standardised, as the so-called 'Agency mortgage pools' were largely predominant. Afterwards, a number of new, differentiated instruments, increasingly tailored upon investors' needs, started circulating. Moreover, it was not uncommon for such a derivative to be collateralised again, and repeatedly, in an attempt to diversify away the interest default risk posed by the original borrower's inability to fulfil its obligations. Within such "enveloped" debt, we may find instruments like the collateralised debt obligations (CDOs) or the financially simpler yet opaque credit default swaps (CDS), the latter representing the purchase of insurance against an obligor's default. After the short crisis occurred at the beginning of the Millennium, they experimented a take-off. In 2006, 'Agency' ABS had already been surpassed—in market share terms—by 'private label' ones, i.e. those stemming from financial innovation and more closely addressing the counterparties' needs.

At that time, however, not only home prices turned out being a bubble and, thus, collapsed due to insufficient demand: the same occurred in ABS markets—and, more intensely, in 'private label' ones, as investors started realising how poor was the quality of underlying debtors. It was ultimately exposed what had been a despicable attitude to ignore the intrinsic riskiness of lending, because of the 'systematic' underestimation of default probabilities (Foote et al. 2008; Gennaioli and Shleifer 2010).

This perverse financial mechanism, which for the most is at the root of the GFC, has been the result of several determinants and wrong incentives which are clearly resumed in the contribution of Rajan (2006). Note that this paper helps drawing a picture of the dissemination of risks before the GFC became known to the financial world.

This phenomenon would have not taken place so broadly and rapidly without the role played by technology and financial innovation (see par. 3 which deepen this topic). Regulators are often "followers" of financial markets when addressing new issues which emerge spontaneously, merely as a result of market forces. This latter, for example, is the case of 'high frequency trading' (HFT), arisen thanks to the outstanding progress experienced by computer science in the last forty years, starting from a time in which the dematerialisation of securities was still quite limited. Nowadays, all transactions are executed on digital platforms; conversely, paper has almost completely disappeared from financial markets (at least in developed economies).

An essential point regarding the dissemination of risks in the system is then represented by the wrong incentives given to insiders, so as the poor control by the outsiders (and sometimes by regulatory authorities). They are basically driven by compensation policies. Incentives to the management (e.g., the delivery of stock options, or even the reverse link between competitors' results and compensation) have made bank managers orient their choices toward high-risk, high-return investments. Although the US legislator had already faced this issue via the 2002 Sarbanes-Oxley Act—enacted in the wake of the Enron scandal, the GFC showed that short-termism, labelled *the infant illness of capitalism* (Onado 2017), had not been over yet. The unescapable trade-off between immediate good performance, on the one hand, versus sound and prudent management over a longer horizon, on the other, seemed to have been addressed by ignoring lessons from the past and stubbornly following the latter, which might bring benefits to the management but, also, is more likely to impair shareholders' wealth in the future. Therefore, short-termism has to be deprecated not only from an 'institutionalist' standpoint, which regards firms' primary objective as that of serving some social purpose (Asquini 1959), but, also, from an approach inspired by the Chicago School thinking, which deems a firm's objective to be value creation for its owners (Friedman 1962).

The relation between incentives and controls deals more generally with corporate governance issues (among which executive compensation), but deepening such issue is outside our scope. Nevertheless, all the major issues related to the business of financial intermediaries are significantly affected by corporate governance and, also, can trigger governance changes (Dyck et al. 2008). This may be true in general, for each kind of firm; in the financial industry, however, this holds a fortiori, as regulators are often endowed with the duty of overseeing the internal governance of supervised entities and might eventually be regarded as a "third party" interposing between the two traditional sides (that is, the principal and the agent). In respect of this, the alignment of incentives is clearly the ultimate objective. The literature has widely investigated the differences between banks where managers hold little stakes and those where they are, conversely, large shareholders, thus being more akin to behave in an aggressive, profit-maximising way (Saunders et al. 1990). The GFC has shed a sinister light on this issue. Even the "golden age" of GM, already doomed by the Enron scandal, was marred by some 'incentive misalignment' cases. They show how Rajan (2006) was right—at least partially—in viewing increased riskiness as the dark side of financialization. At the same time, we should not forget the good brought by such phenomenon, which—by allowing for more largely available information, greater standardisation within contracts, and higher diversification between them—may be summarised into enhanced lending and entrepreneurship—in turn yielding faster growth—and reduced transaction costs (Jayaratne and Strahan 1996, 1998; Black and Strahan 2001). The overall result is increased profitability for financial intermediaries but, also, a growing 'commodification' of transactions (Jagannathan et al. 2013).

While denouncing wrongly-designed compensation, Rajan (2006) issued another warning on how the 'perfect storm' in the financial sector was actually imminent. In his view, which would have proven right, managers were strongly subject to the so called *herding behaviour*. In such case, the irrational component is so prevalent that business psychology, though well aware of the problem, fails in dissuading decision-makers from following their peers. In a period in which stock markets are not particularly bullish but do preserve investors' wealth by ensuring long-term upward trends (such as those to which we refer in this chapter), imitating others' choices is not only aimed at seizing good returns by bearing relatively low risk: also, it describes an optimising strategy under a game-theory framework, as otherwise losses would be severe.

By looking at interest rates rather than stock returns, Rajan (2006) also noted that the most dangerous situation is the one in which a period of high rates, like the one ignited by oil crises and subsequent inflationary spirals during the Seventies and early Eighties, gets followed by times in which rates become significantly lower, like during the GM. In fact, on the one hand, this is an incentive to 'searching for yield', clearly pursued by bolder risk taking; on the other, it pumps asset prices up, thus prompting a sharp and messy realignment to fundamental values. This might theoretically occur in a very short time: the GFC showed that it required something like twenty years to fully deploy its effects; yet—with the benefit of hindsight—no one can deny that Rajan's (2006) warning has shown close correspondence with reality.

Another "big issue" is the one of liquidity, whose creation is universally regarded—at least from an 'institutionalist' point of view—as one of intermediaries' major roles in the financial system. Nowadays, in particular, liquidity creation is no more at a "local" level, but—thanks to the free circulation of capital—has rather surged at a global one. It is no doubt that the GFC has somehow impaired these mechanisms, mainly because of the increasing opaqueness of credit institutions' balance sheets. Moreover, such problem is self-propelled: more "complicated" assets—e.g., those originated by securitising debt—discourage shareholders from exerting due control upon the management, who is responsible for them; in turn, this lack of control de facto increases the likelihood that the latter be tempted to undertake risky operations (Diamond and Rajan 2009).

Another issue which has characterised financial markets during the 'easy credit' period is the substantial failure in efficiently transferring risk. As a matter of fact, the reduction in certain kinds of risk—e.g., borrowers' default one—cannot be pursued fully, but inevitably copes with the reality of undiversifiable, "physiological" remaining portions. Moreover, banks might even be willing to retain some of that risk: e.g., for 'signalling' purposes, related to both asset quality and the commitment to closely monitor the obligor. As evidence of such failure, Rajan (2006) found that banks' earnings' volatility decreased only in the first half of the Nineties, after which it started surging, and eventually peaked during the early-Millennium crisis; conversely, looking at long-term trends in many advanced economies, the 'distance to default' comprehensively shrank over the whole GM horizon.

Also, the growing riskiness of financial markets has directly stemmed from the 'reintermediation' process. Still nowadays, banks are leaving room to investment firms or they are enhancing and enlarging their asset management divisions. In fact, the provision of asset management services by larger firms shows clear advantages in terms of economies of scale. In that industry, the close link between managers' compensation and assets under management has been proven to act as an incentive to risk-taking. The market had already warned the asset management industry well before the GFC broke out. In mid-Nineties, for instance, market mutual funds mainly invested in derivatives had been hit by a materialisation of tail risk: they had exposed themselves to it by selling guarantees against companies' default, something which eventually occurred when the Fed tightened its monetary policy.

At the end of the GM, Rajan (2006) had already understood how, at that time, the situation was closely resembling the events of a decade before. In fact, the actual size of risks incurred by protection sellers was widely underestimated. Nowadays, the increase in the world's riskiness may be summarised by looking at how forecasting future 'states of nature' in financial markets is becoming extremely difficult (or, at least, much harder than in periods when the economy was not as "financialised" as today). Correlations that may seem very trivial, intuitive, or established in market mechanisms, might rapidly turn to unexpected, surprising, counter-intuitive relationships when the trend gets reversed.

Very few voices—like Rajan (2006)—had been raised against many asset managers' choice to bet against insolvencies, often regarded as events with almost zero probability. We are now aware of the tails being much fatter vis-à-vis the pre-crisis era. Between 2007 and 2008, however, too many retail investors—not fully aware of the bold strategies pursued by the funds in which they had put their money—discovered such dismal reality at their own expense. As of the relationship with the clientele, the lack in transparency exposed by large financial conglomerates—suddenly come on the brink of default—is one of the topics most widely addressed by the Package. Also, it is tackled by other fundamental pieces of EU legislation like Directive 2011/61/EU, commonly known as 'UCITS V'.

2.3 The Reaction of Authorities: Shaping a New Regulatory Framework

The idea of a growing divergence between the evolution of financial markets, on the one hand, and of regulation, on the other, is nowadays largely accepted. It is probably the result of years in which, given the GM macroeconomic framework, many authorities had perceived the financial environment as relatively safe and, thus, needless of potentially distorting interventions. At a European level, the most evident result of this approach is probably the Directive 2004/57/EC, commonly known as 'MiFID I'. Come at the end of a decade in which the EU legislator had made various efforts in an attempt of regulating a growing industry, it was mostly welcome as the definite, liberal-oriented, soft-handed innovation against many domestic laws, still anchored to a very restrictive view of financial intermediation. The subsequent decade has instead witnessed the opposite approach, plainly due to fading GM and mounting GFC.

It is no doubt that a sound institutional environment, whereby minority shareholders—as well as creditors in general—be adequately protected, is particularly beneficial to financial markets. In fact, it helps reducing moral hazard in many principal-agent relationships: as a result, only "physiological", undiversifiable ones continue affecting the industry. The efficacy of institutional elements in lowering risk—both at an idiosyncratic, *micro-* level and a systemic, *macro-* one—has become increasingly lower over time. We reviewed the mechanisms which have ended that beautiful 'alchemy', to use a phrase from a former Bank of England governor (King 2016).

First of all, as highlighted by Kim et al. (2013), we should try to correctly define what happened in the economic system, well beyond the generic and simplistic 'crisis' label. Out of the three types of crisis that can be detected—namely, the 'banking', the 'currency' and the 'debt' ones—Eurozone countries (actually, with large variability between them) have experienced the first and the third one, while being spared from the second thanks to the monetary union. In general, globalisation, which means growing economic interdependencies, has made somehow more difficult to disentangle the actual characterisation of a period of financial turmoil—whether of banking, currency of debt origin, as the three may well overlap and come as closely intertwined. This probably occurred with one of the heaviest economic troubles of the last two decades: namely, the Argentinian crisis. Although financial innovation has significantly exceeded the industry's expectations, the regulatory burden on financial entities has been growing over time. We can easily infer this by looking at the various rounds of the Basel Accords, sponsored by the Bank for International Settlements (BIS).

Kim et al. (2013) found that traditional prudential regulation measures, such as capital and entry requirements, actually succeed in reducing systemic risk by lowering the likelihood of banking crises. The dark side of the story, however, is that currency crises become a higher threat wherever this kind of restrictions get applied. This is also the result of credit institutions being held by the Government, which is an indirect blow to the free circulation of capital and, thus, yields an inefficient allocation of resources. Such mechanisms are somehow opposite to those ignited by financial innovation, which—by opening immaterial borders to new products and markets—exerts a moderating effect on the probability of a currency becoming either too scarce or too common in respect of the actual needs. This helps keeping the currency's value around its 'equilibrium price', given by the "true" interactions between supply and demand in international markets for funds. Conversely, ad hoc powers attributed to supervisory authorities seem to be beneficial, provided they are not used in excess of what is needed: lest, there would be no difference vis-à-vis 'structural' supervision, i.e. the one endowed with the right of deciding how to shape the market structure.

As far as capital requirements are concerned, the Basel ones have given birth to a large debate over the issues of their procyclicality. In fact, as banks are more likely to experience troubles in periods characterised by excessive risk-taking, they also have to set apart substantially higher regulatory capital when they would be more in need of it. Conversely, although good performance is more likely associated with a prudent approach to credit policy, it may often come along with lower levels (or even quality) of regulatory capital. Of course, these tendencies harden difficulties and enhance the goodness of a bank's financial results, with the overall effect ranging from a presumably strengthening of the 'savings glut' during booms and a severe credit crunch during busts. The GFC has dramatically exposed the drawbacks of such procyclicality, and regulators have intervened to heal it. The Basel III Accords show a focus on preserving a credit institution's liquidity as well as countering the procyclical effects of regulation by means of an ad hoc capital buffer. It is intended to mitigate the macroeconomic spill-overs onto banks' profitability—but, also, the economy as a whole—stemming from resources being driven away from investments to fulfil regulatory obligations. Of course, this negatively reflect onto business which finance themselves mainly via the banking credit channel.

Anyway, the third round of the Basel Accords is not the only source of soft law in respect of liquidity, as the Committee of European Banking Supervisors (CEBS

2007) swore to establish a framework of sound and prudent management in respect of it, centred on liquidity buffers and—most importantly—contingency plans to be enacted in case of deteriorating conditions. In this regard, central banks have come to play an increasingly wide role: for instance, the ECB is allowed to act as a 'liquidity provider of last resort' in case of severe banking crises, when the sudden shrinking of liquidity may put the whole economic system into serious trouble. This precisely occurred in Greece at the beginning of summer 2015, when the ECB opted for mobilising its Emergency Liquidity Assistance (ELA) tool to momentarily fund Hellenic credit institutions, while negotiations went on at a political level.

Nevertheless, a study like Kim et al. (2013) should be taken with caution for various reasons. First, that study focussed on banks exclusively and, also, it did not account for the possible time lag between banking and debt crises. Moreover, the intertwining of different aspects and kinds of crises yields quite contradictory analytical results, which do not design any clear empirical evidence but should rather be taken into consideration along with specific countries and times, as contingent factors may exert great influence over a single trouble regardless of longer-term trends. In particular, debt crises may be linked to very long-dating causes, often dealing a lot with the country's economic history and structure and a little with political decision making. Hence, there is no easy answer at all, a fortiori if we consider that regulation is not a time-invariant factor, and that EU harmonising endeavours have not completely succeeded in creating a 100% level playing field: domestic frictions still remain, though being lower than in the past. In fact, Kim et al. (2013) found that one single prudential measure might be useful to pursue the intended objectives, whereas the simultaneous enactment of different ones may actually backfire.

In summary, regulators are exposed to the risk of unintended consequences yielded by their actions; and the more pervasive their role, the greater such risk. Of course, the opposite situation—namely, the absence of regulation or a very soft one—is likely to inject systemic risk onto the financial environment. In respect of this, remarkably significant is the role played by the so-called 'shadow banking', whereby institutions tend to exhibit high leverage because of the regulatory "light touch" they enjoy vis-à-vis banks but, also, because of the business they are usually involved with (e.g., issuing securitised debt). In particular, the EU legislator has its own responsibilities not to have stopped such a widening phenomenon, as no harmonising legislation has ever been passed. The securitisation industry, along with a relevant portion of the shadow banking universe, are currently subject to domestic rules only. Hence, EU supervisory authorities are not endowed with adequate tools to avoid the proliferation of systemic risks onto different segments of the financial system, first, and the economy as a whole, then.

As we shall discuss later, the Package shows a remarkable commitment towards limiting financial transactions executed over platforms which do not ensure minimum transparency requirements (e.g., so called 'dark pools', as well as OTC markets). Conversely, it has substantially renounced to intervene on an entire industry, whose existence is fundamental to the *smooth and orderly functioning* of the financial system, but which are increasingly becoming a problem, given their exploitation of large regulatory arbitrage opportunities. More in general, Kim et al. (2013) show that low regulation disciplining the entry of a new institution in the market may ultimately be detrimental to stability. This view has been much more commonly expressed after the GFC; in contrast, the GM literature had showed a completely opposed conviction, especially in respect of the association between entry requirements, on the one hand, and efficiency as well as competition, on the other (Shleifer and Vishny 1998).

As far as the efficacy of regulation is concerned, what we should duly take into account is, also, the so-called 'financial structure' of a country or a group of countries. This mainly relates to Levine (2002) classification as 'bank-based' *versus* 'market-based', depending upon the role attributed to the different types of intermediaries. Of course, from a quantitative analysis standpoint, it would suffice to look at total assets held by each category of financial entities (that is, monetary and financial institutions—abbreviated as MFIs—versus others). However, this would probably fail to catch the characteristics shown by a financial system where one funding channel is favoured over the other, yet the two coexist. This is plainly the case of every advanced country, as only a few underdeveloped ones are nowadays closed to financial markets and, thus, exclusively rely on credit.

There are many benefits associated with firms issuing debt and capital instruments rather than applying for loans: most importantly, they relate to greater incentives to transparency, good internal controls, wise investment decisions, greater financial reliability, and so on. Nevertheless, market-based systems—*rectius*, entities—show less "committed" shareholders because of the smaller stakes they hold, as well as—conversely—more powerful managers, more likely to become 'entrenched'. If we turn this problem to the financial industry, we may easily understand how relevant it is.

Kim et al. (2013) shed a sinister light, also, on the role of financial innovation in terms of systemic stability. In fact, while it reduces the likelihood of currency crises as it clearly helps mobilising capital by narrowing information asymmetries, it also enhances the likelihood of banking crises. This is due to its role in determining excessive risk taking via loose credit policies, which ultimately increase leverage. In the abovementioned study, the drawbacks of a market-based capital structure are evident in respect of currency crises: they are thought to yield sudden, large shocks to capital flows, such that subsequent adjustments do not manage to fully absorb them and stop the propagation from exchange markets onto other segments of the financial industry. Lestano et al. (2003) have also shown that a rapid growth in savings and liquidity is, still, more likely to determine a speculative attack onto the currency in which bubbling assets are denominated.

The idea that the GFC has not been the consequence of inherent weaknesses within the free economic system, but rather of some regulators' failure, is well rooted in the extant literature (provided that "ideology" be subjected to crude data, as it always should). Other than an improper design of incentives—which clearly played a significant role in yielding those unintended consequences which we had referred before, some authors underline the striking 'lack of expertise' on the supervisory side (Moshirian 2011). The focus of the Package—and, in particular, the Regulation—onto coordination between authorities, their enhanced powers, and the stress on people's individual requirements to play direct roles in financial oversight, describe the attempt to solve the issues dramatically exposed by the sequence of troubled intermediaries. Unfortunately, this is consistent with Gordon's (2000) view that *regulation comes after disasters*. For most of the time, the isolation of such rules at a national level had diminished the strength of the global response to a global turmoil. Although the EU regulatory framework—based upon a financial 'single rulebook'—was partially ongoing, and in spite of the American efforts at a federal rather than a State level (not unlikely what had been done during the Thirties), there was a faint global coordination. The G20 summit held in Pittsburgh (26–27 September 2009), though efficaciously tackling the matter of derivatives markets from a systemic stability standpoint, may be regarded as just a "late" response to a crisis which had already transmitted onto the so-called 'real economy'.

The lack of worldwide "integration" has left the financial system exposed to regulatory arbitrage phenomena, which can be something "ordinary" under a liberal international regime but is nowadays regarded with much greater suspect and might give rise to "retaliatory" actions by domestic authorities. In fact, before the GFC, regulatory competition was mainly "downwards": that is, jurisdictions battled over granting foreign investors looser rules, especially in case of large multinational conglomerates. The first seminal piece of EU legislation addressing banking subjects (namely, Directive 1989/626/EEC), by introducing the principle of mutual recognition coupled with home-country control, was undoubtedly reflective of such approach. After the GFC, this trend looks completely reversed. While a consistent supranational regulatory framework has not been achieved yet, competition between regulators has taken the opposite direction vis-à-vis the pre-crisis era. As a matter of fact, even the country which par excellence pursued deregulation—namely, the United Kingdom—has been discussing on which kind of regulatory approach to adopt once Brexit becomes effective. For the moment being, the two alternatives—a more investor-friendly environment versus strengthened requirements—are almost equally probable, in absence of clear indications regarding the overall direction to take. In a sense, the UK situation may be thought to resemble the one of the entire world, as protectionism is regaining ground in trade matters, yet many steps in that direction—aimed at rebuilding ancient commercial barriers—still look too dangerous to be definitely made.

Although many industries (e.g., food and beverage) are commonly deemed to suffer from "unfair" foreign competition due to excessive deregulation both domestically and abroad, financial services are even more intensely attacked by 're-regulators', as much of the criticism does not make any difference based on the "nationality" of financial entities. Hence, it does not come as a surprise that the area to which MiFID II is mainly addressed turns out being the relationship between intermediaries and their clients, shaped under the investor protection framework, rather than the increasingly cross-border business of many intermediaries. Conversely, supervisors seem to be still widely aware of the importance of keeping the cross-border operations of financial intermediaries as easy as they are nowadays, for a financial system segregated at a national level cannot be envisaged anymore. Interconnectedness between intermediaries is growing along with interbank markets, notwithstanding the scandals that have recently affected the formation of the major reference point for not only interbank transactions but, more broadly, a large number of contracts: namely, the London Interbank Offered Rate (LIBOR). Historian Alan Ferguson (2018) provided a thorough representation of how the 'Wall Street network' was established, prospered, and ultimately fell in a framework where networks are deemed to play a large role in many of the most significant events in human history. Anyway, while Ferguson (2018) claims that networks have been meaningful in a few moments over time, and almost silent or less significant in much longer periods, some adopt a view which holds them as more pervasive, though not always with the same strength. In particular, Moshirian (2011) notes that *unlike the past, when all roads led to Rome, in the 21st century, not all roads lead to Wall St.*, meaning that idiosyncratic shocks due to the circulation of toxic assets are still possible, and the self-adjustments yielded by investors' mobility might be not enough to avoid them.

Moshirian's (2011) view of a sort of "stagnation" in the freedom of capital flows is not isolated in the literature. For instance, this is a case made by Obstfeld and Taylor (2004), who noted that, over a century, the exchanges between advanced and developing economies had significantly grown, whereas those within first-world economies had conversely shrunk. Such trend, however, was already slowing and raised some concerns over the future. In that study is noted, also, that the GFC has added on these concerns: for the slowing trend we should blame *the absence of an integrated, cohesive, and inclusive global financial system*, clearly needed to overcome those national-level frictions which exacerbate the negative spill-overs yielded by financial turmoil. Actually, as Moshirian (2011) acknowledges, the European Union has shown the good will to counteract that trend. From a regulatory point of view, the enactment of the European System of Financial Supervision (ESFS) represents a commendable step forward. Moreover, even the fiscal convergence—which was still in fieri at that time—is nowadays regarded as one of the major steps to take for levelling the playing field, albeit some continues to see competition between Member States as much better than complete harmonisation. The overarching goal is that of making the euro even more pivotal in global currency markets, something which would foster the EU's appeal to investors, ultimately benefiting the economic union (other than the monetary one).

In the international arena, some good steps have been taken, but they still appear largely insufficient: as a matter of fact, the "perfect" world whereby capital flows freely is still yet to come and, as we have seen above, a reverse trend is now taking place. For instance, the abovementioned Pittsburgh G20 summit established the Financial Stability Board (FSB)—replacing the former Forum, endowed with limited yet significant regulatory powers. For instance, it is now committed to overcoming the weaknesses of the Basel Accords via the design of a new capital requirement; namely, the *Total-Loss Absorbing Capacity* (TLAC). Beyond such direct role, it represents the "venue" at which worldwide regulators can meet to discuss financial stability issues from a global perspective. Still in respect of regulators' role, Moshirian (2011) notes that one of the inefficiencies which mostly contributed to the propagation of the GFC should be found in the 'overconfidence' of many national regulators towards the American ones. Given the role played by the United States in financial markets worldwide, many authorities simply expected that US overseers would have done something like *whatever it takes* to prevent global turmoil from spreading. Such confidence was probably not fully deserved, if we consider the substantial inability of US regulators in stopping the 'easy credit' bubbling spiral, or even their support to such pernicious policy. The GFC has clearly shaken this rooted conviction; therefore, it is reasonable to believe that the catastrophe has now prompted regulators to become more committed to ensuring systemic stability. This deals not only with coordination between supervisors but, also, with the tasks they are charged with, as monetary policy decisions and oversight functions are increasingly concentrated in the hands of a single authority (the SSM is a clear step in that direction). Hence, it should be noted that, other than imposing more targeted requirements in the exercise of prudential regulation, many central banks—including, recently, the ECB—have growingly purchased assets from the financial sector, injecting liquidity into it (the most radical version of such programmes is often labelled as 'quantitative easing'). However, although there is almost no doubt over the immediate effects—that is, in the very short term—of this kind of interventions, their long-term efficacy and sustainability (in absence of structural reforms) is harshly debated.

The discussion has rapidly extended onto the duties of central banks in general, as nowadays most of them are endowed with inflation targeting purposes, something which many see as a limit, even if it were to be applied in a 'flexible' way (Demirgüç-Kunt and Servén 2009). In fact, the generally-agreed opinion is that, during troubled times, it would be particularly useful to have central banks available as lenders of last resort. The ECB—*rectius*, the EU supervisory architecture as a whole, in particular via the European Stability Mechanism (ESM)—has de facto played this role following the GFC outbreak, in the light of its relevant role for some fragile countries like Greece and Cyprus, kept away from defaulting on their obligations toward international creditors. More in general, notwithstanding the possible overlap with the duties of governments, it has been the BIS itself to assess that the role of central banks is widening for the purpose of defending systemic stability. The same authority has been endowed with the task of working with the FSB to develop adequate macro-prudential tools.

The problem of lacking global coordination between supervisors has been addressed by the International Monetary Fund (IMF). While relieving some of the guilt from regulators, that institution blamed—along with the former—markets themselves, which had revealed not to be sufficiently responsive. In particular, these allegations were referred to the risks posed by huge off-balance-sheet exposures, as well as intense dealing with over-the-counter transactions—marred by heavy counterparty risk—and the uncontrolled spread of the shadow banking system. In fact, the main feature of the latter has always lied in excessive leverage; hence, it has always exerted a negative contribution to systemic stability. Many ideas have come out of regulators, worldwide, when pressed by the need of finding not only solutions to new problems (never observed before the GFC) but, also, more effective answers to issues that had been very well known but never adequately addressed: for instance, how to exert due supervision over intermediaries engaged in cross-border operations, how to deal with intermediaries—and, in particular, banks—that were *failing or likely to fail*, how to protect the weakest parties in a financial transaction, and so on. The EU legislation had attempted giving an answer to these fundamental issues, which tackle the raison d'être of supervision itself. Discussing them in detail would be outside the scope of this work, but we shall consistently refer to them when analysing the content and the rationale of MiFID II, as far as investment services/activities are concerned.

2.4 Why Banks Got into Trouble

As we have previously noted, although financial intermediation had expanded well beyond what one could have imagined just a few decades before, the GFC brought trouble to credit institutions much more than other players. Banks suffered deeply, along with their stakeholders: inter alia, sovereign States relying upon them for their bond issuances being underwritten. We have already suggested how such distress—sometimes propagating at a systemic level—could be summarised: too much leverage; too little liquidity. We have also highlighted the supervisory responsibility not to have stopped a very dangerous trend, as denounced by the advocates of 'excess elasticity' of the existing monetary and financial regimes as the origin of the GFC (Borio and Disyatat 2011; Shin 2011).

A very insightful analysis on the causes of many banks going into trouble is the one made by Cabral (2013), who looked at different indicators on the "health" in an attempt to clarify how economists could have foreseen the tide and, thus, avoiding being hammered by Queen Elizabeth II with that unescapable question: *How come did nobody notice?* In his analysis, Cabral (2013) tries to disentangle maturity risk—i.e. the one represented by cash flows more distant in time—from the other sources: as of risk premia, this requires separating 'term spreads', which are due to the former kind of risk, from the others. This helps us avoiding taking into account what should rather be seen as 'confounding effects', because they contribute setting up a more "aggressive" risk/return profile in "ordinary" times, characterised by physiological operations.

Cabral (2013) moves from a twofold paradox: first, in 2006 and the first half of 2007—that is, when the GM was already fading away and the first symptoms of the GF were coming to the surface, banks were still highly profitable in respect of both GDP and banking assets; second, margins were quite low at that time (these two evidences are even contrasting one another). Hence, argues the author, we need a more detailed insight on banks' balance sheet to fully understand what actually stirred the disaster. In particular, between 2002 and 2007, he observed a significant decline (as a proportion of total assets) in two of the major outflows for a credit institution: namely, allowances for losses on loans and leases and non-interest expenses. However, these trends cannot explain the upward one in profits: as a matter of fact, spreads for a given asset-liability mismatch in terms of default or maturity risk actually shrank. This might be seen as the signal of enhanced asset quality, unlike the simple widening of a bank's size: this last expands output but not necessarily its quality, and may ultimately get impaired if credit standards are loosened. The underlying economic phenomenon may be easily detected: derivative exposures, which by their nature exploit widening mismatches, had been substantively growing.

Enlarging balance sheets, coupled with more pronounced asset-liability mismatches, should theoretically improve a bank's margins: yet, if we look at the NIM, the reverse occurred. Such contradiction is not easy to explain, and probably requires the introduction of more theoretical microeconomic arguments regarding the formation of profits, commonly known to be diminishing along with increased inputs. If widening balance sheets and quality improvements (under a 'product differentiation' strategy) are pursued by many intermediaries at the same time, the overall effect—as Cabral (2013) argues to have occurred at the end of the GM—are shrinking spreads and, thus, lowering profitability. In summary, the abovementioned study deserves our attention due to its effort to correctly identify the microeconomic roots of the GFC, i.e. those not stemming from wrong incentives by monetary policy or regulation. Anyway, such *macro-* aspects are not neglected at all: for instance, some early bank runs—e.g., the one occurred at Northern Rock—aggravated the industry's liquidity hardships, for interbank markets act as transmission channels.

Regulation—as we have repeatedly underlined—has not helped banks pursuing a sound and prudent management able to face systemic threats. Basel I, still quite distant from the everyday reality of banking business, was faulted with perverse incentives to pursue arbitrage: e.g., regarding the treatment of loan loss provisions. Paradoxically, the overall result was not a reduction in risk-taking, but rather an awkward boost to balance sheet growth via increased leverage (regardless of the trends experienced by asset quality, on which looking at crude figures might be not exhaustive at all). Conversely, we should consider how techniques to assess creditworthiness were strikingly inadequate. Basel II—which introduced the element of externally-assessed credit ratings and allowed for banks to compute their credit risk exposure by internally determining at least the investor's probability of default—was agreed upon at a time in which distorted incentives had already been acting for too long time, and eventually came into force in January 2008, when it was too late. In fact, the perverse mechanism which ultimately led to the GFC was already working, as the spread of credit—in other words, the expansion of banks' balance sheets—ultimately ends up posing pressure onto reserves. In turn, this is an incentive to leverage up by means of capital requirements arbitrage strategies (Cabral 2013). This strengthened the call for a constraint on leverage: it will be imposed only by the third round of the Basel Accords, progressively implemented throughout the post-crisis period.

However, the global banking industry would have not suffered so intensely had the two utter crises not broken out: namely, the fall of the "house of cards" represented by securitisations, in the USA, and the sudden worsening of public finances—severely hit by the 'real economy' recession—in many EU peripheral countries, including some (e.g., Ireland) that a little time earlier had been universally acclaimed as champions of fast growth, driven by innovation and high-value-added sectors. How that contributed to banking crises worldwide is almost self-evident in modern finance, as cross-border operations allow large conglomerates to spread instability due to their excessive leverage (Shin 2011).

Basel III ultimately came to 'close the stable door after the horse had bolted'. In addition to new requirements designed to deal with the issues of leverage and liquidity, a thorough revision of risk weights—aimed at reversing the wrong incentives which had accrued over the previous years and, thus, limiting the spread of systemic risk—was eventually carried out. In fact, we may easily spot that liquidity constraints are the liability-side counterparty of those on credit on the asset side, and in such way have been intended by regulators throughout history. Yet, criticism was moved to Basel III as well as to the previous versions (Scott 2010; Rochet 2010). Besides, even the new rules on liquidity were generally not welcome in the literature: they seemed to address a very hot topic by the same out-dated approach inspiring the rationale behind mandatory reserves, at the dawn of central banking. Actually, empirical evidence seems to suggest that in history, contrary to common intuition, bank runs have occurred at times of high reserves, not low ones (Feinman 1993). Therefore, the anti-bank-run purpose of stricter liquidity requirements appears quite misplaced, and probably driven by an "emotional" reaction to the crisis of Northern Rock and large US conglomerates (all facing liquidity hardships), much more than the result of a wise cost/benefit analysis of the proposed rules.

Among the several concerns raised over the new standards, some lament that liquidity requirements are too overarching to clearly show actual differences in liquidity between banks. In fact, a credit institution might fulfil such requirements by exhibiting very different kinds of items—even very illiquid ones—in their balance sheet. Some others, in the literature, questioned the leverage ratio for being too low, and both the LCR and the NSFR as too high. In summary, the problem with Basel III was not different from the one with the first round of the Accords: banks can reach their targets, set by supervisors, by pursuing radically different strategies and, thus, substantially cherry-picking the composition of their balance sheet for regulatory purposes. This endangers the transmission of benefits from the *micro-* level, of credit institutions' sound and prudent management, to the *macro-* one, of systemic stability.

The United States experienced a significant regulatory overhaul when the Dodd-Frank Act (DFA) was enacted in 2010. Although it encompassed only a handful of really meaningful provisions (yet, it is extremely lengthy and complex overall), its relevance in the history of financial legislation can hardly be denied. In fact, while ending three decades of deregulation, it substantially ignited the opposite trend by posing many decisions under regulatory agencies. Before the reform, these last ones either had much less power or did not exist and, thus, were created for the specific purpose of tightening oversight over financial institutions. Other than these "architectural" changes, the DFA encompassed a very restrictive provision—known as the 'Volcker Rule' from its "father", namely the former Fed chairman, which prohibited banks from engaging in proprietary trading *tout court*, without any discernment between different kinds of products or instruments. In contrast, EU rules of this kind are much more "friendly" and do not envisage any full prohibition. The esprit of that radical DFA provision—though having its supporters in Europe—has ultimately failed to pervade continental jurisdictions. Anyway, there are some noteworthy similarities between the two legislations. For instance, in the DFA is acknowledged the need to impose a more stringent regulation on those intermediaries which pose systemic risk because of the extent of their activity, and therefore can be charged with additional requirements by federal authorities.

More in general, Cabral (2013) discusses, also, how monetary policy contributed to yield *micro-* changes in the banking industry and, thus, originate the GFC. First of all, there is a close correspondence between interest rate decisions and the shape of the yield curve: whenever reference rates get lowered (raised), long-term investments become relatively riskier (safer) and, thus, the curve steepens (flattens). This results in a modification of term spreads and, clearly, the profitability (cost) of a bank's assets (liabilities). However, we should also consider that the effect on liquidity premia is not as large as that explained with maturity, for investors are able to discount the exogenous, artificial effect stirred by monetary policy from the "natural" one, due to actual changes in market fundamentals. Given the easy predictability of monetary policy decisions during the GM—often inspired by the so-called 'Taylor rule', such effects had never represented a serious issue before the GFC outbreak. At that point, however, rate increases by the Fed could be blamed for having "crowded out" investors' expectations, as a flattening yield curve makes it more difficult to appreciate any shift in the intrinsic riskiness. In simpler words, we might say that, when it was purportedly ended by the same monetary authority—namely, the Fed—which had initiated it, the GM backfired, as investors well not well "trained" to interpret the central banks' signals different from a plain, direct response to changes in macroeconomic indicators like inflation and output growth. At that time, in fact, these two did not show any significant drifts from their long-term trend.

Anyway, as far as banking is concerned, we could go backwards and ask even "bigger" questions, dealing with the structure of the industry rather than the operations carried out by credit institutions. First, as observed by the European Systemic Risk Board (ESRB 2014), the 'old continent' is the only area of the globe whereby banking has steadily increased its relevance—in respect of the financial system as a whole—since the Seventies, with the degree of concentration growing over time (Onado 2017). Moreover, if we broke down the dynamics of banks' balance sheets, we could easily spot the structural change in the functions they serve. Moreover, if we gazed the dynamics of banks' balance sheets, we could easily spot the structural change in the functions they serve. More surprisingly than anything else, extending credit to firms and households is no more the prevalent activity in European banking, despite the remarkable boost to credit yielded by the currency unification.

After the GFC outbreak, some voices have raised to support the case for a de facto reversal in the evolution occurred to banking over the last decades, with a comeback to the fundamental function of raising funds from the public of savers and extending loans to subjects in *deficit*. This is the kind of banking commonly known as 'commercial' in opposition to the investment activity, nowadays often allowed in conjunction with the former. Besides, many are the advocates of an increasing separation between the two, albeit this claim is put forward for very different reasons. On the one hand, this is intended as a measure aimed at reducing risk-taking by restricting certain activities to banks which had been established to pursue basic commercial tasks; on the other, some argue that deposit insurance funded by taxpayers' money should be balanced via a mandatory reduction in the "aggressiveness" of banking business. Re-establishing a certain degree of separation would also reinstate the old 'originate and distribute' model, where market-oriented intermediation is endowed with a smaller role vis-à-vis client-oriented one, focussed on performing more traditional activities. Ackermann (2008) rebukes at these convictions, highlighting that *these good old days [of purely commercial banking] were far from good*. Less advanced business models were clearly unable to efficiently diversify some risks away, especially in geographic terms (a virtue described as 'flexible risk') but rather favoured their concentration, and eventually allowed despicable capital management practices.

Nowadays, capital allocation is more efficient and pricing—though far from perfect—relies upon more solid assumptions, which may easily be checked in the light of market conditions. The punctum dolens of modern banking, however, remains securitisation practices; especially—this is the warning by Ackermann (2008)—if originators forcedly had to keep the first-loss tranche. This clearly prevents proper risk transfer from occurring and, instead, reduces the entire operation to something which is good only for funding purposes and perhaps, in a certain regulatory framework, even capital arbitrage.

2.5 Transparency and Intermediary-Client Relationships

As we have already pointed out, 'overconfidence' was the real problem—at least from a behavioural economics standpoint—behind the inability of financial intermediaries to face the crisis when it showed its first signs. In particular, liquidity is the area in which divergence between an idealised view of markets, on the one hand, and a dismal reality, on the other, was most evident. In fact, notwithstanding the skyrocketing growth in transactions yielded by the large availability of liquid funds on financial markets as a whole, many assets eventually turned out being largely illiquid. This was a fortiori the case when they were exposed as relying too much on the occurrence of very unlikely events (e.g., a subprime obligor paying its debt back). Of course, very limited was the awareness on what was going on before market conditions openly became "pathological": between 2001 and 2006, reports Ackermann (2008), the subprime segment had risen from 6 to 15% of total outstanding mortgages. When the tide of favourable monetary policy retired, uncovering what had been concealed for such a long time, the American economy found out how irresponsible had credit policies been over recent years. Among the many awkward problems that had affected loan instructor procedures, the most shocking ones were the lack of adequate documentation and the benign attitude towards 'no income, no jobs, no assets' (NINJA) people.

So weak basements are certainly the most evident reason why that "house of cards"—created via securitisations—ultimately collapsed. When default rates reached a historical low, the path undertaken inevitably appeared as the right one. This reflected that basically Keynesian view according to which loose policies do not harm the finances of those which implement them (being either a sovereign State or a financial entity), as they are able to spur growth and, thus, allow the counterparties to fulfil their obligations, whereas stricter policies would harm them, jeopardising their viability. As a way of thinking, such belief dated back well before the 'Keynesian revolution' in economic science, as denounced by Bastiat (1850) in his 'parable of the broken window': that is, the idea that an ostensible individual damage turns out spreading real benefits for those who participate in a given economic environment. Unlike the Keynesian doctrine, which advocates deliberate deficit spending by governments, those criticised by the great French economist used to believe in the thaumaturgical effects of unintended damage, such as a window accidentally broken by a child playing with a ball.

This 19th-century approach is even closer to the paradoxical 'financial folly' of GM years: that is, accruing liquidity by creating illiquid assets. Yet, other than a very generic political project, there was often little awareness of the risks actually faced when trusting NINJA people or other subprime borrowers. The 'alchemy' would have created gold by poor materials, thus allowing repayments which would have not been rationally possible if looking at the situation from a "static" viewpoint (i.e. ruling out any changes over time). The 'alchemy' ended—with a dramatic reversal in the "transformation" process—when the Fed started gradually raising interest rates in mid-2004. Several weak entities, in both the financial industry and elsewhere, have remained on the ground. Many issues have been faced over subsequent years: some with adequate strength; some others by just showing good will. Nevertheless, many structural problems remain outstanding.

Ackermann (2008) ask whether accounting rules could have played a role in fuelling the credit bubble. They argue that, although the 'fair value' criterion is still deemed to be the most transparent—hence, at least theoretically, the most investor-protective one—it makes a lot of difference based on how it is actually intended. In fact, marking asset prices to the market is uncontestably "fair" by definition, whereas using internal models to make valuations clearly is not. Moreover, estimates are by construction even less affordable at times in which assets have become substantially illiquid and, thus, there are no "active markets" where they can be efficiently dismissed. Hence, third parties will find significant difficulties in making their own valuations, a fortiori if they are companies used to different accounting standards, as this kind of rules are often fine-tuned by regulators along with the characteristics and the needs of respective economic players.

This issue is particularly concerning in respect of financial instruments. The classification of a financial instrument—which gives rise to diverging accounting treatments—has to be done at the initiation of the transaction, whereas a subsequent amendment is prohibited under IFRS but theoretically possible under US GAAP. Such difference opens huge room for regulatory arbitrage, which clearly makes the playing field less 'level' than it should be; moreover, this would eventually harm systemic stability, as it is a blow to that 'certainty' consistently required by investors for any long-term commitment. Moreover, fair value accounting is procyclical by definition: asset values soar over booms and decline over busts. While this was plainly welcome during GM years, when many European accounting legislations were redefined in accordance with that principle replacing the older one (namely, the 'historical cost' approach), it became a remarkable source of concern once the GFC broke out. A decade later, the new IFRS 9 represents a major innovation in that realm: enacted starting on January 2018, it has tackled the issue of loan losses in a context whereby asset impairment has become increasingly relevant to banks' profitability as well as stability.

From a risk management standpoint, recent years have witnessed a growing attention devoted to culture, which should reasonably be regarded as the primary defence against loan delinquencies, representing the basis of a sound credit policy. This implies that financial institutions should rely not only upon third parties when assessing a counterparty's creditworthiness, but rather conduct their own "due diligence", the most thorough and objective as possible. This should be done regardless of the role played by CRAs: ratings have to be intended as a complement, rather than a substitute, for internal assessments (Ackermann 2008). While this might seem theoretically easy, as it appeals to what common sense would suggest as of managing a financial firm, it is much more difficult to be put into practice. In fact, pricing risk has become a very challenging task, as large portions of it might actually be hidden like an iceberg's body. This is the result of financial instruments becoming more complex, so that payoffs might not be fully known a priori but cash flows get often triggered by the occurrence of different events, whose likelihood is also difficult to assess with certainty.

In addition to this, many assumptions that used to be made during GM years with a forward-looking approach would have soon turned out being unrealistic. As if such inconvenience had not been enough, the excessive convolution of many mathematical models has certainly played a role in lowering the investors' ability to understand how credit policies are implemented in the entities whose stakes they hold, thus diminishing the shareholders' right to signal the right track to the management. Of course, this is a graver problem in public companies or, more in general, to those institutional framework—for instance, of Anglo-Saxon origin—where the agency divide between owners and managers is wider than elsewhere. It is inevitable, therefore, that in financial entities located in countries with a lower degree of separation between ownership and control there is, also, lower opaqueness of assets, as investors tend to value clarity. The same cannot be told of risk, as a stricter control of owners onto managers is tendentially associated with higher risk-taking. Yet, complexity is only one of the several elements contributing to an asset's riskiness and is almost never taken into account for pricing purposes. We shall come back on the role of "complexity" in Chap. 6, where we discuss investor protection issues.

Internal models did not turn out being the solution but may rather have aggravated the problem. The role of CRAs has been subjected to even harder scrutiny in the GFC years, despite substantially lacking oversight during previous ones. In particular, the fact that CRAs get hired by the same under their assessment has always represented a source of concern over the independence of such relevant players in global financial markets. Moreover, the timing of credit rating announcements is often subject to very strong criticism: on the one hand, news regarding the viability of a company as assessed by external professionals may easily turn out being self-fulfilling; on the other, this reinforcing mechanism might sometimes fail, so that the company shows a path actually inconsistent with recently-released ratings. Lehman Brothers is the most famous example of this last inconvenience.

2.6 Issues Left Outstanding by MiFID I

It was an unfortunate coincidence that the entry into force of MiFID I—whose delay had relied upon reasonable concerns over the market's reaction—occurred when the "perfect storm", which had already shown its first symptoms, was on the brink of deflagrating. Therefore, between 2008 and 2010, the European legislator was committed to fixing the awkward fragilities of the EU financial system much more than performing a thorough assessment of MiFID I's actual impact. Anyway, if we ever suspected that piece of legislation to have been repudiated too quickly and in a substantially unfair manner, the very utter situation of that-time financial environment would refute such hypothesis. A posteriori, no one could blame either Directive 2004/39/EC or the two subsequent 'implementing' pieces of legislation (namely, Directive 2006/73/EC and Regulation 1287/2006) as wrongly-designed or ill-intentioned. Conversely, they had actually represented a very "liberal" innovation at a time in which, notwithstanding the significant improvements that markets had already self-developed, rules still often appeared as old-fashioned and inadequate. However, the very bad macroeconomic conjuncture exposed—and, presumably, magnified—many of the flaws of MiFID I. By taking into account the *Impact Assessment* document released by the European Commission on 20 October 2011, when proposing a new Directive, let us review the points which needed an amendment.

First of all, one of the most overarching objectives of MiFID I was acknowledged to be far from being achieved: despite all efforts, a 'level playing field' could not be observed yet in EU financial markets. Had a satisfactory degree of far, balanced and efficient competition been reached before the GFC broke out, we would have never witnessed the turmoil propagating so deeply and rapidly. The Commission—which has been endowed with substantive regulatory powers, following the Lamfalussy reform—makes a timid attempt to forgive itself by attributing such failure in levelling the playing field to the surge of *new players and new trading techniques*. Nevertheless, this phrase should be read as the admission of supervisors being unable to discipline the upcoming novelties. Such mea culpa becomes evident when the Commission advocates a complete overhaul of supervisory practices, blamed to be 'inconsistent' with the underlying principles, and identifies *the lack of sufficient information* as the main problem. This is coupled with financial markets being not enough transparent to their participants, something which—if we look at how many new provisions on transparency have been included in MiFID II—has been regarded as MiFID I's greatest fault. Actually, 'information' entails something more "granular" and wide than 'transparency': in fact, it is not limited to the communication between market participants, market operators (or investment firms), and regulatory authorities. Conversely, it should be extended to the importance that the public of investors gets reliable knowledge over the universe of tradable instruments, including—under the 'best execution' principle—that information which should trigger the choice between different entities providing the same investment service or performing the same investment activity (e.g., venues competing for executing orders).

If these are *macro-* issues, the *micro-* ones—that is, those more closely related to the everyday business of intermediaries and their relationships with clients—are no less concerning and worth addressing. The first to be listed as a serious problem left on the table by MiFID I, according to the Commission, is *difficulties for SMEs to access financial markets*. This phrase confirms that the EU system is, still nowadays, centred around banks: since credit institutions represent the main source of funding for many small and medium-sized enterprises (SMEs), as well as households, and they have been gravely hit by the GFC, this latter has shed a light on the importance for debt and capital markets to become increasingly open to retail investors. As we shall see, this is an objective which the EU legislator has certainly set up when drafting the Package, but which it may have not pursued at the fullest of its possibilities. Instead, the ECB has done an outstanding job to counter the credit crunch: first, by conditioning its open-market operations on the beneficiaries conveying credit to the so-called 'real economy'; then, by directly purchasing corporate bonds and other instruments issued by companies. However, one might object that the latter kind of intervention has actually benefited large entities, already active on financial markets, much more than SMEs coping with insufficient funding from channels other than the banking one. This is a largely accurate observation; anyway, a regulatory intervention on the structure and the functioning of financial markets would not suffice to allow SMEs collect the amounts of money required to undertake profitable investments, without a tantamount legislator's endeavour to lift the fiscal and the bureaucratic burden charged on external financing. A EU-driven harmonisation on this latter issue is still yet to come in a substantive manner.

Finally, remaining within the *micro-* flaws exhibited by MiFID I, the Commission acknowledged that many market participants had shown *weaknesses in some areas of the organisation, processes, risk control and assessment*. In short, they have failed to successfully do their job, destabilising markets and, thus, contributing to turmoil at a systemic level. When discussing the onset of the GFC, we have already pointed out what these 'weaknesses' actually are. However, the Commission made a step further by stating that not only such frictions had been a blow to confidence, which is fundamental to the orderly functioning of markets;

but, also, that these inefficiencies had yielded negative spill-overs—labelled as *deficiencies*—onto investor protection, which is the supreme goal of current financial legislation in the *micro*- realm (equivalent to systemic stability in the *macro*- one). Hence, it is no doubt that the public of investors had been profoundly shaken by the GFC, after which it found itself more unsafe about choices to be made, more exposed to sudden shocks in market conditions, and more doubtful about the efficacy of intermediation itself. This trend is a very dangerous one: when it started, right after the early cases of large and once-reliable institutions collapsing, some worried that the steady long-term expansion in financial activities experienced over the last three decades could have come to an end, raising concerns over the sustainability of financial capitalism per se. A decade later, we have fortunately seen that this has not been the case. The economic system, partially reformed, has proudly survived. Yet, this does not automatically ensure that every single amendment has been a worthy one. In this work, we review what has been done by the EU legislator and attempt providing a reasoned judgement over it.

Before moving onto a detailed discussion of the purposes set out by the MiFID II legislator as an improvement over pre-existing rules, we should first clarify the mutual connections between the abovementioned issues and how they yielded negative effects onto financial markets. The Commission's *Impact Assessment*, summarises these mechanisms (Fig. 2.1).

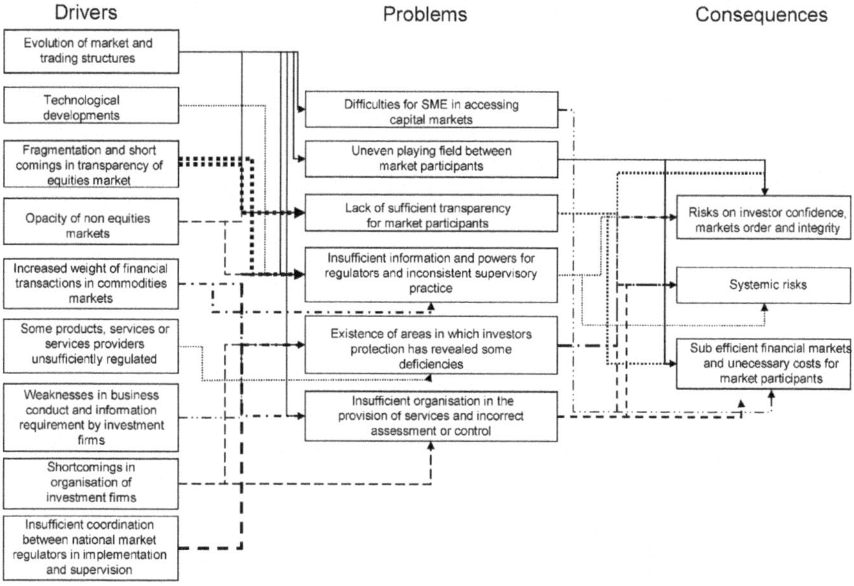

Fig. 2.1 The Package's rationale: drivers, problems detected, and expected impact. *Source* http://eur-lex.europa.eu, © European Union, 1998–2019

Among the 'drivers' of such troubled conditions, we have:

- Technological disruption, often resulted in the opaqueness of assets;
- an overly spread of dematerialised financial transactions, often OTC, coupled with an inadequate regulatory framework;
- players' deficiencies, regarding business as well as their internal organisation, such as in the risk management function;
- supervision lacking effectiveness and coordination between different authorities.

What is grouped under the label 'problems' is clearly the result of these flaws jointly deploying their effects: we have discussed these issues above. During the GFC years, also, the 'consequences' of those imbalances have become increasingly clear: plummeting investor confidence, disorderly markets, the infrastructure—a concept closely associated with transparency, as we shall detail in Chap. 5—losing its 'integrity'; and, at an upper level, the survival of the system being either in jeopardy because of systemic risk, or—if crumbling gets avoided—obtained at the cost of inefficient capital allocation and higher burdens borne by its participants. Having clarified this approach to the issues tackled by the Package, let us circumscribe them in a clearer manner.

(A) **An imperfectly levelled playing field**

It is a striking evidence that technological progress favours competition, but—at the same time—it not always manages to enhance its "fairness", intended as market participants having the same opportunities and no one holding any dominant position. This is exactly what has recently happened: over the last twenty years, we have witnessed the surge of new types of trading platforms challenging the traditional, MiFID I-compliant ones; yet many of these newcomers—largely unregulated—are endowed with very low transparency requirements, or even waived from them. It is the case of the so-called 'dark pools' and 'broker-crossing networks' (BCNs), on which we shall come back in detail.

However, the Commission acknowledged that supervisory concerns were not exclusively referred to the galaxy of bilateral, discretionary matching outside "classical" trading venues. In fact, even multilateral trading facilities (MTFs), which MiFID I had conceived as the less burdensome alternative to regulated markets (RMs), had stirred suspicion about a regulatory framework which was allegedly too lose to be effective against macroeconomic turmoil. We shall review the main features of MTFs in Chap. 4; for the moment being, however, we report the Commission's fear that even this kind of venues could have contributed to 'market fragmentation', i.e. a situation in which the same instrument may be exchanged over significantly different platforms, established in abidance by very different rules and provided with very different characteristics, in a blow to the principle of a clear, safe, and consistent regulatory framework. In a fragmented market, arbitrage opportunities are more frequent and more easily exploitable, as what is denied over a certain platform (e.g., a RM or even a MTF) can be pursued elsewhere (e.g., over-the-counter).

Of course, considering such unregulated entities as a threat to systemic stability has its roots in some alarming empirical figures. The Committee of European Securities Regulators (CESR)—established as part of the Lamfalussy's 'comitology' and now turned into an authoritative research institution—has found that the proportion of transactions executed over BCNs had doubled in a few months at the onset of the GFC, as they moved from 0.7% of total EEA trading at the beginning of 2008 to 1.5% in the first quarter of 2010. The European legislator foresaw what could have happened without any decisive regulatory intervention: at the end of 2010, in the USA, 'dark trading' accounted for more than 13% in respect of equities and was projected to exceed 15% by the subsequent year. Of course, such levels would have never been reached in Europe, where financial transactions have historically been subjected to much heavier oversight and, thus, have never witnessed such a decline in transparency requirements. Nevertheless, the trend was too frightening to be ignored. It was clear that, given the plummeting profitability of trades executed over "classical" venues—due to the joint effect of macroeconomic hardships and stricter supervisory control, investors were increasingly fleeing RMs and MTFs to search for better results in a completely different financial environment, where very low transaction costs would have offset the increase in settlement risk. American regulators were already reacting, especially in respect of derivatives trading (the culprit of the GFC); and European ones had no other choice than following them.

As of derivatives and their 'clearing', the EU legislator seems particularly concerned about coordinating different pieces of legislation. In Recital 37^{R} is clearly stated that the *European Market Infrastructure Regulation* (EMIR, No. 648/2012) sets forth clearing obligations—with different thresholds applying to different instruments—for OTC derivatives. This is done to prevent *competitive distortions*, which had marred MiFID I. This is done by setting up free access in a twofold direction: on the one hand, trading venues will have a non-discriminatory access to central counterparties (CCPs) that perform centralised clearing, whereas the latter ones will have a non-discriminatory access to the so-called 'trade feeds' of trading venues. In the light of this, Recitals 38^{R} and 40^{R} insist on the removal of any obstacles to the access to post-trade infrastructure, envisaging that other *commercial barriers in the clearing of financial instruments*, harmful to competition, be tore down.

The disruption of the level playing field—which, actually, had never been established—should be associated, also, with the spread of algorithmic (*automated*, in the Commission's wording) and high-frequency trading (denoted by 'AT' and 'HFT' acronyms respectively). These are tools that—by definition—do not let human traders reflect on the action to take in case of an adverse scenario suddenly materialising, but rather replace them in decision-making and may eventually trigger severe liquidity crises. The two noteworthy events of this kind—that we mentioned before—prompted the EU legislator to take a tougher stance on the issue. Of course, as we shall underline in Chap. 4 when detailly discussing the topic, generally, AT and HFT are highly beneficial to the orderly and efficient functioning of markets in terms of liquidity. In fact, they facilitate posting, matching, and executing orders, such that their role may be appreciated by looking at narrowing bid-ask spreads. Again, however, the issue should be seen in terms of tail risk: with regard to the events of 6 May 2010, the Commission reported the American authorities' claim that, *even if HFT firms may not have been the cause of this crash, the way and the speed of their reaction has greatly amplified it*. Like 'dark trading', still nowadays, HFT is much more relevant—in terms of high-frequency trades over total ones—in the USA than in Europe, where it nonetheless represents a growing phenomenon. Because of such upward trend, many regulators feared that it might have become a threat to the efficiency of price formation, because of distorted incentives to market participants. A similar concern was about OTC transactions, especially those in derivative instruments, due to the well-known systemic stability issues that the GFC had dismally exposed.

(B) **Frictions in accessibility to markets and the trouble for SMEs**

The common belief of European markets often tells that 'small is good', mainly referring to business profitability. Notwithstanding the fact that size is a harshly debated issue and its association with a firm's results is often unclear, SMEs may actually hold some competitive advantages over larger companies, which have to deal with a complex organisation and, thus, are more likely to be sclerotic and inefficient. When the talk is turned to the financial structure, however, conclusions are strikingly different. In fact, it is neither a surprise nor a recent discovery that SMEs face greater trouble in raising external capital, mainly because of the higher impact of fixed transaction costs, of which compliance ones represent a significant share, along with the lower bargaining power vis-à-vis the involved counterparties (investors, investment banks serving as coordinators and/or underwriters, and so on).

As was easily forecastable, the credit crunch experienced during the GFC hit SMEs much more severely than larger companies. The ad hoc platforms set up in certain jurisdictions to enhance the funding of smaller entities did not manage to counter the very negative trend. According to the Commission, this mainly occurred because of national rules being too different one another and, thus, wide arbitrage opportunities marring otherwise useful provisions. Therefore, further European harmonisation was reasonably desirable, along with greater interconnectedness between markets whereby the instruments issued by SMEs (mainly shares) are listed. In particular, the latter objective could have been reached by allowing those securities traded on an MTF to be automatically traded on another one. This was theoretically possible given the repeal of the so-called 'concentration rule', but MiFID I had not envisaged it. Finally, the Commission denounced the *disproportionate costs* charged on SMEs to get listed. This plainly contributed to an inefficient, suboptimal allocation of capital, as often listed companies were not representative of the universe of firms and, thus, of investment opportunities. instead, they generally reflected the *premium* segment only, which is not necessarily the best one from the investors' standpoint (at least in the short term).

As we have seen, however, the Package more extensively focusses on the functioning of trading venues. In particular, Recital 13[D] tackles the emergence of new exchange platforms, as the EU legislator was interested in creating *a coherent and risk-sensitive framework* as of execution-only arrangements, along with the recognition of *a new generation of organised trading systems alongside regulated markets*, to be treated carefully not to allow any regulatory arbitrage. The 'consistency' of the regulatory framework is advocated, also, in Recital 6^R, where a seminal principle is stated: *any trading in financial instrument is carried out as far as possible on organised venues*, which should therefore be *properly regulated*. In order to deliver on that, Recital 7^R circumscribes the scope of the Package to exclude certain operations from being carried out in a manner which would be opposed to the investor-protective purposes of the new legislation. This is the case of dealing on own account—that is, exchange platforms executing orders against proprietary capital—for both market operators (on RMs) and investment firms (on MTFs).

Under MiFID II, those markets where SMEs can issue financial instruments to collect monetary resources are MTFs and known as *SME growth markets*. However, asking to be registered as such is just elective (Recital 134^D), considering that an obligation might unintendedly yield negative consequences onto the market operator. Of course, there are precise requirements to be fulfilled in order to get the abovementioned registration (Recital 135^D): first, *at least 50% of the issuers whose financial instruments are traded on a SME growth market should be SMEs*, though such threshold *should be implemented in a flexible way*: that is, a "grace period" should be allowed to the operator in the case the condition be temporarily violated (deregistration should not be immediate) and, also, the registration should not be refused if the applicant *has a reasonable prospect of meeting the 50% criterion from the subsequent year*. In general, MiFID II provisions are plainly applicable to SME growth markets, as this is intended as a way to lift their visibility and, thus, improve their efficiency. The EU legislator claims that further law-making should make these exchanges more appealing to investors, so that SMEs—being subject to smaller regulatory burdens—will have an incentive to recur to markets for their funding purposes. In order to achieve such liberalising objective, *sufficient flexibility* is necessary: in fact, these markets should not to be segregated on a national basis, but rather work all across the EU. This would also help reaching an optimising balance in the trade-off between higher investor protection and softer regulation (Recital 133^D).

(C) **Transparency: the hardest lesson from the GFC**

In a globalised world, no one dares to downplay the importance of information, from which everything descends: technological progress, for instance, is often driven by the need to overcome barriers in communication, as undoubtedly occurred in the financial industry. Therefore, reducing asymmetries—in other words, increasing transparency—is pivotal to ensuring an orderly functioning of markets. In fact, an enhanced ability to take financially sound decisions yields positive spill-overs onto systemic stability, as it results in better capital allocation. However, notwithstanding the innumerable improvements that had occurred to transparency thanks to technical and infrastructural advancements, the GFC showed that the status quo was far from flawless (*in both the equities and non-equities markets*, stated the Commission).

By looking at MiFIR, we may notice that the EU legislator explicitly mentions *harmful socioeconomic effects* (Recital 1^R) among the possible spill-overs of lacking transparency in financial markets. In light of this, the voice for a 'single rulebook' becomes even stronger than before. However, current threats are not only macroeconomic distress and legal uncertainty: although multiple parties had called for stricter regulation as a response to misconduct-based systemic turmoil, Recital 3^R advocates *less regulatory complexity* as a goal worth pursuing for the sake of efficiency and competition in trading. In fact, regulatory complexity had revealed not to be a valid countermeasure against some phenomena which had marred financial markets and, thus, magnified the GFC.

First of all, the spread of dark pools and BCNs was a major blow to transparency: when the Commission released its *Impact Assessment*, this kind of trading accounted for roughly 7% in the EEA as a whole. Coupled with 38% represented by OTC transactions, it summed up to an astonishing 45% of exchanges done without abiding by basic transparency requirements. While this was welcome by market participants, which had to devote less resources to the abidance by strict pre-trade requirements, investors started complaining, as lacking information was often associated with burdensome costs. Furthermore, even in "classical" trading venues where transparency obligations have always been in place, information did not flow as plainly as a well-functioning system would have required. In fact, while equities had been harmonised by MiFID I, non-equity instruments had not, and remained subject to domestic rules, usually very different one another. Moreover, these latter instruments are more commonly traded in a 'bilateral' way—that is, orders directly flow between a counterparty and a 'dealer'—rather than in a 'multilateral' one, which is instead more akin to equity ones. This mainly occurs in primary markets, whereas secondary ones are much less developed: as a consequence of these features, while counterparty risk is reduced thanks to the presence of dealers, settlement one gets increased. Hence, for the purpose of mitigating it, transparency surges to an even greater role.

The EU legislator caught such asymmetries, and attempted removing them, by providing a detailed comprehensive framework on pre- and post-trade transparency requirements for both equity and non-equity securities. Anyway, such a heavy regulatory intervention was pursued with a "moderate" approach, not to impose excessive burdens on market participants: that is, by means of waivers and deferrals. While calibrating the an and the quando of reporting information in accordance with the subjects and the instruments involved in the transaction, the EU legislator has endeavoured to thoroughly discipline the quomodo. This was done to overcome those many concerns regarding the quality of information, raised following MiFID I. Both 'consolidation' (i.e. the collection on an aggregate basis) and 'dissemination (to the public of investors) have been significantly enhanced by the Package, which has tackled the issue of transparency in financial markets far more seriously than other pieces of legislation (either at a EU or a domestic level). The response to the flaws exposed by the GFC might have been disproportionate, yet its utmost urgency could not have been ignored.

(D) The efficacy of supervision

Although they have historically been among the first to be established, commodity markets had started representing a source of serious concern to regulators, mainly because of their volatility. In fact, the public of investors interested in commodities had significantly changed over time, due to financialization itself. Once, it was largely made by subjects with "commercial" purposes, willing to acquire those materials to conduct their business; as time passed, however, the presence of "professional" traders—acting as "pure" financial investors—had significantly increased. Moreover, argued the Commission, the strong interaction between different commodity markets called for a reinforced cooperation between supervisors, including physical ones (i.e. those charged with setting quality standards to traded materials).

When the GFC broke out, commodity markets were largely unregulated, yet this is much less surprising if we think of the fact that most of such transactions occur by means of derivatives. However, the EU legislator's concerns were not exclusively referred to the functioning of markets, but to the operations carried out by players as well. Although once was common opinion among regulators that these subjects did not pose any relevant systemic risks, regardless of them being "commercial" or "specialist" investors, this was no more the case during the GFC: exemptions had gone too far. Of course, re-regulation has its dark sides, as the Commission acknowledged that—for instance—agricultural firms active in the oil market, though performing a non-core activity by trading in those commodities, actually provided an investment service which was essential to their stakeholders (e.g., when provided by cooperative firms on behalf of their farmers), especially for hedging purposes. As we can see, the debate could easily shift onto the raison d'être of derivatives as financial instruments, because of their historical origin as the assets underlying many contracts of this kind.

Recital 9 of the Directive marks a noteworthy difference from the previous approach: in respect of commodity derivatives is stated that *those contracts being financial instruments, financial markets law requirements would apply from the onset*. A logical follow-up of the EU legislator's intent is encompassed by Recital 10, where—in the light of a new kind of trading venues, namely OTFs, being introduced—is highlighted that *the limitation of the scope concerning commodity derivatives traded on an OTF and physically settled* should be reduced *to avoid a loophole that may lead to a regulatory arbitrage*. This would be secured by means of an accurate definition of what is a physical settlement, i.e. *the creation of an enforceable and binding obligation to physically deliver, which cannot be unwound and with no right to cash settle or offset transactions*', though relevant waivers are allowed (*in case of force majeure, default or other bona fide inability to perform*).

At the GFC outbreak, emission allowances were another type of instrument whose discipline—though some relevant regulation was already in place—was in urgent need of an update. They had been "created" by means of Directive 2003/87/EC, best known as *EU Emissions Trading Scheme* (EU ETS), implemented starting from 2005; yet their categorisation had remained ambiguous and they could have been regarded as either financial instruments or physical commodities. MiFID I had already covered these instruments, but actually in a partial, inconsistent manner: in fact, its provisions did not apply to secondary trading of spot emission allowances but did apply to every primary segment, including derivatives (in particular, futures). The result was that different kinds of allocation—whether 'free' or via an auction—took place in different segments of the same market. Since this was a new-born, rising one, such regulatory confusion was particularly concerning and—as acknowledged by the Commission—exacerbated the risk of market abuse, leaving the door open to price manipulation or other misconduct.

Along with emission allowances and derivatives, Recital 8^{R} lists bonds and structured finance products as the securities that can be traded on OTFs. There is a largely understandable rationale behind the enactment of stricter rules on the abovementioned instruments, a fortiori in the aftermath of the GFC. In Recital 11^{D}—with a reprise in Recital 45^{R}—is acknowledged that *a range of fraudulent practices have occurred in spot secondary markets in emission allowances (EUAs) which could undermine trust in the emissions trading scheme*. This raised the concern that, *in order to reinforce the integrity and safeguard the efficient functioning of those markets, including comprehensive supervision of trading activity*, the measures provided for by EU ETS Directive should be complemented *by bringing emission allowances fully into the scope* of the forthcoming Package.

In fact, such market segment had raised several concerns during the GFC. Recital 29^{D} denounces that some recipients of EU ETS legislation (e.g., local energy utilities) had *bundle[d] and outsource[d] their trading activities for hedging commercial risks to non-consolidated subsidiaries*. However, these latter ones did not provide any proper investment service (no any other service at all) and, thus, in abidance by the principle of substance prevailing over form in commercial law, have been excluded from the scope of MiFID II. While this apparently creates room for regulatory arbitrage (two connected firms are de facto subjected to diverging disciplines), it should be regarded as the enactment of a sharp separation between financial companies performing investment activities, on the one hand, and different entities not engaged in such business, given that the GFC had shown how pernicious—from a systemic stability standpoint—were the connections between these two types of firms.

As of transaction reporting, the EU legislator had to consider the interaction between MiFID I and the *Market Abuse Directive* (MAD, No. 2003/6/EC): in fact, further legislation on that issue—namely, the MAD II/MAR package—would have been passed in 2014, in a timely connection with MiFID II and MiFIR. Results obtained at that time were not satisfactory at all, as the Commission claimed that *the existing reporting requirements fail[ed] to provide competent authorities with a full view of the market, because their scope is [was] too narrow*. In particular, the degree of harmonisation was too low to ensure the effectiveness of transaction reporting for the sake of market integrity. The Package intervened on this subject with all its "fire power" by reshaping the whole of market infrastructure and, in particular, pre-and post-trading industry. It is even more significant that such wide reform has been encompassed mainly by MiFIR, as this ensures greater harmonisation and a more effective implementation of the novelties.

Of course, this objective cannot be pursued without strengthening the action pursued by regulators, another topic addressed by the Regulation more extensively than the Directive. On this issue, the path undertaken by the EU legislator has followed a trail which had already been blazed throughout previous years, when the supervisory architecture had been reshaped (that is, starting from Lamfalussy and Wright 2001). In turn, this had been a follow-up on the objectives set forth in the Maastricht Treaty to achieve the economic and monetary union. Domestic authorities are still nowadays empowered with very different tasks, and a greater harmonisation is timidly taking place, as a result of the "nudge" included in the Package. At that time, when the GFC outbreak exposed many cases of *mala gestio*, the vast majority of domestic authorities still had no power to directly impose sanctions onto supervised non-bank financial entities. Such inconsistency across the Union was seen as a serious blow to the functioning of the Single Market, especially because this determines higher compliance costs for those firms engaged in cross-border operations.

Also, MiFID I had failed to harmonise other fundamental activities performed by investment firms: an example is represented by the underwriting and placing of securities, now encompassed within the scope of MiFID II. Finally, the Commission wished that the forthcoming reform could trigger a 'proportional' supervisory action—that is, with a lighter touch by a more powerful regulator—and abide by the principle of subsidiarity, which values the reduction in the distance between the supervisor and the overseen subject. In particular, a regulatory action is deemed to be 'proportional' if it takes into account *the right balance of public interests at stake and the cost efficiency of the measure*; that is, if it is implemented by considering *the specificities of each asset class and possibly of each instrument*. This requires calibrating the requirements charged upon them, to accomplish a mission based upon three pillars: investor protection, the efficiency of markets, and the costs borne by the industry. Hence, the role of the new authorities—especially those endowed with micro-prudential duties—has been significantly strengthened. In fact, it is coessential to the advancement towards a level playing field disciplined via the 'single rulebook' in financial legislation. ESMA, in particular, has taken powers that it had never held before the enactment of the Package (especially in terms of product intervention).

(E) **Investor protection**

Some serious damage, occurred to many retail investors in the wake of the GFC, gave rise to the belief than MiFID I provisions on that issue—the first significant novelty following the *Investment Services Directive* (ISD, No. 1993/22/EEC), focussed on admission to trading—were substantially inadequate to ensure the desirable level of protection for the market's weakest parties. In particular, the Commission noted that some MiFID provisions were not charged on intermediaries which provided investment services at a national level exclusively: it warned that these exemptions could have represented an undue burden on certain investors, subject to less protection vis-à-vis the others. The distribution of financial products is, also, an issue which regulators are increasingly addressing, as a variety of new types of packages—satisfying different investors' needs—are nowadays on the market.

In particular, the GFC seems not to have weakened the favour toward products which unify features usually linked to various types of instruments, such as—for instance—banking and insurance ones. Moreover, there is growing interest toward securities which encompass even a portion of uncertainty, given by their payoffs being somehow marked-to-market. Instead, complex products have been spreading over time. Therefore, the EU legislator has intervened with various measures devoted to the category of Packaged Retail Investment and Insurance Products (PRIIPs), the latest ones being MiFID II and MiFIR as well as the *Insurance Distribution Directive* (IDD, No. 2016/97/EU). Recital 87[D] is devoted to *investments that involve contracts of insurance*. In this realm, levelling the playing field is the main concern, which the EU legislator claims to be achievable only by tightening regulation (something actually done with the passage of IDD). In the same Recital is also expressed the "wishful thinking" that further EU pieces of legislation about insurance intermediaries and undertakings *appropriately ensure similar investor needs and therefore raises similar investor protection challenges*. We might extend to supervision this call, addressed to lawmakers: hence, we may read that MiFID II wording—explicitly referred to the *conduct of business* issue—as the hope for closer cooperation between ESMA and EIOPA.

Within the residual category of 'complex' instruments—notwithstanding the narrow difference between 'instruments' and 'products'—structured deposits are among the most relevant ones. While left uncovered by MiFID I, they have been encompassed inside MiFID II. Recital 39[D] acknowledges that they *have emerged as a form of investment product* (this wording plainly evokes their 'complexity'), though being almost completely unregulated at that time: therefore, harmonisation—coupled with stronger investor protection—was absolutely needed. Anyway, apart from specific categories of products, the topic of the separation between issuing and distributing financial products, and to which extent the different stages of a product's lifetime should be regulated by supervisory authorities, are deeply rooted in the EU legislator's attitude.

The regulator was concerned, also, that even the provision of execution-only services might actually conceal larger risks to investors than what was assumed at that time, under MiFID I, for non-complex products. In that case, the appropriateness test—that is, the assessment of whether investing in a specific product is the best choice for a given, individual investor—was waived, and only the 'suitability' one—that is, a check of the consistency between the investor's profile and the type of product, without any regard to the contingent decision-making—was preliminarily mandated. The GFC reality, however, proved to be strikingly different from the "perfect world" envisaged by the MiFID I legislator, i.e. the one whereby there is a clear correspondence between an investor's awareness of his/her own knowledge of economic mechanisms (and his/her own financial conditions, too), on the one hand,

and his/her answers to the appropriateness and suitability tests, on the other. Unfortunately, various cases all over the world have proven this assumption to be distant from reality, though fully legitimate and—most importantly—consistent with the Western judicial tradition, where *ignorantia (legis) non excusat*.

Other than this "cultural" issue, the EU legislator had additional worries. First, after years of 'easy credit', leveraging up was a common practice even at a retail level, as many small investors used to get indebted to purchase financial investments, though mainly non-complex. Moreover, the classification of instruments into one of the two categories—where 'complex' is residual, thus having a wider extent and strengthening the degree of protection overall ensured in the financial system—needed a revision. In fact, the Commission had noted how stakes held in 'undertakings of collective investments in transferable securities' (UCITS), technically defined 'units' and labelled as 'non-complex', might actually hide the fact that the collective investment scheme holds risky assets in its portfolio. If this were the case, the intermediation by a subject which would otherwise be classified as 'professional'—namely, the investment company, which manages the fund—would not succeed in adequately reducing the risk borne by unitholders. Besides, the Commission reported that many retail investors had complained regarding the way in which their portfolios had been managed.

Investment advice is another service/activity that the Package has widely addressed, as a response to the many flaws come to the surface when the GFC resulted in a serious blow to many retail investors' wealth. In fact, these last ones had trusted some pieces of advice which, though based on bona fide assumptions, would have soon be overhauled by a sudden turnaround in market trends. In respect of this, the discipline of inducements was blamed to have been distortive, as it might have prompted advisors not to act *in the best interest of the clients*, to use MiFID II wording. In particular, the Commission acknowledged that disclosure of inducements could have been, actually, not as *clear and articulated* as it should have. In particular, coupling the existence of inducements with a declaredly 'independent' advice could reasonably have led to suboptimal choices, de facto annihilating the benefits yielded to investors by independence. Finally, even independence per se was a source of trouble, mainly from a transparency standpoint, as seminal information was consistently missed when disclosing trading data. Of course, this might impair price formation, with a series of pernicious waterfall consequences to investors. The link between transaction reporting, on the one hand, and investor protection, on the other, is often remarked throughout the Package provisions devoted to transparency issues.

Another potential threat to competition and investors' wealth was represented by cross-selling practices, defined as the situation in which two or more financial services are bundled together in a package while the separate selling of at least one of them is not available (Recital 81^{D}). The arguments against such practices do not differ from those applying to markets for goods and non-financial services: by endowing the seller with market power, they drive *surplus* away from the buyer. In Recital 81^{D}, the European legislator warns that—although they are *a common strategy for retail financial service providers throughout the Union* and might eventually turn out being beneficial—their consideration of the client's actual interest could be insufficient; hence, they might yield negative spill-overs onto competition and the investors' *ability to make informed choices*. Besides, though less risky than "pure" cross-selling, those cases in which at least one of the bundled products can be purchased separately might yield the same negative effects on both competition and customers; yet, since they *leave choice to the client*, they are less alarming from a regulatory standpoint.

Another relevant issue for investor protection purposes is that of position limits to trading. They are envisaged for a wide range of instruments; in particular, they apply to the riskiest ones, such as derivatives. By pursuing this objective in conjunction with market efficiency, in Recital 130[D] is underlined that *the methodology used for calculation of position limits should not create barriers to the development of new commodity derivatives*'; but, equally importantly, *the development of new commodity derivatives cannot be used to circumvent the position limits regime* (ESMA is in charge of preventing circumventions from happening).

Other important changes recognised by MiFID II deal with 'alternative investment fund managers' (AIFMs), which represent the main subject of Directive 2011/61/EU (best known as AIFMD). In fact, beyond collectively managing alternative investment funds, the Member States—pursuant to the abovementioned piece of legislation—may allow AIFMs to provide multiple different services. Since all the latter are harmonised at a EU level, the principle of mutual recognition does not encounter any obstacles to working fully; therefore, AIFMs authorised by their home competent authority do not have to submit any additional requests in order to be authorised to provide the abovementioned services. However, in order to truly levelling the playing field and removing any obstacles to the cross-border provision of services, such mutual recognition might be not enough. In Recital 162[D], therefore, the EU legislator explicitly states its commitment toward removing those provisions mandating AIFMs to comply with national rules in the host countries where they are willing to operate (with or without *the establishment of a separate legal entity*), in clear abidance by the principles encompassed by the fundamental EU Treaties.

(F) Financial firms' individual requirements and algorithmic/high-frequency trading

The EU legislator was highly aware that many financial entities had acted, for a very long time, without obeying very basic rules of self-discipline, dictated by common sense in advance of regulation. The GFC had spared no area of management and business organisation; therefore, significant amendments were required as of compliance, risk management, and internal audit, especially in dealing with new products and services whose actual risk might be not fully known before it gets dismally exposed (for instance, this occurred to derivatives originated by debt securitisations). Therefore, by helping financial firms developing sounder policies, the EU legislator would have avoided *detrimental practices toward clients*.

As we have discussed above, one of the most urgent concerns for the EU legislator was represented by algorithmic and high-frequency trading (the latter being a subset of the former), which are strictly connected with the sound and prudent management of financial firms and, thus, investor protection. Recital 59^{D} plainly acknowledges that an increasing number of transactions are executed without any human intervention, merely in a computerised manner. Hence, an update in regulation had become absolutely undelayable: in fact, stated Recital 62^{D}, the main systemic threat was represented by *the risk of the overloading of the systems of trading venues due to large volumes of orders, but also risks in algorithmic trading generating duplicative or erroneous orders or otherwise malfunctioning in a way that may create a disorderly market*, or even by *algorithmic trading systems overreacting to other market events*, with the result of higher volatility in the case of a *pre-existing market problem*. In addition to this, as highlighted still in Recital 62^{D}, HFT *may also, because of the information advantage provided to high-frequency traders, prompt investors to choose to execute trades in venues where they can avoid interaction with high-frequency traders*. This is the reason why in the same Recital is advocated *particular regulatory scrutiny* to counter such risks, even overriding the case in which, to escape from the scrutiny, high-frequency traders deal on own account.

Recital 59^{D} clarifies that *the use of algorithms in post-trade processing of executing transactions does not constitute algorithmic trading*. Leaving this apart, the main concern is about discerning the cases where algorithmic trading is used to pursue a market-making function and where it is not, having regard to the relevance of such continued trading as a proportion of *the trading venue's trading hours* and, at the same time, *taking into account the liquidity, scale and nature of the specific market and the characteristics of the financial instrument traded*. Secondary EU legislation—namely, some Regulatory Technical Standards (RTSs)—is charged with detailing the issue of such *self-assessment* to be executed by trading venues, which holds a pivotal meaning for regulatory purposes.

A feature of HFT—one that actually makes it possible and, also, has triggered the evolution in business models over time—is the *close physical proximity* between market participants and the *matching engine* (Recital 62^{D}). Since this is extremely relevant *in order to ensure orderly and fair trading conditions*, the European legislator is particularly concerned about trading venues providing *such co-location services on a non-discriminatory, fair and transparent basis*. This not only helps levelling the playing field: in fact, a decent degree of fair competition yields positive spill-overs onto the functioning of the whole of the financial system, in terms of *wider participation (…), increased liquidity, narrower spreads, reduced short term volatility and the means to obtain better execution of orders for clients*.

References

Ackermann, J. (2008). The subprime crisis and its consequences. *Journal of Financial Stability, 4* (4), 329–337.

Asquini, A. (1959). *I battelli del Reno*. Milano: Giuffrè.

Bogle, J. C. (2008). Black Monday and black swans. *Financial Analysts Journal, 64,* 30–40.

Bastiat, F. (1850). *Which is seen, and that which is not seen* [original French: *Ce qu'on voit et ce qu'on ne voit pas*]. Translated by Patrick James Stirling.

Black, S. E., & Strahan, P. E. (2001). The division of spoils: Rent-sharing and discrimination in a regulated industry. *American Economic Review, 91*(4), 814–831.

Borio, C., & Disyatat, P. (2011). *Global Imbalances and the Financial Crisis: Link or no link?* BIS Working Paper No. 346.

Cabral, R. (2013). A perspective on the symptoms and causes of the financial crisis. *Journal of Banking & Finance, 37*(1), 103–117.

Caporale, G. M., & Kontonikas, A. (2009). The Euro and inflation uncertainty in the European Monetary Union. *Journal of International Money and finance, 28*(6), 954–971.

Committee of European Banking Supervisors, *First part of CEBS's technical advice to the European Commission on liquidity risk management: Survey of the current regulatory frameworks adopted by the EEA regulators,* 15 August 2007.

Committee of Wise Men on the Regulation of European Securities Markets, Lamfalussy, A., & Wright, D. (2001). *Final report of the Committee of Wise Men on the regulation of European Securities Markets.*

Demirgüç-Kunt, A., & Servén, L. (2009). *Are all the sacred cows dead? Implications of the financial crisis for macro and financial policies.* The World Bank.

Diamond, D. W., & Rajan, R. G. (2009). The credit crisis: Conjectures about causes and remedies. *American Economic Review, 99*(2), 606–610.

Dyck, A., Volchkova, N., & Zingales, L. (2008). The corporate governance role of the media: Evidence from Russia. *The Journal of Finance, 63*(3), 1093–1135.

European Commission, *Impact assessment accompanying the Proposal for a Directive of the European Parliament and of the Council on Markets in financial instruments [Recast] and the Proposal for a Regulation of the European Parliament and of the Council on Markets in financial instruments.* SEC (2011) 1226 final, Commission Staff Working Paper.

European Systemic Risk Board, *Recommendation of 18 June 2014 on guidance for setting countercyclical buffer rates* (ESRB/2014/1).

Ferguson, N. (2018). *The square and the tower: Networks and power, from the freemasons to Facebook.* London: Penguin.

Feinman, J. N. (1993). Reserve requirements: History, current practice, and potential reform. *Federal Reserve Bulletin, 79,* 569.

Foote, C. L., Gerardi, K., & Willen, P. (2008). *Negative equity and foreclosure: Theory and evidence.*

Friedman, M. (1962). *Capitalism and freedom: With the assistance of Rose D. Friedman.* University of Chicago Press.

Fukuyama, F. (2016). American political decay or renewal: The meaning of the 2016 election. *Foreign Affairs, 95,* 58.

Gennaioli, N., & Shleifer, A. (2010). What comes to mind. *The Quarterly Journal of Economics, 125*(4), 1399–1433.

González-Cabanillas, L., & Ruscher, E. (2008). *The Great Moderation in the euro area: What role have macroeconomic policies played?* (No. 331). Directorate General Economic and Financial Affairs (DG ECFIN), European Commission.

Gordon, J. S. (2000). *The great game: The emergence of Wall Street as a world power: 1653–2000.* New York: Scribner.

Jagannathan, R., Kapoor, M., & Schaumburg, E. (2013). Causes of the great recession of 2007–2009: The financial crisis was the symptom not the disease! *Journal of Financial Intermediation, 22*(1), 4–29.

Jayaratne, J., & Strahan, P. E. (1996). The finance-growth nexus: Evidence from bank branch deregulation. *The Quarterly Journal of Economics, 111*(3), 639–670.

Jayaratne, J., & Strahan, P. E. (1998). Entry restrictions, industry evolution, and dynamic efficiency: Evidence from commercial banking. *The Journal of Law and Economics, 41*(1), 239–274.

Keynes, J. M. (1936). *The general theory of employment, interest and money*. London: Palgrave Macmillan.
King, M. (2016). *The end of alchemy*. London: Little Brown.
Kim, T., Koo, B., & Park, M. (2013). Role of financial regulation and innovation in the financial crisis. *Journal of Financial stability, 9*(4), 662–672.
Lestano, L., Jacobs, J., & Kuper, G. (2003). *Indicators of financial crises do work! An early-warning system for six Asian countries*. CCSO Working Paper 2003/13, University of Groningen, Netherlands.
Levine, R. (2002). *Bank-based or market-based financial systems: which is better?* (No. w9138). National Bureau of Economic Research.
Mitchell Waldrop, M. (1987). Computers amplify Black Monday. *Science, 238*(4827), 602–604.
Moshirian, F. (2011). The global financial crisis and the evolution of markets, institutions and regulation. *Journal of Banking & Finance, 35*(3), 502–511.
Obstfeld, M., & Taylor, A. (2004). *Global capital markets: Integration, crisis and growth*. Cambridge: Cambridge University Press.
Onado, M. (2017). *Alla ricerca della banca perduta*. Il Mulino.
Palumbo, M. G., & Parker, J. A. (2009). The integrated financial and real system of national accounts for the United States: does it presage the financial crisis? *American Economic Review, 99*(2), 80–86.
Rajan, R. G. (2006). Has finance made the world riskier? *European Financial Management, 12*(4), 499–533.
Rochet, J.-C. (2010). The future of banking regulation. In M. Dewatripont, J.-C. Rochet, & J. Tirole (Eds.), *Balancing the banks: Global lessons from the financial crisis*. Princeton, NJ: Princeton University Press.
Saunders, A., Strock, E., & Travlos, N. G. (1990). Ownership structure, deregulation, and bank risk taking. *The Journal of Finance, 45*(2), 643–654.
Scott, H. S. (2010). Reducing systemic risk through the reform of capital regulation. *Journal of International Economic Law, 13*(3), 763–778.
Shin, H.-S. (2011). Global banking glut and loan risk premium. In: Mundell-Fleming (Lecture), *12th Jacques Polak Annual Research Conference*, International Monetary Fund, Washington, DC.
Shleifer, A., & Vishny, R. (1998). *The grabbing hand*. Cambridge, MS: Harvard University Press.
Turner, A. (2017). *Between debt and the devil: Money, credit, and fixing global finance*. Princeton, NJ: Princeton University Press.

Chapter 3
Relevant Changes from MiFID I

Abstract The chapter highlights how MiFID II differs from MiFID I, with regard to trading venues, instruments and entities affected by the new legislation, as well as the changes to the supervisory architecture. This is done by describing the legislative path undertaken and explaining the three-pillar content addressed by the Package (product governance, product intervention, rules governing the interaction between intermediaries and clients). We investigate how said EU legislation deals with specific issues, highlighting which rules are applicable to certain recipients and which are not, with a view to the issues of practical enforcement. In particular, the latter is addressed by explaining the rationale of including certain rules into the Directive rather than the Regulation, or vice versa. Moreover, we focus on the provisions entailing a close cooperation between different supervisory authorities. Finally, we discuss corporate governance and risk management issues, as well as those dealing with investor protection and transparency toward clients, which are highly significant in order to ensure an efficient implementation of the principles inspiring the Package.

3.1 How the Package Approaches Regulatory Issues

According to Di Noia (2017), the goals of the Package may be divided into (a) product governance, (b) product intervention, (c) rules governing the interaction between intermediaries and the clientele.

The difference between product ‘governance’ and ‘intervention’ may roughly be spotted by looking at the meaning of the two words. Although they both contribute to shaping the current supervisory framework, the former is more (but not completely) in line with the ‘prudential’ approach to overseeing financial services and activities. Conversely, the latter might somehow be viewed as a step backwards, stemmed from the turbulences of the crisis: it is much closer to the old view that empowered regulators with the duty, rather than the faculty, to enact direct measures aimed at healing distortions in the market and preserving systemic stability.

M. Comana et al., *The MiFID II Framework*,
https://doi.org/10.1007/978-3-030-12504-2_3

As we read in the wording of the Directive, however, product governance has been practically interpreted in a more "interventionist" fashion than one could have expected. Di Noia (2017) noted that the provision disciplining product governance par excellence—that is, Recital 71^{D}—designs a framework where the lifecycle of the product is regulated in its entirety. It reflects a 'cradle-to-grave' approach which in fact has been transferred onto the investor worth protecting, as if the Package had been introduced for "welfare" purposes in respect of a category conceived as a "weak", endangered one.

In Recital 71^{D}, it might be read the prescription that the Member States not only ensure that investment firms act in accordance with the best interests of their clients and comply with what is provided for by the Directive. Also, those entities must *establish and review effective policies and arrangements to identify the category of clients to whom products and services are to be provided.* More in detail, the reference is to both the "manufacturers" and the "distributors" of the products, such that is possible to *meet the needs of an identified target market of end clients within the relevant category of clients.* Moreover, a periodic review of these subjective characteristics of the demand side, as well as the performance of marketed products, is invoked.

To a careful reader, the wording of Recital 71^{D} might seem to have been designed in order to explicitly establish a comparison between the provision of investment services to retail clients, on the one hand, and consumption as a whole, based on the sale and purchase of non-financial products, on the other. In fact, consumer-protective discipline often unfolds in a remarkable *corpus*, especially in civil-law countries with a French-like juridical framework. First, the pronoun *whom* is generally referred to physical persons, rather than entities, albeit there are other cases where such "personification" is made in respect of firms: e.g., as for the best execution provisions contained in Article 27, par. 6. Second, the verbs *manufacture* and *distribute* are much more akin to describing the lifecycle of a material good rather than that of a financial product. In this case, these two clues—evaluated in light of the goals of the Package—may well be regarded as a proof.

Specific attention is due in the case the manufacturer and the distributor do not coincide (of course, nothing a priori prevents the two from being the same) and, thus, a third-party product is offered or recommended. However, this is explicitly labelled as something different from the 'suitability' and 'appropriateness' tests, which address the personal 'needs, characteristics and objectives' of investors. Hence, as we may notice, this wide-ranging principle does not discern between the three typical categories of investors—namely, retail clients, professional clients and eligible counterparties—circumscribed by MiFID I. As a result of such approach, the investor-protective measures that have to be mandatorily put in place are actually made of a double layer: one is related to the appropriateness and suitability —in respect of the end client—of the service itself; the other applies whichever product and type of investor be concerned, on the basis of a close correspondence between the product and its target market.

Anyway, this does not exhaust product governance. Additional provisions apply to the management body of the intermediary by charging obligations on the supply side, in order for the demand one to be protected. This is clearly stated in Article 9^{D}, pursuant to which the abovementioned body *defines, oversees and is accountable for the implementation of the governance arrangements that ensure efficient and prudent management of the investment firm.* The EU legislator has carefully opted not for leaving this provision so generic, but rather providing some details: the above-stated goal has to be pursued by the twofold means of *the segregation of duties in the investment firm and the prevention of conflicts of interest.*

This is likely to yield positive spill-overs not only onto the company's financial conditions but also—and most importantly—onto 'the integrity of the market' and 'the interest of clients'. This double reference to the broader objectives set forth by the Package clears away any doubt on whether these requirements applying to the management are subordinated to those charged on the firm as a provider (performer) of investment services (activities). The answer is negative, as the two "declinations" of product governance, though rooted one in the Recitals and the other in the Directive itself, are absolutely on the same level; hence, they must be pursued with equal commitment.

Product intervention is per se a concept worth detailing in legislation, lest there would exist some margins for supervisory authorities to act arbitrarily. As a result, the long-standing question *Quis custodiet custodes?*—which no regulatory environment could avoid dealing with—would remain unanswered. Therefore, the provisions contained in the Package itself define the "rules of engagement" of this regulatory reaction against the harmful consequences of the crisis. In Article 42^{R}—headed *Product intervention by competent authorities*—some essential elements are laid down: pursuant to it, relevant authorities in any EU country may restrict *the marketing, distribution or sale (...) of certain financial instruments (...) in or from that Member State.* The scope of application is potentially wide, yet specific conditions must be met: they range from the duty to consult other authorities to the avoidance of negative unintended effects, from the inadequacy of existing supervision to the attention not to act in a discriminatory manner. More specifically, intervention is allowed if:

(a) there are 'orderly functioning and integrity' or 'stability' concerns regarding various financial instruments—including structured deposits, which were not covered by MiFID I—or 'detrimental effect on the price formation mechanism' in markets for those assets underlying a derivative contract;
(b) some "regulatory failures" have occurred in other Member States, such that the 'supervision or enforcement of existing requirements' does not manage to properly address the issue;
(c) 'the action is proportionate' in light of a careful cost-benefit analysis;
(d) foreign EU competent authorities which may be 'significantly affected by the action' have been consulted;
(e) no 'discriminatory effect on services or activities provided from another Member State' arises;
(f) in the case an agricultural derivative be concerned, the oversight bodies in charge of the physical agricultural markets *de quo* have been consulted.

Finally, when looking at the innovations brought by the Package, we should not avoid seeing how a remarkable harmonising effort has been carried out. For instance, the so-called 'self-placement' of financial products by the companies "manufacturing" them had been a source of great debate all across Europe. In fact, it was not clear whether it could have been classified as an investment service or not. Such question has been answered by MiFID II, whereby the execution of orders is treated uniformly without any discernment based upon the issuer's identity.

This choice should probably be attributed to the legislator's intent of widening the scope of application of the extremely relevant rules about 'best execution'—i.e. a general principle which has always represented one of the strongholds of MiFID legislation—and the placement of orders, either under a firm commitment obligation or without it (both types are included within the range of investment services). For instance, in Italy, where many intermediaries are used to distributing to the clientele their own products, Article 25-bis of the code on financial intermediation (TUF) had already solved the previous uncertainty by encompassing the self-placement into the category of investment services, thus anticipating what would have been definitely ruled in MiFID II. In particular, is explicitly stated that some preceding provisions apply to a previously-defined set of instruments in the case they are 'issued by banks', too. Such a restrictive choice, theoretically excluding intermediaries other than credit institutions, might reasonably be questioned. However, this ostensible flaw should be related to the specificity of the Italian financial system, where (commercial) banking is largely prevalent. The rationale followed in other EU Member States is similar, as the underlying structure of the financial system is often the main driver behind the legislator's choice.

The relevance of best execution—that we are going to discuss—may well be regarded as the trait d'union between the two souls of the Package, namely investor protection and the organisation and functioning of markets. The idea of executing transactions in the best interest of the client was one of the most powerful innovations carried by MiFID I. It may be read in Recital 91^{D} (reprised from Recital 33 of MiFID I), where is stated that firms must *execute client orders on terms that are most favourable to the client*, in the case the counterparties be bound either by a contract or an agency relationship. With a view to enacting such principle, which prescribes to take *all reasonable steps to obtain the best possible result for its clients taking into account the execution factors*, some transparency rules are set forth by the Directive: in Article 27^{D}, par. 6, is stated that—in abidance by the ad hoc requirements laid down by the Member States—investment firms *summarise and make public on an annual basis, for each class of financial instruments, the top five execution venues in terms of trading volumes where they executed client orders in the preceding year and information on the quality of execution obtained.*

Other MiFID II provisions lato sensu aimed at enhancing the best execution of orders may be identified with those disciplining the pivotal issue of conflicts of interest, which firms are called to 'prevent or manage'. Again, such a relevant obligation should be particularly wide-ranging in order to be effective; hence, the legislator has stated that it applies *in the course of providing any investment and ancillary services, or combinations thereof, including those caused by the receipt of inducements from third parties or by the investment firm's own remuneration and other incentive structures*. These provisions have not changed from MiFID I to MiFID II. Anyway, second-level regulation is strongly empowered with the duty to determine how conflicts of interest may be concretely addressed. Some particularly remarkable rules—developed by ESMA, and implemented by the Commission in its delegated acts—are those contained in the *Technical advices* published on 19 December 2014. In it, the management of risks potentially arising to the client, the organisational provisioning to be put in place, the "physical separation" between analysts and different personnel within investment firms (so-called 'Chinese walls'), as well as the extension of conflict-of-interest rules to marketing communications, are dealt with.

In relation to conflicts of interest, inducements and independent advisory—*rectius*, 'advisory performed on an independent basis'—are really critical. Pursuant to Article 24^{D}, par. 2, in order for that label to apply, advisory must be directed to a wide range of instruments, with a sufficient degree of diversification: that is, it must not be circumscribed to the products issued by the firm exclusively, nor exclusively take into account those issued by *entities having close links with the investment firm or any other legal or economic relationships, such as contractual relationships* in a way that would seriously diminish the degree of independence.

Inducements received *from third parties or by the investment firm's own remuneration and other incentive structures* must be thoroughly managed in order to prevent conflicts of interest from arising, as they might be one of the most significant means by which information asymmetries are transferred onto market distortions: in fact, any incentive—either of monetary or non-monetary nature—given to the firm is likely to drive the recipient's effort away from acting in the client's best interest. Pursuant to the rules proposed by ESMA and adopted by the Commissions, inducements are forbidden if they do not bring any benefits to the investor: if this is the case, no condition—e.g., the provision of an additional service, maybe on an ongoing basis—could ever legitimise the settlement of any incentives.

Finally, we should analyse the novelties brought by the Package into market infrastructure. In respect of algorithmic and high-frequency trading, new rules have been driven by "technical" needs of an up-to-date legislation. Previous legislation used to generalise and label as 'algorithmic' every automated trade; conversely, nowadays—in the wake of the Package and its related second-level regulation—the situation has been clarified. For instance, the cases in which automation is used to transmit orders to one or more trading venues, or to determine trading parameters, or for post-execution purposes, are excluded.

In Article 17^{D}, the systemic concerns raised by the GFC are explicitly addressed, as is required that algorithmic systems be 'resilient' and have 'sufficient capacity', with specific 'thresholds' and 'limits' being carried out, in order to *prevent the sending of erroneous orders or the systems otherwise functioning in a way that may create or contribute to a disorderly market*.

However, this does not exhaust the innovative extent of the Directive. Between MiFID I and II, in fact, the whole system of exchanges underwent a severe reshaping, trying to bridge the divide between the two opposite types: namely, informal, bilateral facilities, based upon the "direct" matching of the counterparties' mutual needs, on the one hand; "traditional" venues—such as regulated markets (RMs) and MTFs, introduced by MiFID I, on the other. In relation to the latter, "formality" and the multilateralism of exchange are among the most prominent characteristics. The first one is especially relevant in respect of the price formation process, which is subject to strict disclosure requirements.

As a result of such polarising realignment, whose most evident consequence was the increasing number of trades fleeing the latter and reaching the former, the European legislator conceived a new category of trading venues, somehow "median" between the two, showing features attributable to either: namely, the OTFs, whose operator (generally an investment firm) is not obliged—unlike the other types—to match the submitted orders. In other terms, it is allowed to act in a 'discretionary' way, something which cannot occur in other markets; moreover, it can trade against its own ('proprietary') capital, which is otherwise forbidden to other operators in order not to endanger the stability of the system, which would be at risk if the entity governing the infrastructure were exposed to the uncertainty of getting impaired. Furthermore, under MiFID II, some MTFs may even be registered as 'SME growth markets' and, thus, play a noticeable role in supporting the access of small and medium-sized enterprises to capital markets, a phenomenon which is still quite uncommon in many EEA countries.

Before moving to the issue of reporting, it should also be highlighted that systematic internalisers (SIs)—which, however, were not significantly reformed by MiFID II—play a seminal role in respect of the creation and maintenance of liquidity in a market. However, they cannot be classified as trading venues but rather treated as a counterparty (actually, they act *on an organised, frequent, systematic and subsequent basis*, outside trading venues). This reinforces the idea—largely prevalent in literature—that they should be regarded as counterparties, rather than trading venues. Besides, be aware of the fact that OTC transactions—which are not concluded on trading venues stricto sensu, of course—are not wholly excluded, for certain classes of them are actually mandated to abide by such clearing obligation pursuant to EMIR. With regard to SIs, Recital 17^{D} helps clarifying their subjectivity. Moreover, they should not be confused with the post-trade role of 'central counterparties' (CCPs), which are the entities presiding over the mandatory clearing set forth in MiFID II, as the absence of such obligation was blamed for having de facto favoured the global amplification of the GFC. In this sense, the obligation for trades to be centrally cleared was one of the most remarkable recommendations encompassed by the final statement at the G20 summit in Pittsburgh (2009), which prompted many legislators worldwide to act in order to address the systemic threats (potentially) hidden in derivatives markets.

Finally, MiFID II has codified the so-called 'data reporting services' (DRSs) and envisaged that entities might be authorised as providers of them (DRSPs). Such discipline is carefully laid down in Articles 64^{D}–66^{D}. While the previous Directive had substantially avoided dealing with such a detailed classification, the new legislation adds new categories on the so-called Trade Repositories (TRs), established by EMIR in relation to OTC derivatives (whose transactions, often deemed to be opaque, are extremely sensitive to information being reported, for the negative spill-overs of the rise of information asymmetries represent the greatest threat to those markets).There are multiple detailed rules governing this category; however, here we just mention the rough discernment between the entities authorised to publish reports—submitted by investment firms—regarding transactions that have already being concluded, namely under 'approved publication arrangements' (APAs) and '*approved reporting mechanisms' (ARMs), on the one hand; and those which collect the information (...) consolidate it into a continuous electronic data stream and make the information available to the public as close to real time as is technically possible, on a reasonable commercial basis*—that is, the Consolidated Tape Providers (CTPs)—on the other, with the 'collection' role being played in respect of either RMs, MTFs or OTFs.

3.2 Topics Addressed by MiFID II

The changes occurred in the method used to transact assets and monies are addressed by MiFID II through a reorganisation of the legislation on trading venues, which is now shaped in three main types, plus a fourth—namely, SIs—whose actual nature is highly debated.

1. Regulated Markets (RMs);
2. Multilateral trading facilities (MTFs);
3. Organised Trading Facilities' (OTFs).

The major differences among them can be found with regard to: the instruments that are allowed to be traded on them; the owner of facilities (a market operator properly said, or an investment firm); the non-discretion in the 'multilateral matching'; the possibility for traders to use their own capital. As well as MiFID I had introduced MTFs, MiFID II created OTFs: they are thought for non-equity instruments, can be owned by an investment firm, are not subject to any non-discretion obligations and their traders cannot use their own capital for transactions. However, this last provision seems to be quite controversial and—due to a de facto restriction in the resources that can be mobilised in exchanges—has raised concerns about a theoretical liquidity shortage affecting the functioning of OTFs.

Furthermore, MiFID II introduces a trading obligation for shares and *derivatives which are eligible for clearing under the European Markets Infrastructure Regulation [EMIR] and are sufficiently liquid*. Since OTFs may give rise to liquidity concerns, MiFIR *ensures that investment firms operating an internal matching system which executes client orders in shares, depositary receipts, exchange-traded funds, certificates and other similar financial instruments on a multilateral basis have to be authorised as a multilateral trading facility*, whereas systematic internalisers are dedicated to bilateral transactions (Recital 11[R]). In fact,

SIs are intended to operate in an ad hoc manner to guarantee an adequate level of liquidity—and, one could say, depth and thickness—in the market. MiFID II substantially innovates them: they are now subject to stricter transparency rules, for they are mandated to apply them not only in respect of equity instruments (shares or other), as already stated in MiFID I, but, also, to a wide range of non-equity ones *traded on a trading venue and for which there is a liquid market* (Recital 18[R]).

Since they constitute the trading venues which are doubtlessly subject to fewer compliance requirements, OTFs may be regarded as the legal tool designed to confer a more solid structure and a higher degree of transparency to those transactions that would normally occur OTC, i.e. outside regulated platforms. Since most of these operations encompass derivatives (e.g., swaps), one could easily spot how OTFs are consistent with the general purposes of MiFID II. In fact, it has been noted how in response to the GFC, the Package's legislator has redefined the organisation of the trading function as far as derivatives are concerned. This has been done under the perspective not to protect the retail investor from capital risk, but to achieve a regulatory scenario serving the establishment of a "rational" market, able to express the price of the product, which is reflected by the market quote of the risk of the underlying asset (Lucantoni 2017).

However, the consensus on a tighter regulation on derivatives seems to have been enacted all around the world, as a result of a general awareness on that lack of transparency which had played a major role in propelling he GFC. As a proof, one should look at the statement by the G20 leaders gathered in Pittsburgh in September 2009, underling that *all standard OTC derivative contracts should be traded on exchanges or electronic trading platforms, where appropriate, and cleared through central counterparties by end-2012 at the latest*; and also that *OTC derivative contracts should be reported to trade repositories (TRs)* and that *non-centrally cleared contracts should be subject to higher capital requirements*. Also called 'swap data repositories', TRs are entities which centrally collect and maintain the records of derivatives. According to ESMA, *they play a central role in enhancing the transparency of derivative markets and reducing risks to financial stability*. Their main source of law is represented by EMIR: by passing it, the European legislator in fact abided by the 2012 deadline by definitely disciplining the topic of OTC derivatives in a way actually compliant with the spirit of Pittsburgh. Besides, said issue seems to have been fully encompassed in the debate around the revision of MiFID I.

The iter of the new Directive also carried an opportunity to rethink the infrastructure of financial markets, of course for the whole EU. This had clearly been the core content of EMIR, which constituted a valuable tool to address an issue that is per se pan-European: especially nowadays, when markets are deeply interconnected and none of them can be said to be 'segregated' from others. For systemic stability purposes, it requires a high level of harmonisation, which can be granted more by a Regulation than a Directive. However, once an immediately enforceable piece of legislation like EMIR had already been in charge, some issues regarding the duties of trading venues could have been addressed by MiFID II (whose scope covers many financial instruments, not merely OTC derivatives). In particular, trading venues are now *required to provide access, including data feeds on a non-discriminatory basis*, to those CCPs that are willing *to clear transactions executed in different trading venues subject to certain well-defined conditions being fulfilled.* These conditions entail that the access arrangement do not require an 'interoperability' one (that is, CCPs are not obliged to connect one another and perform the so-called 'cross-margin', i.e. the mechanism that allows to transfer margins from the accounts in *surplus* to those in *deficit* fallen below the 'maintenance margin', which is the *minimum* required).

This has also to do with 'fungibility', i.e. the circumstances under which contracts may be subjected to netting or cross-margining: a CCP cannot deny access by referencing to absence of fungibility. In order to create a coherent regulatory environment, the provisions of MiFIR regarding access—which are intended to *prevent discriminatory practices and help remove barriers that hinder competition in the clearing of financial instruments*—have been fully harmonised with those of EMIR. As far as access is concerned, there was a chance that exchange-traded derivatives—i.e. instruments whose value is based upon the value on another instrument and are traded on a regulated exchange—be exempted from these requirements for a 30-month (maximum) horizon. Such exemption had to be declared by the European Commission—once accounted for possible negative spill-overs at a systemic level—within 6 months before MiFID II come into force: had the Commission not found any valid reason for such a waiver, CCPs and trading venues would have still been allowed to ask for an exemption. The principle of non-discriminatory access applies to benchmarks used to construct derivatives, too; for new benchmarks, a similar 30-month "grace period", following the first use, is allowed.

As far as new instruments on which MiFID II sets provisions are concerned, two main categories are worth investigating: commodity derivatives and energy contracts. With regard to the former, 'European emission allowances' (EUAs)—that is, tradable securities entitling the holder (generally a manufacturer firm) to reach higher levels of polluting substances that otherwise would be prohibited—are included. The *Memo* published by the European Commission underlines that *the extension to EUAs will introduce greater security for traders of EUAs but without interfering with the purpose of the market, which remains emission reduction.* With regard to energy contracts, initially all commodity contracts, exchanged on any venue and that could be physically settled, were intended to fall within the scope of MiFID II. Unlike the proposal, the final text of the Directive excludes wholesale energy contracts, which a different piece of legislation is specifically devoted to: namely, the *Regulation on the Integrity and Transparency of the wholesale Market Integrity and Transparency* (REMIT, No. 1227/2011).

Inter alia, the Directive covers physically settled contracts on oil and coal; nevertheless, since at present day they are not cleared, EMIR will apply to these types of contracts traded on OTFs starting by six years after MiFID II will come into force. Moreover, it will be possible to extend the period once by two years and once by one year, after the Commission will have assessed the impact of these deferrals on prices and the changes in the configuration of counterparty and systemic risk. This is to say that, although the most relevant and common energy contracts are covered by MiFID II, we shall not be able to properly assess the impact of regulation on this segment of financial markets before several years (at most, by 2028), when the EU legislation on derivatives and commodities might well have been changed. Such concern is fuelled by the significant volatility of these instruments, deeply connected with macroeconomic factors.

Pursuant to MiFID II, in an effort to tighten regulatory requirements for such a crucial category of systemic relevance, fewer commodity firms will be exempted from the Directive when they deal on their own account or provide investment services in commodity derivatives on an ancillary basis as part of their main business, and when they are not subsidiaries of financial groups. Moreover, for such category of instruments, supervisory powers and a harmonised regime on position limits are enhanced in order to *support orderly pricing and prevent market abuse*, so that supervisors can intervene when *there are concerns in terms of market integrity or orderly functioning of markets*. Other obligations are charged to trading venues, for position management controls on their platforms must be 'transparent and non-discriminatory'. In addition to this, venues can ask the holders of these instruments *to reduce or terminate positions or to provide liquidity back into the market*. Furthermore, *pre- and post-trade transparency requirements are extended to derivatives traded on trading venues, including commodity derivatives*. Finally, *mandatory trading on organised venues will apply to commodity derivatives*.

By keeping discussing instruments, a very widely debated issue addressed by MiFID II refers to the 'packaged retail investment and insurance-based products (PRIIPs), which 'are often complicated and opaque'. For those PRIIPs that are 'financial instruments or structured deposits', the Directive creates 'a robust and coherent framework in the areas of information about the product to clients and the rules governing the sales process (e.g., conduct of business and conflicts of interest). These measures are obviously complementary to the "standard" MiFID ones on investment advice and sales services.

Another important issue addressed by the Directive is transparency, that had been previously conceived in relation to equity instruments only. In this context, a very relevant topic—surged in recent years—is the one of the so-called 'dark pools'. This phrase refers to those cases in which there is no such thing as a 'bid-ask spread' acting as a reference price for the instrument, for it encompasses the vendors' (minimum) willingness to accept (i.e. the ask or 'offer' price, which will be paid by anyone on the demand side) and the purchasers' (maximum) willingness to pay (i.e. the bid price, which will be received by anyone on the supply side). Of course, in order to prevent riskless arbitrage opportunities from arising, in "normal conditions" the ask price will be higher than the bid one, so that the spread—computed as the difference between ask and bid—turns out to be positive. It may also be used as a proxy for market liquidity: the smaller the spread, the greater the liquidity. Generally, the price of a certain instrument is taken at the midpoint of the 'European best bid and offer' (EBBO), i.e. halfway between the highest bid and the lowest ask. Nevertheless, with growing frequency, transactions are carried out at non-public prices and instruments themselves are not publicly priced: dark pools are *platforms where trading interests interact without full pre-trade disclosure to other users or the public.*

In particular, *MiFID II continues to allow waivers from pre-trade transparency, but only as long as they do not cause competitive distortions and reduce the overall efficiency of the price discovery process.* Waivers are still allowed in the following cases:

(a) the transaction is "large" vis-à-vis the 'normal market size' ('large-in-size waivers');
(b) the price is determined by reference to the one generated by another system ('reference-price w.');
(c) the systems involved formalise negotiated transactions, provided they meet certain criteria ('negotiated-price w.');
(d) orders are held in an order management facility of the trading venue, pending disclosure ('order management w.').

However, the Directive introduces a so-called 'double volume cap mechanism' for the first waiver: in terms of monetary amount, the reference-price cannot exceed 4% per venue and 8% globally. Unlike this, large-in-size waivers are not furtherly restricted, the rationale being that, if investors selling large amounts had to disclose a great amount of data, prices—in markets which are far from frictionless, in reality—would be negatively affected and driven down. Moreover, *pre-* and post-trade data are required to be available *on a reasonable commercial basis and through the establishment of a consolidated trade mechanism for post-trade data*, whereas before MiFID II there were substantial incentives to deviate from the "reasonableness" invoked above. Under the objectives pursued by MiFID II, the issue of 'reporting, publication and consolidation of trade data' turns out to be a major one, for it regards 'formatting, cost, quality and reliability': indeed, increasing consistency and reducing costs are two of the main aims of MiFID II.

In accordance with G20 commitments, the Directive also reshaped the regulatory requirements for commodity markets. As a result of this, the supervisory powers in charge of ESMA turn out being expanded: *Inter alia*, said authority is now entitled to set the methodology for calculating some position limits that must be obeyed, each category of trader having a position-reporting obligation. In order for investor protection to be furtherly enhanced, other provisions introduced by MiFID II *strengthened conduct rules such as an extended scope for the appropriateness tests and reinforced information to clients.* This has brought to substantive amendments to the requirements to which advisers are subject: the category of 'independent' advice is now more effectively isolated. One major element of separation is the reception of 'inducements' and commissions on exchanges. In accordance with the *Commission Staff Working Document Impact Assessment* that accompanies the Commission Delegated Regulation supplementing MiFIR, 'inducements' is *a general name referring to varying types of incentives paid to financial intermediaries in exchange for the promotion of specific products or flows of business.*

However, transparency—even if largely addressed by MiFID II—is not the only concern for the European legislator. Since investor protection—and, thus, the stability of the whole financial system—would not be properly fulfilled if the degree of competition in trading and clearing were not sufficiently good, the principle of non-discriminatory access to trading venues and CCPs, as well as to the benchmarks set for trading and clearing purposes, is regarded as one of the pillars of the Directive. Little transitional waivers, designed to ease the impact of these requirements, are granted to smaller venues and newcomer CCPs. Another relevant issue is the one of algorithmic trading, which MiFID II intends to regulate in a more decisive manner, especially to the extent that liquidity is assured in the market-making process. Besides, *investment firms which provide direct electronic access to a trading venue will be required to have in place systems and risk controls to prevent trading that may contribute to a disorderly market or involve market abuse*.

In the past, algorithmic trading was mainly a "shadow" area of exchanges, for both agents and strategies were often unknown and the available information set was very poor. Conversely, at present-day, MiFID II provisions are aimed at bridging the operational cleavage between those players which use algorithms and those which do not. For this purpose, they impose tighter checks on the arrangements by the means of which a firm is admitted to direct electronic access to public markets. Moreover, *algorithmic traders must be registered as an investment firm and have in place effective systems and risk controls* (Article 17^{D}, par. 1). Nevertheless, apart from a greater concern on the riskiness they spread, they are not intended to be "other" than ordinary traders: in fact, *when engaged in a market making strategy they are required to post quotes at competitive prices to provide liquidity on a regular basis which will contribute to more orderly trading*. Such "order" ensured by the Directive also mandates that venues *be able to halt trading in case of significant price movements*, negatively affecting the "natural" flow of capital. A mechanism like this is referred to as a 'circuit breaker'.

3.3 Interactions Between Directive, Regulation and Supervision

As we have mentioned above, supervisory micro-prudential authorities are endowed by MiFID II with new powers. Pursuant to Article 40^{R}, ESMA can now *restrict (a) the marketing, distribution or sale of certain financial instruments or financial instruments with certain specified features; or (b) a type of financial activity or practice*. Pursuant to Article 41^{R}, EBA can do the same in respect of structured deposits. To be precise, these last are 'products' rather than instruments, and constitute peculiar financial accounts whose funds are directly invested in derivatives (thus having an underlying asset).

For instance, ESMA will play a fundamental role in evaluating the applications submitted by venues willing to recur to pre-trade transparency waivers, acting as a dark pool. Moreover, said authority currently holds the duty to coordinate NCAs in dealing with this subject. Of course, the Directive strongly interacts with market abuse legislation, nowadays represented by the *Criminal Sanctions for Market Abuse Directive* (CSMAD, No. 2014/57/EU) and the *Market Abuse Regulation* (MAR, No. 596/2014): reporting information on a transaction is mandatory for all investment firms, including the case in which other instruments exchanged on a trading venue underlie investments. In simple words, this means that the reporting obligation applies regardless of where the trade takes place.

In order for the whole compliance and penalty architecture to be internally consistent, the requirements set forth by MiFID II mirror those of MAR. As already underlined, MiFID II is designed to encompass the widest possible range of financial instruments, except for those instruments which are not susceptible to or could not be used for market abuse (Recital 32[R]). Moreover, since reporting requirements currently differ on a national basis, MiFIR becomes very salient, too. Thus, said Regulation ensures a higher degree of harmonisation, especially with regard to *the information that identifies who is trading and for whom a trade is being executed*. Moreover, ESMA is required to draft some RTS to furtherly enhance harmonisation.

Of course, MiFID II aims at improving efficiency in reporting, for a better quality of data will certainly have positive spill-overs on the functioning of markets. This means that some provisions are designed to avoid overlaps in reporting. For instance, reporting to trade repositories, different from the one mandated by the Directive (so that ‘double reporting’ would be obtained), is deemed to be sufficient; no other reporting obligations arise and, thus, ‘double reporting’ would be avoided.

Additional valuable interactions are those between MiFID II and *Undertakings for Collective Investments in Transferable Securities* (UCITS), i.e. substantially the legislation on investment funds (other than ‘alternative’ ones) and their managers, represented by different Directives amending the previous or introduced ex novo. The latest one (No. 2014/91/EU) is labelled ‘UCITS V’, albeit there have actually been four pieces of legislation (in fact, UCITS II has never come into force). As may clearly be understood, financial instruments are the “content” of collective investments: hence, MiFID II fully covers investment services related to them. An important issue addressed by the Directive—other than the classification of instruments between ‘complex’ and ‘non-complex’ ones—is the ‘execution-only’ regime, i.e. the one in which the firms providing investment services only execute their clients’ orders, without any deeper involvement, thus being subject to looser regulation (e.g., no appropriateness test is required). This applies to non-complex instruments: up to now, all UCITS have been classified as non-complex; nevertheless, there is a growing number of structured ones, whose mechanics is not so immediate to understand (notably in respect of the pay-off). This is the reason why MiFID II introduces the notion of ‘structured product’, regarded as complex, which do not entail exceptions on the appropriateness test for clients (even in case of execution-only transactions).

In order to overcome fragmentation in the regulatory environment (as the *De Larosière Report* had highlighted), some important issues are addressed by the Regulation rather than the Directive. They may be summarised as follows:

(a) disclosure of data (on trading activity, to the public; and on transactions, to regulators and supervisors);
(b) mandatory trading of derivatives on organised venues;
(c) enforcement of competition, achieved by removing barriers between trading venues and providers of clearing services;
(d) specific supervisory actions regarding financial instruments and positions in derivatives.

In contrast, the Directive deals with those topics in which an intervention at a domestic level may result useful: for instance, the role of NCAs and Member States, including their powers of sanction. Finally, one of the greatest innovations carried by MiFID II is the harmonisation of rules regarding the access of extra-EU investment firms to the Single Market. Although it is often referred to as a market for goods with no customs tariffs or barriers, the Single Market also entails the free provision of services, including financial ones. This is evident from the words used in the Treaty on the Functioning of the European Union (TFEU), which mandates that restrictions to both the free provision of services and capital movements be prohibited not only within Member States, but also—under an ad hoc ruling by European institutions, in accordance with the ordinary legislative procedure—*in respect of nationals of Member States who are established in a Member State other than that of the person for whom the services are intended* (Article 56 TFEU); and *all restrictions on the movement of capital between Member States and between Member States and third countries shall be prohibited* (Article 63 TFEU). In fact, MiFID I had not ruled this topic, thus leaving a remarkable wound in the construction of a level playing field.

The European Commission is entitled to take so-called 'equivalence decisions' on the access of third-country investment firms operating on their own behalf or on that of their professional clients and eligible counterparties: that is, they have to assess an effective compatibility between the EU legal regime and the jurisdiction to which the investment firm is subject. These definitions had been originally provided by MiFID I and are reiterated by MiFID II. We shall clearly analyse them in detail when discussing client categorisation. For the moment being, it is worth noting that professional clients are those possessing a high investing expertise (e.g., financial firms), thus in need of a lower degree of protection; eligible counterparties represent a subset of the former, and they can be classified in that way only by submitting explicit request. Clearly, in absence of an equivalence decision, the so-called 'passport' cannot be recognised: it would entail the possibility for a firm to provide investment services in other EU countries, without establishing any branches there, once authorised by its NCA. The equivalence decision process is ignited by the Commission, but a Member State may recommend initiating the procedure in respect of those countries that it would like to be granted a recognition. It is worth noting that the assessment should not be done on a "line-by-line" basis, but rather looking at the whole of the jurisdiction. Once the decision has been adopted, the competent authority in the applicant country stipulates a cooperation agreement with ESMA, so that third-country investment firms will have to refer to said micro-prudential body—as if they were based in the Union—regarding the provision of services inside the E.U.

Notwithstanding this framework, domestic rules still apply to the provision of services to retail clients, though MiFID II sets standard requirements for a third-country investment firm to be authorised by the NCA. Despite being no full harmonisation, this is doubtlessly a valuable step forward with the potential to curb the regulatory burden surrounding the decision by an extra-EU investment firm to provide retail services inside the Union. This would eventually enhance the compliance of the regulatory environment with Articles 56 and 63 TFEU. More in general, it would more closely resemble the spirit of the Treaties (thus, being more in line with the overall acquis communautaire), which shapes not only the relationships between Member States but, also, the attitude of the EU toward external countries.

3.4 The Path Towards the Package

MiFID II explicitly repeals MiFID I, which is partially recast into it: the new Directive is not only innovative in substantial parts but presents some of the already-stated principles under the new, more "investor-friendly" framework (which is, also, more consistent with the current state of financial markets). Actually, MiFID I had already been amended four times (see Annex III, Part A). In respect of such legislator's activism, Recital 1 of the new Directive settles that, *since further amendments are to be made, it should be recast in the interest of clarity*.

The Directive found its legal basis in Article 53 TFEU, par. 1: although the choice is not so straightforward, that paragraph (albeit referring to intellectual property) is about the legislative procedure that was actually followed, namely the 'ordinary' one—commonly known with the old phrase 'co-decision', abandoned in the Treaty of Lisbon's wording—and, also, about mutual recognition. This last is an important principle shaping not only that piece of legislation, but the whole of the EU legal system. On 20 October 2011, the first draft was adopted by the Commission—once the Directorate General for Internal Market and Services had drafted the Commission's proposal—and transmitted to the Parliament and the Council. On 10 February 2012, the European Data Protection Supervisor released its *Opinion* on the topics dealing with data protection issues. On 22 March 2012, the ECB issued its *Opinion*, supporting the proposal. Frankfurt adopted a favourable stance because, inter alia, it foresaw an *[increase] in the legal certainty by limiting Member State options and discretion*, something theoretically apt to *reduce the risks of market distortion and regulatory arbitrage*.

Another *Opinion* was issued by the European Economic and Social Committee (EESC) on 25 April 2012. It was a more complex statement, even comprising some criticism with regard to the 'legal bases' in the light of the Treaties: in fact, it would have been much more logical to indicate a different one in the same chapter (e.g., the more general Article 50, par. 1), which deals with the right of establishment. The EESC observed that '*the proposal [achieved] the goal of strengthening the EU financial market and making it more integrated, efficient and competitive, combining greater transparency with greater consumer protection, reducing areas of unbridled speculation*, especially as far as OTC derivatives are concerned.

The first reading by the European Parliament ended on 26 October 2012 with a referral back to the competent parliamentary committee. The European Council discussed the draft in its meeting on 21 June 2013 and the Parliament finally passed the text, with amendments, on 15 April 2014. The Council proceeded with its approval on 13 May and the Directive was finally adopted—i.e. co-signed by the heads of both the Parliament and the Council—on 15 May 2014, which is the date referred in the header of the piece of said legislation.

The Regulation—whose legal basis is Article 114 TFEU, another one with a strongly harmonisation-oriented purpose—followed an almost-identical path, apart from a couple of 'rectification proposals' submitted on 11 November 2011 and 27 June 2012 respectively.

3.5 The Scope of MiFID II and MiFIR

As is quite common in legislative technique, in Title I^D is clarified the scope of the Directive and provided the definitions that should be followed in interpreting and applying that piece of legislation. Article 1^D, par. 2, sets out that *the Directive shall apply to investment firms, market operators, data reporting services providers, and third-country firms providing investment services or performing investment activities through the establishment of a branch in the Union.* Thus, it states the aim of determining a level playing field not only for the financial players in the EU but, also, in relation to the external ones that are willing to access the Single Market by means of a branch. In fact, it is common that, despite freedom to provide services in the Union being granted even in absence of the establishment of a branch, the Single Market and its rules have proven to be so attractive that various financial firms have decided to open EU branches.

Article 1^D, par. 2, enumerates the subjects in relation to which the Directive sets out specific requirements:

(a) authorisation and operating conditions for investment firms;
(b) provision of investment services or activities by third-country firms through the establishment of a branch;
(c) authorisation and operation of regulated markets;

(d) authorisation and operation of data reporting services providers;
(e) supervision, cooperation and enforcement by competent authorities.

The declared 'subject matter and scope' of MiFIR is obviously quite similar. Article 1^R, par. 1, enumerates the following topics addressed by the Regulation:

(a) disclosure of trade data to the public;
(b) reporting of transactions to the competent authorities;
(c) trading of derivatives on organised venues;
(d) non-discriminatory access to clearing and non-discriminatory access to trading in benchmarks;
(e) product intervention powers of competent authorities, ESMA and EBA and powers of ESMA on position management controls and position limits;
(f) provision of investment services or activities by third-country firms following an applicable equivalence decision by the Commission with or without a branch.

Moreover, the Directive encompasses provisions that *shall also apply to credit institutions authorised under Directive 2013/36/EU, when providing one or more investment services and/or performing investment activities* (Article 1, par. 3). The referred piece of legislation is commonly known as the *Capital Requirements Directive IV* (CRD IV, No. 2013/36/EU): although currently undergoing revision with a view to passing a CRD V legislation, it is the main source of law for compliance and supervisory purposes in respect of financial firms. It is worth noting that, even if the wording of the abovementioned paragraph may suggest that there is a difference between investment services and activities, this is not the case; actually, CRD IV uses the phrase 'investment services and activities' to denote the same kind of operations (e.g., asset management), as well as various national supervisory bodies do.

Such a provision seems to envisage a type of regulation which could be defined as 'operation-based': rules apply to certain recipients not because of the intrinsic features of their juridical form (in fact, credit institutions are not mentioned in par. 1), but to the extent that they are involved in certain operations. This approach is becoming increasingly common in the whole EU acquis: also, it is sometimes referred to as 'supervision by activity'. The provisions applying to those credit institutions—defined pursuant to the CRD IV definitions—are the following ones.

Article 2^D, par. 2, enhances the ban on monetary financing entailed by Article 21 of the Statute of the European System of Central Banking (ESCB), which prohibits central banks from directly providing funds to credit institutions. In fact, is stated that *the rights conferred by this Directive shall not extend to the provision of services as counterparty in transactions carried out by public bodies dealing with public debt or by members of the ESCB performing their tasks (...) or performing equivalent functions under national provisions.*

In Article 9^D, par. 3, the widely-recognised principle of sound and prudent management (along with its 'effectiveness') is underlined regarding the maintenance of systemic stability, for 'the integrity of the market' is directly related to 'the interest of clients'. Furthermore, is stated that—pursuant to Article 88 CRD IV, par. 1—the abovementioned ‘arrangements’ will make ‘the management body define, approve and oversee’ organisational and investment measures, along with remuneration policies. Another provision of Article 9^{D}, par. 3, applies to credit institutions: it is about the management body being granted an *adequate access to information and documents which are needed to oversee and monitor management decision-making*.

Article 14^{D} refers to the duties which financial firms are subject to; namely, for investment ones, the obligations stemming from Directive 1997/9/EC (on investor compensation schemes) and, as far as credit institutions are concerned, the membership of a ‘deposit guarantee scheme’ (DGS), i.e. a fund—created through the mandatory contributions charged upon the banking industry—that will be used to protect depositors in the event of a financial distress and, specifically, a resolution procedure: e.g., a DGS subrogates (in their claim on the failing intermediary) to those persons whose deposits at that bank are below € 100,000, in case of bail-in). The functioning of DGSs is disciplined in Article 109 of the *Banking Recovery and Resolution Directive* (BRRD, No. 2014/59/EU).

Articles from 16^{D} to 20^{D} address the following topics: the requisites—pursuant to the *Capital Requirements Regulation* (CRR, No. 575/2013, bundled in a package with CRD IV)—that investment firms must match in order to be authorised to provide investment services in the Union, thanks to the so-called ‘passport’ (Article 16^{D}); ‘algorithmic trading’ (Article 17^{D}); ‘trading process and finalisation of transactions in an MTF and an OTF’ (Article 18^{D}); ‘specific requirements’ for MTFs (Article 19^{D}) and OTFs (Article 20^{D}) respectively.

Title II^{D}, Chapter II (that is, Articles from 21^{D} to 33^{D}) discuss the ‘operating conditions for investment firms’; however, Article 29^{D}, par. 2, subpar. 2 does not apply to credit institutions. This provision states that *Member States may allow (...) tied agents registered in their territory to hold money and/or financial instruments of clients on behalf and under the full responsibility of the investment firm for which they are acting within their territory or, in the case of a cross-border operation, in the territory of a Member State which allows a tied agent to hold client money*. Therefore, if agents act on behalf of a credit institution, this provision does not apply: hence, they are not allowed to hold money and/or financial investments.

Title II^{D}, Chapter III (that is, Articles from 34^{D} to 38^{D}), on the ‘rights of investment firms’, also apply to credit institutions, but with the exception of Article 34^{D}, paragraphs 2–3 and Article 35^{D}, paragraphs from 2 to 9. Article 39^{D}, par. 2, charges informative duties to *any investment firm wishing to provide services or activities within the territory of another Member State for the first time, or which intends to modify the range of services or activities so provided*. In a clear proof of how the home-country control principle works, these requirements entail to inform the home NCA of the Member State wherein the investment firm intends to operate, as well as to submit to the same authority a ‘programme of operations’ stating which ‘investment services and/or activities’, including ancillary ones, are intended to be provided in that Member State. Moreover, it should be clarified whether tied agents will be employed or not. Article 39^{D}, par. 3, states that the home authority will transfer this information to the host one ‘within one month’; once expired such timespan, the investment firm may commence to provide its 'services and activities' in the foreign Member State. Since this provision is a natural extension of the previous, it does not apply to credit institutions. Article 35^D, paragraphs from 2 to 6, as well as par. 9, contain provisions on the 'establishment of a branch'; hence, following the same rationale as before, their application to credit institutions is denied. Article 35^D, par. 1, underlines the principle of freedom to establish a branch in a foreign Member State: it plainly applies to every financial firm, with no exception. The same holds as for Article 35^D, par. 7, explicitly referred to credit institutions, whereas par. 8—logically joint to the preceding—implicitly does the same. Conversely, par. 9—which is listed among exceptions—makes an explicit reference to investment firms.

Finally, banks are subject to Articles from 67^D to 75^D and Articles 80^D, 85^D, and 86^D. This is a complex set of rules about supervision: the authorities involved, their powers, the sanctions for infringements, the judicial path to be followed, etc. The last two articles outline the 'powers for' and the 'precautionary measures to be taken by' host Member States, mainly in respect of compliance with the Directive.

Article 1^D, par. 4, sets out that some rules apply *to investment firms and to credit institutions authorised under [CRD IV] when selling or advising clients in relation to structured deposits*. Hence, there are two main differences vis-à-vis par. 3: this last provision is addressed to a greater number of subjects, for it is not circumscribed to credit institutions; however, the scope is limited to the activity of advising on, or directly selling, a peculiar kind of financial product. Nevertheless, little changes from the discipline envisaged in par. 3. In fact, pursuant to par. 4, many rules do apply to the abovementioned firms in the same manner as those laid down in the previous. The slight difference between paragraphs 3 and 4 attains with the scope of application of certain rules encompassed by Article 16^D, paragraphs 2, 3, and 6, which do apply only in relation to structured deposits. They encompass the compliance with the Directive (par. 2); the prevention of 'conflicts of interest as defined in Article 23^D from adversely affecting the interests' of the clients of the investment firm (par. 3); the cooperation with supervisory authorities in relation to *all obligations, including those with respect to clients or potential clients and to the integrity of the market* (par. 6).

Additional rules are envisaged in par. 5 with regard to Article 17^D, paragraphs from 1 to 6, on internal controls and compliance requirements for investment firms engaged in algorithmic trading. Furthermore, in said paragraph is stated that Articles 57^D and 58^D do apply even regardless of the exemptions set in Article 2^D, that we shall analyse further. Article 17^D, par. 7, clarifies the application of the Directive in some particular cases:

- there is perfect complementarity between RMs on one hand, MTFs and OTFs on the other: 'all multilateral systems in financial instruments' must follow the provisions on one or another; *tertium non datur* (subpar. 1);
- *when executing client orders outside a regulated market, an MTF or an OTF* (these three exhaust the possible range of facilities, as noted before), investment firms that do this *on an organised, frequent, systematic and substantial basis,*

deal on own account (subpar. 2). This provision clearly aims at reducing risks charged upon investors in those transactions that, being external to regulated exchanges, intrinsically have a greater jeopardising effect on invested capital;
- keeping the *dictum* of Articles 23^{R} and 28^{R} untouched, regarding *trading obligations for investment firms and obligation to trade on regulated markets, MTFs or OTFs,* is stated that—with reference to the previous two subparagraphs —all transactions concluded neither on multilateral systems (i.e. RMs, MTFs or OTFs) nor by systematic internalisers should abide by the relevant provisions of Title III^{R}, encompassing the discipline of transparency for SIs and investment firms trading OTC.

As far as MiFIR is concerned, Article 1^{R}, par. 2, in a much simpler way than the Directive, specifies the recipients of that piece of legislation: in general, it applies to investment firms, authorised under MiFID II, and credit institutions, authorised under CRD IV, *when providing investment services and/or performing investment activities and to market operators including any trading venues they operate.* However, also MiFIR applies in some peculiar cases, explicitly mentioned: they are the following ones.

Title V^{R} (*Derivatives*) 'also applies to all financial counterparties' defined in accordance with Article 2 EMIR, par. 8, as well as *to all non-financial counterparties falling under Article 10(1)(b) of that Regulation*, i.e. the ones that *become subject to the clearing obligation for future contracts (…) if the rolling average position over 30 working days exceeds the [clearing] threshold.* The latter is disciplined in par. 3 of the same Article 10 of said Regulation, where we may read: *In calculating the positions referred to in paragraph 1, the non-financial counterparty shall include all the OTC derivative contracts entered into by the non-financial counterparty or by other non-financial entities within the group to which the non-financial counterparty belongs, which are not objectively measurable as reducing risks directly relating to the commercial activity or treasury financing activity of the non-financial counterparty or of that group.* Title VI^{R} (*Non-discriminatory clearing access for financial instruments*) applies to CCPs and the holders of 'proprietary rights to benchmarks' as well. Title VIII^{R} is about the *provision of services and performance of activities by third-country firms following an equivalence decision with or without a branch.* Therefore, it applies to those firms, based in countries other than the Member States, whose jurisdiction is deemed to be compatible with the rules governing the Single Market through an equivalence decision taken by the European Commission.

Other provisions do not apply in the case of operations whose counterparty is a member of the ESCB or that have *entered into in performance of monetary, foreign exchange and financial stability policy which that member of the ESCB is legally empowered to pursue* (e.g., 'quantitative easing' transactions carried out either by the ECB itself or by national central banks adhering to the Eurosystem). This provision applies to RMs, market operators and investment firms', albeit this is not the case when members of the ESCB act 'in performance of their investment operations'.

3.6 Exemptions to the Applicability of MiFID II

Article 2^D, par. 1, presents a very lengthy list of the exemptions to the Directive's applicability. First of all, the whole insurance field is excluded, also in respect of 'reinsurance and retrocession activities' (letter *a*). As widely known, this is the subject of a different, seminal piece of legislation, namely the Directive 2009/138/EC, commonly labelled as *Solvency II*. Besides, MiFID II does not refer to *persons providing investment services exclusively for their parent undertakings, for their subsidiaries or for other subsidiaries of their parent undertakings* (letter *b*). That is, an investment is considered to be "different" from a standard one when the provider of the service is not fully independent in its investment decisions, i.e. it acts (also on own account, but) executing the instructions of a subject to which it is connected on a 'steering and coordination' mechanism. A similar exclusion is in respect of services provided *in an incidental manner in the course of a professional activity*, as long as the latter is 'regulated' and allowed to perform an investment activity (letter *c*).

A very relevant exemption is set out for those persons *dealing on own account in financial instruments other than commodity derivatives or emission allowances or derivatives thereof.* Here the focus is on 'dealing on own account', for another requirement to be exempted is 'not providing any other investment services or providing any other investment activities in financial instruments other than commodity derivatives or emission allowances of derivatives thereof'. This is to exclude those subjects that do not deal with the most heavily regulated instruments, which MiFID II is particularly devoted to, and—at the same time—whose involvement in other instruments is circumscribed to dealing on own account (letter *d*).

It follows that the Directive applies to those subjects that deal with instruments different from commodity derivatives et similia but perform this not, or not only, on own account (i.e. they trade against third-party capital, at least partially). Yet, there are some other cases to which that provision applies: to operators that are market makers, participate in a RM or an MTF or 'have direct electronic access to a trading venue', or perform high frequency trading, or—most importantly, in a consistent manner with the exemptions' rationale—'deal on own account when executing client orders.' This latter provision might be surprising, for the concept of trading against one's own capital could apparently struggling with the execution of client orders, which is commonly intended to occur against clients' capital. Actually, there is a peculiar form of trading, namely the 'matched-principal trading', which is first regarded as dealing on own account. However, it constitutes a real hybrid between two extremes: *if a firm executes client orders by standing between clients on a matched-principal basis (back-to-back trading), it is both dealing on own account and executing orders on behalf of clients.* Insurance firms, market makers and subjects participating to RMs, MTFs or with DEA to a trading venue do not have to prove the last conditions in order to be exempt.

Other exemptions are for those 'operators with compliance obligations under Directive 2003/87/EC' (i.e. subject to European environmental legislation) that deal on emission allowances exclusively on own account and without using HFT;

for *persons providing investment services consisting exclusively in the administration of employee-participation schemes*, or persons that, in addition to administering them, provide investment services *exclusively for their parent undertakings, for their subsidiaries or for other subsidiaries of their parent undertakings*, consistently with letter *b*.

Other exempt subjects are the members of ESCB 'and other national bodies performing similar functions in the Union', as well as 'other public bodies charged with or intervening in the management of the public debt in the Union' and also 'international financial institutions' for the purpose of *mobilising funding and providing financial assistance to the benefit of their members that are experiencing or threatened by severe financing problems* (letter *h*). These words may relate—for instance—to the European Stability Mechanism (ESM). Of course, since the stakeholders of the EFSF are basically governments—often regarded as 'eligible counterparties', thus needing no sort of protection—, MiFID II provisions do not apply to entities like that.

Exempted are 'collective investment schemes' (CIS) and pension funds, 'and the depositaries and managers of such undertakings'; persons 'dealing on own account, in commodity derivatives or emission allowances or derivatives thereof', or that deal on own account 'when executing client orders' on the abovementioned instruments; or that provide investment services in those instruments 'other than dealing on own account' but 'to the customers or suppliers of their main business'. In fact, these exemptions apply as long as dealing in commodity derivatives et similia is an 'ancillary activity to their main business'. The latter is different from the activities defined as 'investment' ones in CRD IV, or—following the same rationale as before—the subject acts as a market maker, does not use HFT techniques, and correctly notifies the NCA that it is making use of the exemption and the reasons behind it (especially in respect of it being 'ancillary').

With regard to this, ESMA plays an important role: in fact, par. 4 attributes to it the duty to *develop regulatory technical standards to specify (…) the criteria for establishing when an activity is to be considered to be ancillary to the main business at a group level*. These criteria are—at a consolidated level—'the need for ancillary activities to constitute a minority of activities at a group level' and 'the size of their trading activity compared to the overall market trading activity in the asset class'; in this case, *the capital employed for carrying out the ancillary activity relative to the capital employed for carrying out the main business is to be considered* despite this factor being insufficient 'to demonstrate that the activity is ancillary'. However, these three criteria should exclude: '*intra-group transactions (…) that serve group-wide liquidity or risk management purposes; (…) transactions in derivatives which are objectively measurable as reducing risks directly relating to the commercial activity or treasury financing activity; (…) transactions in commodity derivatives and emission allowances entered into to fulfil obligations to provide liquidity on a trading venue*.

On this issue, the ESMA-developed RTS 20—ultimately endorsed by the Commission and become Delegated Regulation 21 March 2017, No. 2017/562. It would be outside the scope of this work to provide detail on these standards;

nevertheless, it is worth noting that there was no reference to the optional capital threshold. Furtherly, the Commission asked the Authority to include 'a capital-based test, where appropriate, for certain firms'; the latter resisted this request (due to the issues of maintaining stability over time and ensuring a level playing field). Anyway, in late May 2016, an ESMA *Opinion* identified 'some metrics' for both the numerator and denominator of such threshold, adding that *in the case where a capital test is introduced, ESMA proposes to allow entities to choose between performing the original main business test based on trading activity or a capital test to avoid putting small and medium-sized entities at a disadvantage*.

Similarly to what is envisaged in letter *c*, other exemptions laid down in Article 2^D are for *persons providing investment advice in the course of providing another professional activity* which is outside the scope of the Directive, jointly with the fact that *the provision of such advice is not specifically remunerated* (letter *k*); for 'associations set up by Danish and Finnish pension funds with the sole aim of managing the assets of pension funds that are members of those associations' (letter *l*); and for agenti di cambio (in the Italian jurisdiction, a residual figure whose discipline dates back to Law 29 May 1967, No. 402) pursuant to Article 201 of the main domestic financial law (Legislative Decree 24 February 1998, No. 58, so-called 'TUF').

Further exemptions (letter *n*) are for 'transmission system operators', explicitly mentioning the pieces of legislation to be referred; for *persons acting as service providers on their behalf to carry out their task*; and for *any operator or administrator of an energy balancing mechanism, pipeline network or systems to keep in balance the supplies and uses of energy when carrying out such tasks*. However, is specified that the exemption applies to the extent that the abovementioned subjects *perform investment activities or provide investment services relating to commodity derivatives*, whereas it does not work *with regard to the operation of a secondary market, including a platform for secondary trading in financial transmission rights*.

Article 3^D sets out some 'optional exemptions' that is possible to envisage pursuant to paragraph 1, stating that a Member State may 'choose not to apply' the Directive to 'any persons' falling under their jurisdiction, *provided that the activities of those persons are authorised and regulated at national level* and other conditions are met. It is important to notice how, as provided for by par. 3, *persons exempt (...) shall not benefit from the freedom to provide services or to perform activities or to establish branches as provided for in Articles 34 and 35 respectively*. We shall clearly come back on these provisions, plainly stemming from the Treaties.

3.7 Corporate Governance of Investment Firms

A reform of corporate governance (CG) requirements for financial firms is not exclusive of the Package; yet, it is encompassed by the most recent developments in legislation: in particular, as far as the CRD IV/CRR package is concerned.

Moreover, even single countries—at a domestic level—have intervened in order to heal the troubles stemming from an unfit shape of the distribution of powers and liabilities within an entity, even outside the financial field. For instance, not only the implementation of CRD IV has subjected to capital, organisational and CG prescriptions also those players which, due to their (relatively) little size, previously had to obey minimal requirements only: at the same time, this has translated into a reinforced supervision to the extent of access to the market, operations and company crises, even by taking into due account the principle of proportionality (Siclari 2016). This last has been envisaged in light of creating a Capital Markets Union (CMU) which should complete and complement the efforts already made in the banking field—through the European Banking Union, of course—and the provision of financial services, harmonised by means of the Package.

Yet, in this context is worth noting how, as the CMU becomes a goal to be adequately pursued, "frictions" in capital markets should be countered by easing the regulatory burden. In fact, there is a reasonable need for cutting-back (in order to achieve a proper 'rationalisation') the huge number of new rules that have been put in place during recent years (Siclari 2016), including those stemming from the Package. They are about 'corporate information and governance', as well as other issues in relation to which the distance between financial and non-financial industries is too large to allow us to talk in general.

Yet, it is no doubt that a reform in CG practices—especially in the financial field—started being widely advocated, after multiple scandals and negative events rapidly unfolded even before the GFC (e.g.). As clearly highlighted in Recital 5^{D}, lots of those 'weaknesses' that have endangered financial markets—as claimed in Recital 4^{D}—should be found in CG ('including checks and balances within them'), as various 'regulatory bodies at international level' agree on this point; hence, they should be treated as 'contributory factors' to the crisis. Therefore, with regard to CG, the aim of the legislator is not simplification: in Recital 5^{D} is also clearly stated that MiFID I *should be supplemented by more detailed principles and minimum standards*, to apply by taking into account *the nature, scale and complexity of investment firms*.

Recital 53^{D} sets out some relevant CG requirements. Several aspects of governance need to be strengthened: *the role of management bodies of investment firms, regulated markets and data reporting providers in ensuring sound and prudent management of the firms, the promotion of the integrity of the market and the interest of investors*. As we may notice from these words, CG is a very wide topic, yielding spill-overs onto different areas and—most importantly—relevant not only at a *micro*- level, i.e. for the single intermediary and its operations but, also (and above all), at a *macro*- one, on the market as a whole. Investors are in the middle: they benefit from the "health" of the firm to which they confer their savings in order to be invested and get money back; but they also benefit from good conditions of the market as a whole and, conversely, are damaged when they deteriorate. This is particularly true for some types of investments, even single assets or asset classes, whose risk is mainly 'systematic' and whose performance is strictly linked to that of wide-ranging benchmarks.

Understanding risks—something which descends from the possession of 'adequate collective knowledge, skills and experience'—is an essential requirement for management bodies. Following a juridical tradition that is deeply rooted in the United States, the EU legislator lays down the reasonable conviction that diversity—with regard to *age, gender, geographic provenance and educational and professional background*—is key in getting 'a variety of views and experiences', thus enhancing the abovementioned skills; hence, of course, *diversity should be one of the criteria for the composition of management bodies*. It is obvious that, among different features to be taken into account in order to set up a sufficiently diverse management body, gender is the critical one: despite different and relevant steps forward having been taken, this still remains one of the most debated issues in industrial organisation. In fact—according to various reports and enquiries—a significant gap between men and women in apical positions continues to be a dismal reality, and the financial industry is not an exception.

As far as investment firms, RMs, and DRSPs are concerned, Recital 54[D] lays down some "good practices" that would be successful in ensuring a sound and prudent management by enabling an appropriate 'oversight and control' activity. First of all, no limitations nor waivers should be recognised to the management body, as it *should be responsible and accountable for the overall strategy of the firm, taking into account the firm's business and risk profile*. That is, not only managers should be judged on the results they yield ('responsibility' stricto sensu, as a synonym of "liability" in both the business and the administrative/criminal realm): also, they should *feel* that responsibility and know that the community of stakeholders will require them to show what they have achieved, without trying to escape such a scrutiny (the more general concept of 'accountability').

Nevertheless, in this realm, the European legislator proves himself to be a wise one, for it does not join the populistic tendency to blame top managers for every negative event associated with the companies they are in charge of, but cleverly circumscribes both responsibility and accountability to 'the firm business and risk profile'. This entails that the evaluation be done by duly considering as a benchmark the ordinary (physiological) activity of the firm, thus paying attention to deviations from it (e.g., in case the firm became involved in operations outside its traditional scope, or even with a higher degree of risk *vis-à-vis* the level usually borne). However, the role of managers is precisely defined, and seems to suggest that no loopholes are recognised in such responsibilities: in Recital 54[D] is stated that they span *across the business cycle of the firm* and are rooted in the areas of *the identification and definition of the strategic objectives, risk strategy and internal governance of the firm, of the approval of its internal organisation*. This last point is furtherly specified: it includes not only 'criteria for selection and training of personnel' but, also, an 'effective oversight of senior management', as well as 'the definition of overall policies governing the provision of services and activities'. Such expression encompasses not only 'the approval of new products for distribution to services', but also 'the remuneration of sales staff', which is central to designing incentives (and, conversely, avoiding distortions). Hence, it contributes to shaping the relations between the firm and its clients (i.e. between the RM, its participants, the companies listed upon it and traders, or between an investment firm and its customers).

A similar concern is raised in Recital 69[D], in which the European legislator considers the possibility that *an investment firm or a market operator operating a trading venue decides to suspend or remove a financial investment from trading*. This normally occurs when the recipient of the suspension has failed in complying with the rules governing the platform. In this case, the avoidance of conflicts of interest and the principle of ensuring certainty to investors require that other venues, if pushed to do so by competent authorities, take a similar measure, *unless continuing trading may be justified due to exceptional circumstances*. Here, the "exceptionality" is not referred to events or situations themselves, but rather to the very limited extent to which this provision applies. In fact, the only reasons allowing for such a waiver appeal to superior interests, such as systemic stability and investor protection. Moreover, in the abovementioned Recital is remarked that no piece of information 'transmitted in the context of a suspension or removal of a financial instrument' should ever be used for 'trading for commercial purposes', and competent authorities are encouraged to exchange information in order to avoid this.

A 'continuous oversight' in relation to these topics, aimed at ensuring that the management be 'sound and prudent', is stated in Recital 54[D]; nevertheless, if a single individual held directorships within multiple management bodies, (s)he would not spend 'adequate time' for a single entity. Hence, *it is necessary to limit the number of directorships a member of the management body of an institution may hold at the same time in different entities*, albeit this rule does not take into account *directorships in organisations which do not pursue predominantly commercial objectives, such as not-for-profit or charitable organisations*. The rationale of these considerations is not particularly clear. In fact, several non-commercial entities are provided with complex organisational structures that require from managers a great commitment in time and personal resources; moreover, trying to go beyond the surface of Recital 54[D] to guess the real intentions of the European legislator (talking merely about 'time' seems to restrict a much wider issue), we should recognise that a purpose like the avoidance of conflicts of interest—which would be very likely to occur when the same individual be a member of different management bodies—is not automatically pursued by allowing to contemporarily manage (e.g.) an investment firm and a charitable organisation, for the scopes of the two might eventually overlap.

In Recital 56[D], the topic of conflicts of interest is more directly addressed by highlighting the opposition between 'different activities' carried out by investment firms and 'the interests of their clients', which—of course—should not be adversely affected. The provision suggested in this Recital—unlike other ones—is very general, merely urging firms to 'prevent or manage' the conflicts and 'mitigate' those risks that might arise. Nevertheless, a 'clear disclosure'—both on the content of the "threat" and the steps to be furtherly made to neutralise it—is what must be done in the case 'some residual risk of detriment to the clients' interests' remains even after the adoption of the abovementioned measures.

Finally, in Recital 55^D is clarified that no CG model (either a 'unitary' or a 'dual' one, like those diffused in the United Kingdom and Germany respectively) is better than another in order to achieve the purposes laid down in MiFID II, nor this piece of legislation actually suggests the adoption of any particular organisational structure. In order to reinforce this concept, is clearly stated that 'no interference' on national company law, to which ruling on CG models is traditionally demanded, should spring from the definitions contained in the Directive. As a proof of the European legislator's unobtrusiveness, no explicit provision about CG is encompassed by MiFIR: if there were, it would have been immediately enforceable starting from 3 January 2018. However, this is not the intention of a legislator whose approach to the issue is by setting general requirements that domestic law is asked to deepen, clarify, and reshape in accordance with the specific context and the existing juridical framework in a given country. To conclude, we may observe that the provisions about CG laid down in the Package—though in the form of mere considerations, as in the Recitals—show more an investor-protective purpose—i.e. the aim of countering mala gestio phenomena—than the orientation to define a precise best practice in relation to the models to be implemented. In fact, there is no agreement on this point. Hence, it seems quite correct to state that each CG model has pros and cons: the differences between the organisational structures of companies likely depend upon which category of stakeholders is the most "influential" one in a certain country or juridical tradition.

3.8 Risk Management and Mitigation

As could be easily guessed, 'risk management' and 'risk mitigation' are very general concepts, for there are multiple kinds of risk that a financial institution has to face. It would be outside the scope of this paragraph to treat them all in detail, also because they are mostly connected not to European-level legislation but to other international standards, sometimes merely of soft-law force (e.g., the Basel Accords), to be furtherly implemented through pieces of domestic legislation.

Toward the end of the Cold War, globalisation started galloping, markets became open like never before and financial transactions gained a worldwide, more easily accessible dimension. At that time, when the first round of the Basel Accords was put in place, the whole of the supervisory architecture was centred around the aim of preventing the regulated subjects from being exposed to unbearable risks (in particular, via the imposition of specific capital requirements in order to avoid any eventualities of loss-related undercapitalisation), for these risks will likely yield negative spill-overs at a systemic level. This concept seems to have been clear only under a theoretical or "academic" point of view, before the GFC dramatically opened the eyes of regulators. Anyway, it is well underlined in Recital 5^D, where is stated that *excessive and imprudent risk taking may lead to the failure of individual financial institutions and systemic problems in Member States and globally*. The use of a conditional mode ('may') would lead to consider risk management and mitigation as a necessary condition for financial markets and intermediaries to be "healthy", but not automatically a sufficient one. In other words, the European legislator seems to acknowledge—with an implicit mea culpa—the possibility that the positive association between risk and return holds consistently over time, without any "breaking point" being reached, making the risk-loving firm a well-performing one, too. In addition to this, however, it seems to admit that financial distress can be due, also, to factors different from 'excessive and imprudent' risk-taking. Nevertheless, the approach first laid down in Basel was deemed to deserve a follow-up in the Package, even if, at present-day, almost nobody thinks that these solutions are able to "work miracles". This is a fortiori true in light of the GFC experience.

The Directive calls for a 'coherent and risk-sensitive framework for regulating the main types of order-execution arrangements' (Recital 13^{D}) but, also, takes into account some practices commonly put in place to hedge against risks. For instance (Recital 22^{D}), is acknowledged that some persons deal 'in commodity derivatives, emission allowances and derivatives thereof', as well as in other instruments, *as part of their commercial treasury risk management activities to protect themselves against risks, such as exchange rate risk* (in fact, most of these instruments are denominated in a single currency, namely the US dollar). Another example is discussed in Recital 29^{D}, where is noted that *some operators of industrial installations covered by the EU Emissions Trading Scheme bundle and out-source their trading activities for hedging commercial risks to non-commercial subsidiaries.* In Recital 50^{D}, counterparty risk is explicitly addressed.

Another source of risks is doubtlessly algorithmic trading (AT), to which Recital 59^{D} is devoted. This *technique* of executing transactions is driving the evolution of financial markets. Here we just underline that in Recital 60^{D} is mandated that 'appropriate systems and controls' be put in place by the firms pursuing a 'market making strategy', an expression which is unbound from other European legislation prior to the Package and explicitly thought to be 'understood in a way specific to its context and purpose'. An additional obligation charged upon investment firms that use HFT for market-making purposes is, of course (by the definition of market making itself), the one to provide adequate liquidity: in relation to this, Recital 113^{D} suggests that this objective be pursued by said intermediaries by means of agreements with trading venues themselves.

However, there is an aspect of risks lying within the algorithmic trading practice that is worth noting: in fact, according to some literature, it has been enhanced by the post MiFID 'competition and fragmentation', which generated arbitrage opportunities. Anyway, while this practice is certainly a benefiting one as far as *deeper liquidity, reduced spreads, and better price alignment across venues* are concerned (albeit some analysts even doubt on the magnitude and the effectiveness of these positive spill-overs), system-wide problems may arise—with particular reference to HFT—in the case of failures, such as those events labelled as 'flash crash' in recent history.

We might just mention a couple of these famous events, affecting two of the largest and most liquid financial items in the world. The first instance refers to the Dow Jones index plummeting on 6 May 2010, when it fell by various points in less than half an hour—rapidly followed by NASDAQ and S&P 500—probably because of the *acme* reached by the crisis of Greek sovereign debt. The second instance is about the path followed by the pound sterling on 6–7 October 2016, probably reflecting the investor's worries about 'hard' Brexit. In the former case, great losses were registered on a single type of futures contract whose huge trading size had been determined by the massive use of HFT, and rapidly spread to other instruments because of the same techniques (SEC 2010). In the latter, the fault for the crash is generally attributed either to the 'fat finger' of a trader or to the wrong interpretation, made by an algorithm, of news reporting of the speech on Brexit delivered by the French then-President, Yet, although this I the most agreed-upon idea, an official investigation failed in identifying a single clear reason for the events (BIS 2017).

Recitals from 63^{D} to 69^{D} design a more effective framework in countering the risks which arise from algorithmic techniques (especially HFT ones). The first answer to these threats (Recital 63^{D}) lies in a greater accessibility to the data produced by trading venues: 'direct electronic access' (DEA) is one of the most important tools that help to curb the distance between the market operator and the players dealing in instruments, thus reducing the difference between HFT and ordinary trading techniques. In fact, DEA is defined (Recital 41^{D}) as *an arrangement where a member or participant or client of a trading venue permits a person to use its trading code so the person can electronically transmit orders relating to a financial instrument directly to the trading venue'*. It should be stressed that, whereas this definition is wide-ranging, trading venues established by different members or participants are very rare in Europe, and especially in the EU (the clearest example being Switzerland), even if such a model—different financial intermediaries coming together to establish a trading venue—is common in other parts of the world (e.g., China). In fact, venues are generally operated by a single company, which is often part of a larger group or conglomerate (e.g., the London Stock Exchange Group, operating venues in London and—through its subsidiary Borsa Italiana—also in Milan) in which 'sister' companies are specialised in the provision of *pre-* and post-trading services.

The same Recital 63^{D} underlines that the obligation to be registered, applying to all firms that make use of HFT techniques, is essential. There are some exemptions that ESMA is called to clarify, along with—and most importantly—an explicit ban, laid down in Recital 66^{D}, on providing DEA to those firms that do not put in place 'proper systems and controls' in relation to such access. Firms are explicitly urged to consider their '*responsibility for trading submitted by their clients through the use of their systems or using their trading codes*: that is, they are generally entitled to get DEA from the trading venue, yet they are also subject to strict compliance requirements when they extend this "right" to third parties, such as clients whose transactions they intermediate.

Nevertheless, DEA would help to assess whether or not they comply with some organisational requirements whose effect is substantially risk-mitigating. In spite of this, the internal measures would not suffice if a proper supervision were absent, as also underlined in said Recital. The aim of both supervision and the requirements charged to firms employing HFT techniques is described in Recital 64^{D} in terms of preventing the creation of 'disorderly markets' and also the pursuit of 'abusive purposes'. Nevertheless, trading venues themselves are charged with important obligations regarding AT: in Recital 64^{D} they are mandated to *ensure their trading systems be resilient and properly tested to deal with increased order flows or market stresses*, including the eventuality in which, *if there are sudden unexpected price movements*, platforms can temporarily halt the trading activity.

In the light of an investor-protective goal, transparency, non-discrimination, and fairness are the objectives set out by Recital 65^{D}. In particular, the European legislator has noted that is *appropriate to allow for trading venues to adjust their fees for cancelled orders according to the length of time for which the order was maintained*. This highlights how a timely intervention on fees—which should reflect the actual volumes and prices in the market—is required to avoid any distortions that would hurt all market participants, either directly or indirectly. In addition to this, the abovementioned Recital envisages, also, that fees have to be 'calibrated', i.e. variable depending upon the trader's "behaviour": if a large amount of orders is cancelled, fees should be higher; and this is particularly true, of course, when HFT techniques are applied.

Recital 67^{D} suggests one of the means that could be used in order to ensure an effective supervision. It is the so-called 'flagging', i.e. the identification of orders generated by algorithms—in a way that enables to 'reconstruct efficiently and evaluate' the strategy put in place by algorithmic traders, for uncertainty on the attribution of orders and the recognition of strategies is per se the source of a risk worth mitigating.

3.9 Investor Protection and Transparency

Information has always been pivotal to the good functioning of any kind of exchanges, whether of material goods or services; and, conversely, asymmetries represent one of the major distortions that an inevitably frictional market fails to erase. This is a fortiori true in the financial system: since practically any instrument encompasses at least an element of 'risk', scientifically defined as either the uncertainty on outcomes or the probability of adverse ones (the most common scenario being the counterparty failing to fulfil its obligation), in order for a market to work in a way which is "fair" for its participants and to establish effective defences against abusive practices, is important that investors be adequately "informed" on the characteristics of the instruments they are going to deal in, especially in relation to the risks they are exposed to and the hypothetical size of losses which they could suffer. Such a protection should be the higher the more "retail" is the investor, that is, the greater the amount jeopardised as a proportion to his/her wealth and the less used s/he is to invest (though we refer to natural persons, it is well possible that a retail investor be a SME or any other little entity).

Recital 83[D] lays down some elements that help to identify such need for protection: even if this might seem silly and perhaps difficult to implement, the first—and simplest—way of evaluating how much an investor has to be protected is by looking at the time it requires in order to read carefully and well understand the features of an investment, before deciding whether to undertake it or not. In relation to this, the time needed will likely be higher if the product is more 'complex' or 'unfamiliar': it seems that 'complexity' be an objective characteristic, rather than a subjective one, whereas 'familiarity' obviously depends upon the investor's 'prior experience'.

Despite the general attitude towards charging intermediaries with duties to provide adequate information to their clients, the European legislator—at least formally—is not insensible to the legitimate claims that over-information is as bad as weak or incomplete one. In fact, it would make investors unable to discern 'relevant' one from what is actually pleonastic and would also make regulation too burdensome to be effective, with the potential risk of yielding depressive effects on investment activity. The idea that information requirements have gone too far is gaining ground in current debate, notwithstanding the appreciable content of Recital 84[D]: in the Directive, *nothing (...) should oblige investment firms to provide all required information (...) immediately and at the same time, provided that they comply with the obligation to provide the relevant information in good time before the time specified* (Recital 84[D]).

The use of *and* in the phrase 'immediately and at the same time' actually makes this principle less strong than it would have been if the preposition *or* had been used. It means that some pieces of information may be required *ad horas* and some other contemporarily instead of sequentially (however, these peculiar duties could be sometimes necessary for special purposes, in extremely urgent cases). Although one of the two characteristics may still be required, it shows a valuable intention by the Package's legislator.

An important distinction to be made—for it shapes the compliance regime that is applicable, and thus the level of investor protection ensured by legislation—is that regarding the provision of services, whether 'at the initiative of a client' or not. Recital 85[D] clarifies the issue: a service is by default considered to be provided at the initiative of a client, albeit such automatism is excluded in the case the latter submits its demand *in response to a personalised communication to or on behalf of the firm*, specifically addressed to it, provided that the reply *contains an invitation or is intended to influence the client in respect of a specific financial instrument or a specific transaction*. Of course, this double specificity—with regard to both the recipient and the content—fails to occur when the advice *by its very nature is general and addressed to the public or a larger group or category of clients or potential clients*. This is another very important discernment made by MiFID II, also separating a traditional service provided by investment firms from another which is merely 'ancillary'. Again, the distinction is made on both a subjective basis (the public instead of specific persons) and an objective one (the generality of the advice, not referred to particular products or investments). The explicit use of *and* seems to suggest that these requisites must hold together, not being sufficient that one holds and the other does not. The rationale of such a restrictive provision can be easily understood, for the classification of a service as provided not at the initiative of a client—but, of course, under the firm's free exercise of an investment activity—is explicitly envisaged as a residual, exceptional one.

The fact that a service is by default regarded as provided at the initiative of a client, thus subjecting the firm to weaker duties in respect of the informative requirements toward the counterparty (e.g., the appropriateness test is not mandatory)—in a manner which is de facto similar to the one envisaged for the execution of client orders—might be surprising. Nevertheless, it should be considered by looking at the whole picture of the Package, which designs a solid protective framework in respect of the majority of investors (as we are going to see). In fact, since more burdensome information duties (vis-à-vis previous legislation) are imposed to investment firms with respect to previous legislation, it is less likely than in the past that a firm seeks to attract investors by explicitly advertising its services. Conversely, it will be more likely to strengthen its reputation in the market and orient its propaganda in an indirect way (e.g., by claiming the successfulness of its business), always kept 'general' and addressed 'to the public', in order to prompt investors to take the 'initiative' and ask for the provision of certain services.

Furthermore, we should note that—regardless of the way in which a firm cares his own advertising and its attitude towards the clientele—is much more likely that the "enterprising" customer is either a 'professional client' or an 'eligible counterparty' (thus needing less protection) rather than a retail one, for the relation between "financial experience" and the "willingness to take the initiative" is—ceteris paribus—self-evidently positive. Anyway, in Recital 85^D—which is introductory to the main investor-protective considerations, made in Recital 86^D, that we are going to analyse—is underlined and applied the principle that the proponent of an investment is less in need of protection than the recipient of it, regardless of how the latter be classified.

Recital 86^D begins with the statement that 'one of the objectives' of MiFID II is 'to protect investors', also assessing the principle that mandates different levels of protection for the three different categories (retail investors, professional investors and eligible counterparties). Anyway, there are "fundamental values" that not only shape legislation in respect of a specific segment but are "universally" valid and help defining the relation between firms and their clients, irrespective of how they are categorised. These "values" are honesty, fairness and professionalism, in order to establish obligations that are 'fair, clear and not misleading'. It is nothing new in the history of contract law; nevertheless, such a principle is particularly important if applied to the financial realm, whereby weaker parties are more susceptible to the consequences of mala gestio than in "real" markets. Moreover, since misconduct toward clients—put in place by exploiting information asymmetries—might lead to the seizure of market power and even the conquest of a dominant position, any wrongdoing in the actions of investment firms is a serious concern under the goal of levelling the playing field.

Therefore, on the financial system as a whole, misconduct—such that providers are able to extract undue profits from the way they relate to their clients—may have a double effect: in a sufficiently or highly competitive market (e.g., asset management), it could theoretically help wrongdoers to build virtual barriers preventing clients from being attracted by competitors, thus being particularly negative for those firms that abide by laws and regulation; in a lowly-competitive one (e.g., investment banking, which is strongly concentrated in a bunch of main players), the fact that firms already hold some market power makes misconduct be extremely harmful for clients. Furthermore, the issues mentioned in Recital 86^{D} directly raise the question of 'confidence in the market' (that is, trust in the fact that markets will fulfil their function of transferring monetary resources from persons in *surplus* to those in *deficit*), which is key to the maintenance of "economic order" and, thus, systemic stability.

A peculiar context in which misconduct might arise if proper regulatory settings were not put in place is what has been extensively labelled as 'bank-insurance', i.e. the even stricter connection—rapidly growing over recent years—between "banking" (*rectius*, investment) and insurance products: the most commonly known items are the so-called 'unit-linked' insurance policies, which rely upon underlying shares in a collective investment scheme ('units', in technical parlance). Recital 87^{D} deals with these situations: for the sake of protecting investors and levelling the playing field, *insurance-based investment products are subject to appropriate requirements*. However, this might not suffice, for such products have their own peculiarity that should be specifically addressed by the comprehensive regulatory framework. In this case—as underlined in Recital 87^{D}—the main reference is Directive 2002/92/EC. Moreover, a close cooperation between EIOPA and ESMA is particularly recommended, as they are the two competent authorities for this (relatively new) segment of financial markets.

Another relevant issue that deals with investor protection is the so-called 'best execution', whose deepening vis-à-vis MiFID I is a consistent novelty carried by the Directive. There is a clear need behind these new rules: in fact, *given that a wider range of execution venues are now available in the Union*, and that there have been significant *advances in technology for monitoring best execution*, there are good reasons for the European legislator to highlight and widen this important point.

Recital 93^{D} specifies what is intended. First, since executing the client's orders makes the investment firm obviously bear some costs, that the latter discharges on the former, is carefully declared that *for the purposes of determining best execution when executing retail client orders, the cost relative to execution should include an investment firm's own commissions or fees charged to the client for limited purposes, where more than one venue listed in the firm's execution policy is capable of executing a particular order*. This is, de facto, a warning on investment firms not to abuse of their position—hence, to keep prices adequately low—when the "market for execution", i.e. the different venues available to execute, is quite competitive. Anyway, these provisions have to be taken into account when the goal is to compare the economic convenience, for the client, to get its order executed on one venue or another. Nevertheless, this does not mean that fees et similia—contributing to the total monetary outflow experienced by the client—can be used to compare different policies implemented by different firms. Furthermore, the European legislator clarifies that, of course, the same investment firm is allowed to apply one policy instead of another, if the service provided is not the same. This sounds particularly consistent with the principle of 'fairness', which—in generic juridical terms—also requires treating different situations in a different manner.

An exemption from the obligation to provide evidence on the costs related to execution is allowed for the purposes dealt with by Article 27^{D}, par. 5: namely, *information on the different venues where the investment firm executes its client orders and the factors affecting the choice of execution venue*, which should be included *in respect of each class of financial instruments* (Recital 94^{D}). However, transparency on fees is clearly insufficient, because—from an investor protection standpoint—is also important that the consumer of investment services not be charged with costs in a way which is damaging for it. To this goal is devoted Recital 95^{D}, where the focus is on unfair discrimination between different execution venues: that is, the case in which the investment firm structures its fees and commissions with a view to favouring one venue over the others and without reflecting *actual differences in the cost to the firm of executing on those venues*. Nevertheless, not the whole of the regulatory burden is charged upon firms: venues themselves—both trading ones and SIs—may have to *make available to the public data on the quality of execution of transactions* on them. Notice that previous Recitals did not mention SIs: in fact, the duty to which a SI is called is neither as related to the execution of orders, nor as investor-oriented, as other venues. Conversely, the role of SIs deals with the "superior" goal of maintaining an ordinate, efficient, well-functioning market.

Specifically, such information obligation applies to the instruments 'subject to the trading obligations' pursuant to Articles 23^{R} and 28^{R}: that is, either the obligation to trade on a RM, unless particular exceptive conditions are met (namely, as stated in Article 23^{R}, to *shares, depositary receipts, ETFs, certificates and other similar financial instruments on a multilateral basis*); or the obligation to trade on RMs, MTFs, OTFs, as well as—in presence of an equivalence decision issued by the Commission and on a non-exclusive basis—also on third-country venues (this provision encompassed by Article 28^{R} basically refers to certain kinds of derivatives). In order to be exempted from the obligation to be dealt on RMs, they have to be

(a) *non-systematic, ad hoc, irregular and infrequen*t, or;
(b) *carried out between eligible and/or professional counterparties* such that they *do not contribute to the price discovery process.*

By continuing in a sort of "flip-flopping" between the creation of an "ideal" regulatory framework capable of adequately protecting investors, on the one hand, and the goal of avoiding a disruption of common, rooted investment practices, on the other, in Recital 97^{D} the European legislator acknowledges that *information provided by investment firms to clients in order to their execution policy often are generic and standard*, such that clients are not able to check whether or not the firm has complied with its best-execution duties or not. Therefore, in order to make such control possible and effective, *is appropriate to specify the principles concerning the information given by investment firms to their clients on the execution policy*. Furthermore, with the rationale that a mere statement of principles might itself remain too generic, there is an additional provision: *to make public, on an annual basis, for each class of financial instruments, the top five execution venues (...) in the preceding year*, measured in terms of volume of executed orders, including it along with *information published by execution venues on execution quality*.

These provisions are followed by technical ones regarding the characteristics of clients and other agents: e.g., the qualification of 'tied agents' is also discussed; moreover, is stated that they are prevented from choosing to be registered in a certain Member State only *for the purpose of evading stricter standards* in place in a different Member State where their activity is carried out in a prevalent manner. An important statement, made in Recital 103^{D}, is that *for the purposes of this Directive, eligible counterparties should be considered to be acting as clients*.

With regard not only to transparency but, also, to the enhancement of the freedoms established in the Treaties to which the whole Package refers, Recital 108^{D} appears as one of the most significant: it states that, *in order to facilitate the finalisation of cross-border transactions, it is appropriate to provide free access o clearing and settlement systems throughout the Union by investment firms, irrespective of whether transactions have been concluded through regulated markets in the Member States concerned*: that is, no barriers to the settlement may be built on a national basis, for this would clearly affect the freedom of investing in the Single Market. Since freedom implies responsibility, the same Recital encompasses the provision that investment firms participating in the settlement systems of different Member States comply 'with the relevant operational and commercial requirements for membership' and, of course, with the prudential measures designed to make the functioning of the market 'smooth and orderly'.

In relation to this goal, the Recitals of MiFID II also address the need for a 'consolidated tape for equities and equity-like financial instruments' (Recital 118^{D}), for this would help creating 'a more integrated European market' and allow market participants to access trade transparency information in an easier way. Although the establishment of a 'consolidated tape' for non-equity instruments is more difficult, notwithstanding such an asymmetry, the legislator does not rule out the possibility to intervene for the purpose of a consolidated tape being put in place for every type of instruments—in respect of asset classes—in the information set available to investors.

Recital 144^{D} deals with the availability of *telephone conversations and data traffic records from investment firms executing and documenting the execution of transactions, as well as existing telephone and data traffic records from telecommunications operators*, which often constitute the only probation elements in the case of an alleged market abuse of other wrongdoing (the reference is to the violation of requirements set forth in the Package) committed by 'an investment firm or credit institution'. It is clear that no criminal inquiry on any infringements could be conducted in an effective manner without the 'assistance and cooperation' of all the authorities involved in a cross-border investigation (Recital 153^{D}), which are thus required to act fairly for such purposes; that is, they basically have to properly manage disclosure and secrecy obligations.

Finally, Recitals 161^{D}–164^{D} specify the role of the managers of alternative investment funds (AIFMs), which is clearly the main subject of AIFMD. In fact, they can be authorised by Member States—as set forth in said Directive—to 'provide certain investment services' outside their ordinary scope, which is the 'collective management' of AIFs: they can perform an ancillary activity, such as the safekeeping, as well as administer 'shares or units of collective investment undertakings' and—most closely to the operations carried out by investment firms—the 'reception and transmission of orders in relation to financial instruments'. Recital 161^{D} underlines the requirement of a single, portable authorisation issued by the NCA, mutually recognised by the supervisors of other Member States, whereas Recital 162^{D} specifies that AIFMs providing investment services must comply with national local rules when operating in foreign Member States. Yet, the freedom to provide services on a cross-border basis—'subject to appropriate notification requirements' and upon authorisation—is reaffirmed as a non-negotiable characteristic of the Single Market for financial services (which clearly applies to AIFMs providing investment services, too). This would imply—and has actually implied—amendments to the AIFMD (Recital 163^{D}), which is clearly outside the scope of this work. Recital 164^{D} explicitly mentions the application of the principle of subsidiarity with the purpose of guaranteeing a deeper integration in the EU financial markets *in which investors are effectively protected and the efficiency and integrity of the overall market are safeguarded*, thus allowing the EU to intervene in the case of Member States failing to establish a common regulatory framework relative to investment firms, regulated markets and trading systems. Nevertheless, such a subsidiary intervention must be conducted in accordance with the principle of 'proportionality', i.e. without trespassing 'what is necessary in order to achieve that objective'.

Prior to conclude the discussion on the main goals of the Package, it may be useful to spend other few words on the investor-protective aspects of SME growth markets. In addition to harmonising a quite fragmented regulatory landscape and fostering the appeal of SME growth markets to investors, the European legislator is quite concerned that 'high levels of investor protection' are maintained (Recital 133^{D}), for they are a basic requirement in order for 'confidence' to be boosted and, thus, keeping the exchanges orderly and efficient. It is easy to guess why 'confidence' is a crucial element, especially for small businesses: SMEs have been severely hit by crisis throughout Europe, with the deterioration of their creditworthiness making much more difficult for them to find financial resources. From a *macro-* standpoint, this is a blow to the pillars of any economy. Hence, SME growth markets may well benefit from a 'lessening of administrative burdens' (Recital 132^{D}); yet, this does not mean that investors dealing in that kind of issuances cannot rely upon the same set of provisions applied to other MTFs. In fact, is easier to be admitted to trading on a 'specialist' market rather than on a 'main' one; however, once exchanges have been initiated, the "rules of the game" are not different and the "playing field" between the two abovementioned categories of markets is substantially levelled.

References

Bank for International Settlements. (2017, January). *The sterling 'flash event' of 7 October 2016.*

Di Noia, C. (2017, June 15). *Hearing at the Finance Committee of the Italian House of Deputies*, Rome.

Lucantoni, P. (2017). Il mercato dei derivati: note preliminari ad uno studio sistematico. *Banca Borsa Titoli di Credito: rivista di dottrina e giurisprudenza, 70*(2), 182–206.

Siclari, D. (2016). European Capital Markets Union e ordinamento nazionale. *Banca Borsa Titoli di Credito: rivista di dottrina e giurisprudenza, 69*(4), 481–505.

Securities and Exchange Commission. (2010). *Findings Regarding the Market Events of May 6, 2010.* Washington, D.C.

Chapter 4
How Exchanges Work: Trading Venues, Algorithmic and High-Frequency Transactions

Abstract The chapter investigates the functioning of exchanges. First, it discusses the features of different types of trading venues: for instance, the role of newly-introduced OTFs. Then, it debates the role of technology underlying transactions, which is increasingly shifting towards algorithmic (AT) and high-frequency (HFT) solutions, widely regarded by the EU legislator as a potential threat to systemic stability. To provide a deeper understanding of what an automated exchange means, the chapter briefly covers the divide between 'electronic communication networks' (ECNs) and 'market makers' in the US jurisdiction, which presents a concerning trade-off under multiple aspects (e.g., efficiency vs. transparency). In addition to merely economic aspects, the most salient regulatory tasks are also investigated: inter alia, the platforms being required to 'self-assess' themselves—and, specifically, their recourse to AT and HFT techniques—by means of a stress test, aimed at identifying and mitigating systemic threats. Finally, we devote some attention to the so-called 'SME growth markets', i.e. a type of MTF specifically designed to trade equities representing small and medium-sized enterprises, for the purpose of sustaining their development.

4.1 Trading Venues as a Critical Issue

Before detailing the organisational and supervisory novelties brought by the Package, it is worth highlighting the relevance of trading venues for an orderly and efficient development of markets. Moloney (2014) defines them as a *critical component of financial market infrastructure*, for they play a number of pivotal roles: permit a mobilisation and allocation of savings towards financial investments, favour liquidity of traded instruments, allow for better trading activity and risk management. Hence, in light of the financial intermediation theory, trading venues are essential in allowing the transfer of monetary resources from the subjects in *surplus* to those in *deficit*. This clearly explains why their regulation is at least as important as that on securities.

M. Comana et al., *The MiFID II Framework*,
https://doi.org/10.1007/978-3-030-12504-2_4

Years before the GFC, trading venues had already experienced disruptive changes affecting their nature and functioning. In general, they had evolved from being "neutral" platforms, designed to merely support and offset the ongoing transactions, to represent perhaps the greatest sources of information and data provision in the financial realm. This has occurred not only because of the increasing 'depth' of markets—certainly driven by technological progress and economic advancement—but, also, thanks to some structural features which have risen in most recent years (Moloney 2014): risk-management products are more standardised; admission to listing and secondary-market trading functions have been separated; the degree of competition has undoubtedly soared. Most importantly, new services have started being provided, such that they are nowadays on the brink of overwhelming—in quantitative terms—the traditional market-operating segment. According to the World Federation of Exchanges (WFE) and its *Costs and Revenues Survey*, in 2012, the exchange industry got 27% of its revenues from trading excluding derivatives (down 6 points from 2011) and 6% from listing (unchanged). Inflows related to derivatives (trading and clearing fees) represented an astonishing 35% of the total (+7 from previous year), whereas 'other services' accounted for 26% (+3), 'financial income' for 5% (−2) and 'other' for 3% (unchanged).

The shift from traditional venues to unregulated ones (mainly OTC)—as highlighted, *inter alia*, by the EU Parliament resolution of 14 December 2010—is not the first historic change faced by stock exchanges. Nor it is the "physical" use of their buildings, which nowadays are increasingly devoted to purposes different from trading. Before the surge in alternative markets, the major evolution undergone in the industry was moving from a "mutualised" model, whereby participants held stakes of the exchange and the latter was somewhat organised as a cooperative firm, to a fully "private" one, not intrinsically different from other companies in the financial realm. Today, the "mutualised" model is still adopted in countries with a broad industry—either by its weight on GDP or its absolute size—like Switzerland and China; yet, the majority of developed nations has already chosen the "private" one.

Operators of exchanges have been often considered as something different from firms stricto sensu. Nowadays, however, they are generally deemed to be companies providing a twofold kind of services, i.e. listing and trading (a third one being settlement, which is often outsourced), for a twofold kind of customers, i.e. firms willing to be listed and intermediaries willing to trade (Di Noia 2001). As a matter of fact, since the liberalising reforms passed during the Eighties in different countries, the exchange industry has been characterised by growing competition (Pagano and Steil 1996) and—more in general—strategic interaction. Besides, remarkable network externalities can be observed: the greater the number of customers, the higher the utility for everyone (Economides 1993, 1996): in fact, liquidity is associated with the attractiveness to clients of any kind. In light of this, a work by Di Noia (2001) applied the externality models by Katz and Shapiro (1986a, b) to competition between exchanges, which may be shaped in accordance with either a 'compatibility' model, which entails both implicit merger (IM)—that is, securities listed on one exchange get automatically listed on the other, too—and reciprocal remote access, on the one hand, or an 'incompatibility' one, envisaging "true" competition instead. IM can be a precise strategic choice, as it likely brings cross advantages in marginal costs, along with higher profits. Of course, it requires strong coordination and a thorough "policy guide" disciplining the business conduct of the implicitly merged exchanges, which might be better achieved if regulators removed barriers to listing and trading, even implementing full remote access (conversely, a protectionist stance would be inefficient and expensive for taxpayers). Also, when one exchange is monopolist but faces lower costs, there would be no need for IM, either from a "social" or a private standpoint. Competition, however, is not necessarily related to prices: it deals with the immediacy of execution, the efficacy of price discovery, the levels of price volatility and liquidity, the enforcement of transparency obligations, and transaction costs.

Looking at their functioning, exchanges can be classified into two major categories: 'quote-driven', whereby 'bid' and 'ask' quotations are inserted by MMs, dealers, or specialists, versus 'order-driven', which instead displays quotations submitted by individual investors. In 1997, for instance, the London Stock Exchange moved its FT100 index from the former kind to the latter one, in a quest for harmonisation to the model prevailing in the EU industry. As for the mechanisms presiding over transactions, in the USA, ATS have been regulated substantially in accordance with the regulatory waves of tightening and loosening. For instance, the framework established by the SEC in 1988 addressed some of the industry's concerns, yet without reforming the 1975 'trade-through rule' (TTR), which will be eventually amended by the 2005 Rule 611. It envisaged that a market, when receiving an order, could not execute it at a price 'inferior' (that is, worse from the customer's standpoint) to any found on another market. In fact, the markets at which orders are eventually sent turn out being slower and manual: hence, the result is that the application of TTR shows a "protective" attitude toward inefficient markets, on the one hand, while burdening investors with opportunity costs associated with the delay in execution, on the other. This is the result of TTR dating back at a time in which the development of HFT was still yet to come. Conversely, repealing said rule would enhance customer choice, speed, certainty of execution, and opportunity for best execution: in spite of the 2005 reform, it is still substantially enforced (Barclay et al. 2003).

During the Nineties, the literature harshly discussed how the exchange industry should have been conceived and, thus, regulated. The *Investment Services Directive* (ISD, No. 93/22/EEC) shared the 'market view' regarding the nature and the functioning of exchanges, seen as somewhat a public good (Pagano and Steil 1996), as opposed to the other ('firm view') deeming exchanges to be firms endowed with a market-making purpose, whereby transacting securities is a "composite good" provided therein. The market view highlights the *macro-* phenomenon of the encounter between bidders and offerors, as all players using the infrastructure perform a risk management function in between lenders and borrowers (Allen and Santomero 2001; Allen and Gale 1997). A third strand of literature, instead, underlined the role of exchanges as intermediaries (Domowitz 1996). Anyway, their profit-seeking attitude has been highly debated, given the "publicness"—at least partially—of the services provided by exchanges, which therefore are not always capable of abiding by a genuine market rationale. For instance, Di Noia (2000) noted that they fail to maximise profits in case of their capital being owned by customers, with different behaviours arising depending on the shares in both the shareholding base and the customer one. In fact, on the one hand, firms contribute to the exchange's profits by paying trading fees; on the other, they consume the exchange's "good" because of the industry's imperfect competition.

In particular, not all market participants seemed able to receive the benefits of competition, whereas market fragmentation had made the trading environment more complex and opaque, especially in respect of the distribution of trading data (Moloney 2014). It mostly arises in case the same instrument be traded across multiple venues: this is due to the fact that MiFID repealed the so-called 'concentration rule', which explicitly denied such opportunity and mandated that stocks of listed companies be exclusively exchanged on RMs. However, it has been argued that, after the concentration rule being repealed, increased competition has *de facto* broken liquidity, with negative implications on the efficiency of the price formation process (Lucantoni 2017).

Concerns arose regarding the possibility that investment firms were operating as MTF in the OTC markets without being subject to the same regulation as the MiFID-compliant venue that they imitated. A serious issue was that of 'broker crossing systems' (BCSs, referred as 'networks', with the acronym 'BCNs', in MiFID II), in spite of their small size in absolute terms. They are defined as electronic matching systems operated by an investment firms to execute orders against other clients' ones, or proprietary orders (CESR 2010). In the wake of the GFC outbreak, to stop the proliferation of BCSs (from 0.8% of total EEA trading in 2008 to 1.15% the subsequent year), CESR had proposed that, beyond a certain trading volume, those systems be forced to become MTFs.

At the same time, even these latter venues were undergoing some notable change. At present-day, many of them offer solely secondary trading; nevertheless, the number of companies fleeing RMs to issue securities on MTFs is growing, attracted by the obligation to disclose fewer information that what RMs require. Nowadays, these are mainly encompassed by Article 53[D], par. 3, applying to subjects different from credit institutions and investment firms, in which is stated that the applicant must have a sufficient level of trading ability and competence, adequate organisational arrangements, and sufficient resources for the role it is to perform.

As regards the structure of the exchange industry, in 2001, many believed that the introduction of the euro would have boosted concentration. Many years later, there is no clear evidence of this having occurred; conversely, we should record the striking failure of an attempted merger between two of the largest EU players: namely, Deutsche Börse (DB) and the London Stock Exchange Group (LSEG). In 2017, mainly because of Brexit-related expected cost increases, they ended their talks for integration: otherwise, they would have led to the business combination of a more traditional exchange like DB, oriented to trading (51.28% of total revenues in 2015, compared to LSEG's 23.28%), with a very "modern" one, whereby information—i.e. collecting data and selling them to third parties—and other services represented the core (42.15%, compared to DB's 16.18%), the two exchanges relying upon similar inflows from clearing and settlement (32.54% for DB, 33.82% for LSEG).

For an exchange, the cost structure is quite complex, as the regulatory burden is particularly relevant and the choice not to charge trading fees, wherever made, might significantly backfire, as well as charging less than the expenditure faced for assessing whether to admit a firm to listing or an intermediary to trading. While these two are "direct" customers, an exchange also interacts with "indirect" ones: namely, all those who submit orders for execution by deciding which intermediary to choose and where to trade. Nowadays, the MiFID framework tends to leave the latter decision to intermediaries themselves; yet, this reflects the evolution of financial markets more than of legislation, given the extent to which collective investment schemes (CIS) are replacing customers' direct choice. Actually, comparisons between different markets are extremely hard to establish (mainly because of their diverging CG structures), unless investors trade in the same instrument and, thus, may observe how it is dealt with on different platforms. Nevertheless, Domowitz (1995) tried to model a "game" with two inputs available to exchanges taking part in it: namely, either the old-fashioned floor trading or the modern automated one. While identifying liquidity creation as a positive network externality, he also found the negative one given by the free riding of innovation or price discovery, eventually leading to inefficient equilibria (i.e. suboptimal prices).

According to Di Noia (2001), frictions might arise if the choice of the venue on which to trade is done in a simultaneous manner, rather than sequentially, as the latter helps selecting the lowest price. For a company, having publicly traded securities per se makes positive network externalities arise: in fact, the value of being listed is higher the more numerous are listed firms and intermediaries transacting on the same exchange. Larger markets do actually succeed in achieving a wide array of conditions: they can provide better services (e.g., clearing and settlement), make more product information available, improve market quality (the larger the share they represent), and even yield beneficial psychological effects. Moreover, the recent development of financial markets has increasingly pursued 'compatibility' as an objective for implicitly merging with bigger venues. By setting up a rigorous theoretical, game-like model, Di Noia (2001) found some interesting propositions related to the structure, the conduct and the performance of exchanges.

First, (1) if exchanges serve areas with cross advantages in marginal costs and a Pareto-inferior equilibrium, IMs have a strictly positive impact on welfare, as well as (2) on total consumer surplus whenever marginal costs of trading and listing exceed the benefits of network externality. Conversely, (3) neither a social nor a private strict incentive to IM would arise if an exchange were 'the only winner' in a perfectly competitive environment, thanks to its capability of better covering costs, whereas the others show both kinds of marginal cost higher than the network effect. Besides, (4) if there is no compatibility between exchanges, the model predicts that, once competition arises (something inevitable in the modern world, as platforms are closely interconnected), only one will survive. The process of merging the trades executed at regional exchanges into the national one—occurred in late-Nineties (inter alia) in Italy, France, and Spain—ruled out the possibility that exchanges remained segmented and, thus, able to exert some kind of market power, leading to suboptimal cost-efficiency in execution. In the end, however, such concentration process might theoretically give rise to monopolies, even across different countries, as the mergers driven out of the market could seek something like a 'unilateral' IM. Another finding by Di Noia (2001) is that (5) in a Pareto-superior framework whereby perfect competition is actually in place, an exchange will have no incentive to pursue IM if it holds both marginal cost advantages, yet both types of its customers—namely, firms willing to list and intermediaries willing to trade—will expand their surplus. Conversely, (6) in a Pareto-inferior setting, an IM would be successful to increasing profits. In a pure-competition setting, instead, there is much larger room for finding equilibria favourable to each party involved (Propositions 7–8).

Anyway, underlines Di Noia (2001), the exchange industry cannot be regarded as a natural monopoly. In fact, even when an exchange remains monopolist, IM keeps alive some price competition. Moreover, specialisation in one of the two major activities—listing versus admission to trading—is not only possible, but beneficial under complete compatibility (that is, IM *plus* remote access). The other side of the coin is that an exchange endowed with a dominant market position will not seek agreements with peers to widen its network, preferring incompatibility instead: the reverse would occur in presence of remarkable cost advantages. Finally, if fixed costs were smaller than profits, some exchanges might seek unilateral compatibility: for instance, it was the case of the London Stock Exchange, which in late-Eighties decided to trade all stocks listed in the EU.

Strictly connected with liquidity is the issue of price formation. The difference between quote-driven and order-driven venues—the former being often "informal" ones, whereby dealers play a salient role—helps us understanding why—in turn—price-formation issues cannot be analysed without considering transparency requirements—mainly in terms of disclosure—substantially diverging between the two "categories", and, thus, affecting their degree of 'efficiency' also thanks to the supervisory activity, which should count on the availability of information in order to correctly identify in advance the emerging risks, eventually preventing them from arising. Nevertheless, some regulatory prescriptions might actually backfire and, in the light of enhancing market efficiency and avoiding systemic disorder, could even be counter-productive: for instance, pre-trade transparency is often deemed to be a potential danger to orderly trading. In fact, disclosure preceding the actual execution might actually yield changes in the behaviour of other investors: hence, by modifying market conditions, it might eventually alter the economic consequences of that investment.

Title III of MiFID II explicitly addresses RMs. First of all, clearly, the RM and its operator must both undergo authorisation, with Member States allowed to differentiate the obligations charged on these two subjects. In the application submitted to the relevant authority, *all information including a programme of operations setting out, inter alia, the type of business envisaged and the organisational structure*, as well as *all the necessary arrangements' in order to comply with any provision of the Directive, must be provided* (Article 7^{D}, par. 2).

The authorisation may also be withdrawn in multiple eventualities, enumerated in Article 7^{D}, par. 5:

(a) in the case it has not been used for twelve months, or has been expressly renounced, or no operation has been carried out in the prior six months;
(b) if the authorisation *has been obtained by making false statements or by any other irregular means*;
(c) if once-existing conditions allowing its release are no longer met;
(d) if the provisions adopted pursuant to the Package have been 'seriously and systematically' infringed;
(e) if the situation *falls within any of the cases where national law provides for withdrawal.*

In Article 47^{D}, 'organisational requirements' are laid down. First of all, Member States must mandate RMs to explicitly envisage the following:

(a) putting in place *arrangements to identify clearly and manage the potential adverse consequences ... of any conflict of interest*, involving the market itself, its owners or its operator, such that the RM's 'sound management' could be endangered;
(b) implementing efficient risk-mitigation strategies and internal procedures, i.e. adopting *appropriate arrangements and systems to identify all significant risks to its operation*;
(c) ensuring a *sound management of the technical operations of the systems*, including the contingency measures to *cope with risks of system disruption*;
(d) having regard to transparency and non-discretionary 'rules and procedures', in a way consistent with the establishment of 'objective criteria for the efficient execution of orders';
(e) pursuing an 'efficient and timely finalisation' of transactions;
(f) holding 'sufficient financial resources' starting from the time of the authorisation, so that they will be able to ensure the 'orderly functioning' of exchanges.

With respect to RMs, important rules are also laid down in relation to the listing (removal) of single financial instruments. In addition to the standard principles set out in Article 51^{D} (paragraphs 1 and 2), a transparent pricing and 'effective settlement conditions' must be put in place in respect of derivatives.

4.2 The Rationale of MiFID II Rules

As already stated, the enhancement of competition between trading venues is one of the major goals set forth by the EU legislator. Nevertheless, some have raised concerns about this objective being achieved or not. In fact, when the Package was still a proposal undergoing discussion, some authors argued that while a previously unlevel playing field between RMs and MTFs would have been healed by MiFID II provisions, OTFs would have revealed to be inconsistent with the other two, in the light of a fair and balanced competition (Clausen and Sørensen 2012). The same orientation—aimed at lowering costs, in a friendly effort towards the financial consumer—had already shaped the official recognition of MTFs in MiFID I. While such facilities had been previously bound to country-specific stock exchanges—that is, subject to national-level rules, today there is appreciable evidence of a decent harmonisation having been reached. For instance, with regard to 'on-book' equity trading, costs have decreased by roughly 60% from 2006 to 2009, moving from 1.18 to 0.47 euros per transaction, though increasing in terms of the value of trading (from 0.43 to 0.49 basis points), as acknowledged in the 2011 Oxera Report. Once combined, these two results suggest that markets have gained depth, with more transactions executed, notwithstanding a narrow increase in the related expenses (a possible explanation being the growing demand for trading).

Altogether, both investors and market operators seem to have achieved monetary gains when acting on MiFID infrastructures, at least in relation to equities. Most importantly, in the wake of the creation of OTFs, 'formal' trading venues have been pushed to differentiate their services, something which in the economic jargon is generally associated to a better 'resource allocation' (and a more widespread participation by investors). As far as financial exchanges and their market infrastructure are concerned, this clearly yields greater stability at a systemic level. Yet, different features of the two types of venue had been accompanied by different regulatory burdens, with MTFs subjected to heavier requirements. As acknowledged by the EU Commission when drafting an EMIR proposal, *the benefits from such increased competition have not flowed equally to all market participants and have not always been passed on to the end investors, retail or wholesale*. In addition to such an unlevel playing field, concerns have also been raised in respect of the possibility for the same instrument to be traded on venues of different type, leading to market fragmentation. As the Commission wrote in the document drafting a MiFID II proposal, said phenomenon *has also made the trading environment more complex, especially in terms of collection of trade data*.

Furthermore, the European legislator has also realised how some MiFID provisions have become "old" and inadequate because of the astonishing rapidity by which markets and technology have changed, with the possible rise of an uneven playing field not merely within RMs and MTFs, but also between trading venues and investment firms, on the one hand, and informal, bilateral facilities, on the other. A third concern highlighted by the Commission was about *weaknesses in the regulation of instruments other than shares, traded mostly between professional investors*; in particular, the *growing complexity in financial instruments* called to update and enhance investor protection. In fact, the increased competition between venues—such that, in 2010, MTFs had peaked to a market share of 25 to 30%—has failed in phasing out the choice for different types of exchanges, which still remains a considerable part of the market. As far as equities are concerned, in 2010 the European Parliament reported that CESR had found the total amount of OTC transactions—i.e. those occurring on *OTC markets, dark pools and other more or less unregulated internal order-matching systems* (Clausen and Sørensen 2012)—represent a share comprised between 30 and 40% of total EEA trading. In particular, 'dark' trading is a 'multilateral' one, in the sense that the venue—or the platform whereby transactions are executed—does not act as an intermediary between the parties; conversely, the venue is one of the parties in so-called 'bilateral' trading, typical of OTC markets and SIs.

Similar concerns as those raised in the USA with respect to TTR have shaped the revision of MiFID I: in particular, this was the case of the 2011 Oxera Report *Monitoring prices, costs, and volumes of trading*, prepared for the EU Commission's DG Internal Markets and Services. One of the main findings was that, under that-time framework, the regulatory burden was not evenly divided, as market fragmentation was a major source of potential turmoil. However, the main reason underlying it—namely, MiFID I having repealed the very old-fashioned 'concentration rule', which was enforced in leading economies like Germany, France, Italy—needed not that Brussels take any step backwards, but rather endeavour to achieve a 'single rulebook' of harmonised financial provisions. As we know, MiFID II is one of the pieces of EU legislation that most contribute to pursuing that goal, and the discipline of exchanges is no exception. Other than repealing the 'concentration rule', MiFID I intended to establish a European regulatory regime for trading platforms different from RMs—namely, at that time, MTFs only—by granting them EU passport. Moreover, it aimed at creating a more coherent basis for investment firms to offer themselves as trading venues. Under the 2004 Directive, the classification of RMs was subject to substantial discretion; yet, apart from "marketing" reasons in terms of reliability for investors, there was no actual difference between RMs and MTFs, which both provided a twofold service: namely, admitting securities to trading and preserving the functioning of the secondary markets on which these securities are transacted following primary issuance. MiFID I had explicitly envisaged that OTC platforms carry out trades above the 'standard market size' set forth by CESR (or ESMA, within the ESFS architecture), with no transparency requirements applying and, thus, such trading being formally 'dark'.

The fact that the industry's playing field was unlevel had many causes. Some corporate finance provisions related to the issuance of capital instruments had worsened the situation: for instance, just to mention one of the most striking ones, the so-called *Takeover Directive* (No. 2004/25/EC, barely contemporaneous to MiFID I) applied to shares listed solely on RMs and not on MTFs. Furthermore, the substantially dualistic nature of systematic internalisers (SIs)—which may be viewed both as intermediaries and venues, this last definition being much less accurate—had not been clarified yet: they were acknowledged as bearing obligations different from those of trading venues and primarily related to transparency, including the mandatory making of firms' quotes. Therefore, while de facto acting as venues, SIs were subjected to a different regulatory framework, such asymmetry contributing to market fragmentation. Hence, the creation of OTFs—encompassing BCSs—represented an attempt to bridge the legal divide between not only trading venues and OTC markets but, also, between the former and "hybrid" subjects like SIs.

In each kind of trading venue, the operator is prohibited from performing proprietary trading, i.e. trading against its own capital. In MiFID II is pointed out that OTC markets, in order to be excluded from the discipline of SIs, must act on a non-systematic, regular basis. It might be theoretically difficult to separate activities carried out under OTF discipline from those which may be performed on OTC markets, the latter being the case of genuine trade execution which, thus, may be kept unregulated. However, the EU legislator is deeply concerned with conflicts of interest, as they could be seen under the lenses of the relationship between a principal (i.e. the customer) and its agent (i.e. the investment firm). In particular, is acknowledged the potential contrast between the objectives pursued by the owners of an MTF/OTF, those trading venues themselves, and their sound functioning from a macroprudential perspective (Article 18^{D}, par. 4). As for the 'discretion' allowed to the investment firm operating an OTF, it arises in two main situations: namely, when deciding either to place (retract) an order on that type of venue or *not to match a specific client order with other orders available in the systems at a given time*, as long as this abides by best execution requirements and follows the client's specific orders (Article 20^{D}, par. 6).

In order to more clearly separate the functions of the various types of venues, the Directive has attributed to RMs the duty of being the primary markets for listed and tradable equities, whereas the others are mainly devoted to secondary trading, though not exclusively: this is the legacy of MiFID I provisions, which circumscribed primary issuances to RMs. These last—unlike MTFs and OTFs, which are waived from them—have to comply with the rules disciplining the admission to trading: heavy disclosure obligations and the duty to verify issuers' own disclosure are in fact envisaged. Nevertheless, as a balance to this "liberal" approach in dealing with investors, non-RM venues are burdened with strict corporate governance (CG) requirements, all aimed at ensuring that the business be conducted in a 'sound and prudent' manner. For this purpose, MiFID II holds the market operator's (investment firm's) management body supremely responsible and accountable for every aspect of the activity de quo. Besides, even the composition of that body has now to comply with some provisions—typical of Anglo-Saxon jurisdictions—designed for the sake of pluralism, intended as the unescapable requisite for managerial efficacy. In particular, it must be adequately diverse in terms of gender, provenance, education, and professional background.

As far as SIs are concerned, we have already mentioned that, notwithstanding their explicit recognition in MiFID I, they had been—and still are—quite marginal venues, for their obligations are mainly related to transparency (for instance, Article 27 MiFID I mandated them to disclose quotes). MiFID II designed OTFs such that they could *capture all types of organised execution and arranging of trading which do not correspond to the functionalities or regulatory specifications of regulated markets and MTFs* (Clausen and Sørensen 2012). Hence, the current tripartite scheme of trading venues is almost exhaustive: the "residuality" of OTFs is evident in light of the fact that their operators are allowed to perform proprietary trading, unlike the other types of venues. Moreover, RMs and MTFs may trade against their own capital merely on a non-systematic, irregular basis. Conversely, SIs are prevented from matching third-party demand and supply: apart from such narrow category (with very few firms belonging to it), we cannot deny that, by introducing OTFs, MiFID II has brought into the realm of regulated activities a large portion of trading previously carried out OTC. In spite of this, not every supervisory loophole has been closed. For instance, it is still difficult to identify OTC transactions performed within the scope of activities that SIs are allowed to carry out, thus subjecting them to MiFID discipline rather than leaving them unregulated. Some legislative advancement has been clearly achieved; however, in relation to supervisory practices, there is still some way to go.

The notion of 'proprietary trading' (or, equivalently, 'dealing on own account') deserves contextualisation. The reference to trades being executed against the investment firm's own capital—in what MiFID II regards as an investment service/activity—has been defined by ESMA (*Consultation Paper Guidelines on transaction reporting, reference data, order record keeping & clock synchronisation*, 23 December 2015) as what takes place *when a firm puts its own books at risk*, though with some exemptions. Within the 'dealing on own account' broader category, we may find two narrower sets of activities: 'matched-principal trading' (MPT), if the firm interposes—with its own capital, of course—between clients, also for the purpose of executing the orders they have submitted; and 'principal capacity', which follows a residual definition. Since it envisages intermediaries using their financial resources to carry out said operations, dealing on own account has been widely regarded as a risky activity, not only at a *micro-* level (as clients not directly involved in trading are nonetheless affected by its related uncertainty) but—much more saliently—from a systemic stability standpoint. This is the reason why, in the USA, banks have been prohibited by engaging in it, with respect to certain securities (not always inherently risky ones), by means of the 'Volcker rule' encompassed by the 2010 Dodd-Frank Act.

In the EU, the Package has not imposed such "extreme" constraints to financial firms; yet, there are MiFID II provisions which actually set forth a stricter regulation of this kind of activities, envisaging at least strengthened reporting obligations to the subjects performing them. A transaction is conducted on a matched-principal basis if the following conditions are simultaneously met (Article 4^D, par. 1, no. 38):

(1) by interposing between the parties, the intermediary ('facilitator') offsets its exposure to market risk;
(2) transactions with different counterparties of the same transactions are executed in a contemporaneous manner;
(3) the facilitator ends up getting no profit (loss) other than *a previously disclosed commission, fee or charge for the transaction.*

MPT is furtherly discussed in Recital 24^D, whereby an investment firm matching orders from different clients with the backing of its own capital (so-called 'back-to-back trading') actually does it on a matched-principal basis and, thus, should be subject to MiFID II provisions on both executing orders and dealing on own account.

An interesting case-study is the one asking whether the investment firm operating an OTF, matching on a matched-principal basis some orders executed on an MTF with others executed OTC, has to include such MPT when computing the parameters aimed at assessing whether it may be regarded as a SI or not, pursuant to the Commission's Delegated Regulation 25 April 2016, No. 2017/565. In our view, the answer would be that only trades executed OTC have to be considered to determine whether the OTF's operator may be regarded as a SI, given the latter's definition of an entity which, *on an organised, frequent, systematic and substantial basis, deals on own account when executing client orders outside a regulated market, an MTF or an OTF without operating a multilateral system* (Article 4^{D}, par. 1, no. 20). This is perfectly consistent with said case, in light of the 'dealing on own account'. One aspect, however, requires our careful attention: including OTC trades in a computation is one thing, but using that computation to declare the OTF as a SI is a completely different story, for *Member States shall not allow the operation of an OTF and of a systematic internaliser to take place within the same legal entity* (Article 20^{D}, par. 4).

In addition to this, we should note that MPT might only occur on an OTF, as the operators of RMs (Article 47^{D}, par. 2) and MTFs (Article 19^{D}, par. 5) are explicitly banned from that. The rationale of this prohibition lies in the fact that, in order to carry out MPT, a certain degree of discretion (even without any discriminatory practices) has inevitably to be exerted, this being allowed—in general, with a few exceptions—to OTFs only. We should also note that MPT is the only kind of dealing on own account which OTFs can perform, in addition to that involving *sovereign debt instruments for which there is not a liquid market* (Article 20^{D}, par. 3), which is allowed in any case, regardless of it being MPT or principal capacity. Moreover, if the subject operating on a matched-principal basis and the OTF's operator did not coincide, the latter would be negotiating no more 'on own account' but on behalf of a third party, in breach of the MPT definition.

With respect to RMs, the provisions on MTFs and OTFs—much more than in MiFID I—expressed remarkable concerns related to the macroprudential effects of how exchanges work. In fact, those organisational requirements that were previously circumscribed to RMs have been extended to MTFs and OTFs: e.g., those envisaged in Article 51 of MiFID I and currently reprised by Article 48^{D}, headed *Systems resilience, circuit breakers and electronic trading*. The rules presiding over how to access markets have been reshaped, too. The obligation to grant access to investment firms from other EU Member States requesting it, either directly—i.e. by establishing a local branch—or by means of remote membership, is charged upon both RMs (Article 36^{D}) and MTFs (Article 38^{D}). A similar rule is not envisaged in case of OTFs, for they are allowed to set forth general rules determining whether a subject is entitled to join the market or not. Nevertheless, said provisions implicitly apply to them, too: if they were actually free to deny access to foreign entities, this would result in a severe breach of the principle enshrined in the Treaties. Hence, nationality per se is not a possible criterion for an OTF to decide which investment firms be admitted to its membership, neither alone nor in conjunction with different ones: in fact, rather than the free exercise of discretion (possible for OTFs but not for the other two), it would abide by a discriminatory approach which is actually banned for each type of venue. Conversely, the simpler condition of establishing a branch is—for instance—one of those which an OTF may charge. Of course, this would probably yield some competitive disadvantage for that venue, as long as granting accessibility to foreign EU investment firms is seen as beneficial to operating efficiency: therefore, an incentive to setting up such a condition would unlikely arise.

Instead, 'discretion' allows OTFs to provide execution services that are, also, *qualitatively* different from those of RMs and MTFs. Yet, the MiFID principle of best execution has brought substantive changes in this realm: some have doubted that the information requirements set forth by the new Directive would have advantaged more liquid and better-established venues or, in a wider manner, incumbent ones vis-à-vis newcomers. However, following the passage of MiFID I, MTFs have been able to attract many trades previously held on RMs, proving these worries to be largely misplaced. Nevertheless, the MiFID II legislator—comprehensively more detailed and precise than in 2004, when it just stated the principle—is particularly concerned with the competition between trading venues. This objective can be pursued only by strengthening the cooperation between NCAs and between them and ESMA, as they are now endowed with far more powerful tools than in the past—including the suspension or removal of an investment firm's board members—to contrast market fragmentation, yet still lacking common "rules of engagement". Besides, in the wider framework of transparency and to detail the content of best execution, is mandated that information be provided to customers on *the top five execution venues in terms of trading volumes where they executed client orders in the preceding year and (...) the quality of execution obtained*, (Article 27^D, par. 6). We shall come back on best execution in Chap. 5.

4.3 ECNs and Algorithmic Trading

Parallelly to trading venues, the USA have witnessed the emergence of two different kinds of trading mechanisms (or, with less accurate wording, 'execution venues'): Electronic Communication Networks (ECNs), having to be registered as broker-dealers under SEC rules, versus market makers (MMs). The former ones showed some appealing advantages to investors: they granted anonymity and higher speed of execution; yet, they were flawed by large information asymmetries and, along with larger trading volumes, higher stock-return volatility, too. Overall, however, their operations were characterised by greater operational efficiency. At the same time, they encompassed lower trading costs, as well as a more favourable "exposure" to position limits, given the peculiarity of trades directly linking one customer to another. Nevertheless, MMs have somehow managed to remain competitive. This is mainly because they interpose themselves between the counterparties by referring to brokers, instead of allowing the former ones to autonomously execute the transaction: therefore, they apply a different business model to different customers.

The dualism between ECNs and MMs has been quite harsh, attracting notable research interest throughout the last two decades. One of the most challenging research questions asked under which of the two frameworks the so-called 'informed trades' are more likely to occur. Since ECNs are prohibited from skimming orders, whereas MMs can preference some trades, a simple idea is that the latter are able to favour the less informed trades—which, in fact, require abiding by fewer and narrower transparency obligations, while the former tend to naturally select the most informed ones, mainly due to the abovementioned advantages that they comprehensively carry. Following the decomposition between 'trade-related' and 'trade-unrelated' components, Barclay et al. (2003) found that—with regard to 150 Nasdaq stocks during normal trading hours in June 2000—*ECN trading explains about two-thirds more of the stock-price variance than market-maker trades*. To rule out some potential collinearity between the two, said authors also found that an ECN trade has an impact approximately 50% higher than a MM one.

Besides, the difference between execution venues tends to reflect onto *pre-* and post-trading transparency costs. Given that small trades are more likely to be less informed, or even totally uninformed, one might think that they face lower costs with MMs than with ECNs. Actually, there is some evidence of this occurring, though with relatively little magnitude. Conversely, the fact that they are governed by informed trades makes ECNs be significantly cheaper vis-à-vis their competitors. Large trades are not shaped by the same rationale. For bigger volumes, the counterparty is generally an institutional investor and, thus, can better negotiate with them and, also, pursue price discrimination strategies enhancing the likelihood for trades to be executed. However, transactions with MMs are found to yield the opposite effect as the ordinary one: that is, purchases drive prices down while sales drive them up. As a consequence of this, realised spreads are larger than "effective" ones. Nevertheless, the mechanism not always works properly. If a small investor demanding liquidity fails to signal that it is misinformed, the MM would not charge lower spreads as usual and, thus, the customer might flee it in favour of an ECN. Actually, a similar choice would be suboptimal, for it entails a trade-off between receiving the bid-ask spread (rather than paying it) and suffering from information asymmetry. Of course, the trade-off is solved in a way which benefits the liquidity trader, provided that adequate information be ensured (de facto in presence of large trades, which are less frequent but may count on lower spreads and are not hurt from an informational standpoint). Empirical evidence showed that the higher the trading volumes, the higher the probability of choosing an ECN, which also increases along with volatility (intended as a proxy of new information being available, in turn defined as the difference between effective and realised spreads). Also, large trades are less likely to occur on ECNs. After controlling for market conditions, comparing trades on ECNs with those on MMs, transactions on the former show larger effective spreads and smaller realised ones in the small segment, and both lower effective and realised spreads in the medium-to-large segment.

More in general, the authors observed that secondary markets tend to skim orders from primary ones by selecting the least informed, which are the most profitable ones. Anyway, there is a clear direct relationship between the degree of information and the overall cost of transactions, as ECN quotes are found to help reducing trading costs. As for tick sizes, ECN quotes are more likely to show odd ticks than MM ones (Barclay et al. 1999); besides, they are more informative than the latter (Huang 2002). Much of the extant literature, however, focuses on quotes rather than the trades actually executed and, thus, cannot be extensively relied upon for policy purposes: that is, assessing whether market making—which ECNs prevent by directly working as an Alternative Trading System (ATS) under US jurisdiction—is actually required for providing liquidity or might be replaced by the automated matching of the parties' orders, with no need of any external intervention.

The origin of ECNs is clear: they were thought as vehicles whereby institutional investors and broker-dealers could have had the trades executed without requiring any disclosure towards the exterior. As stock markets grew, ECNs expanded alongside them, until the point at which they formed lower prices vis-à-vis MMs, despite remaining non-transparent. As documented by Barclay et al. (1999), trading costs fell considerably not only on this segment but on the whole of the market. Quotes from the ECNs executing transactions for less than 5% of a stock's total trading volume may also be hidden from Nasdaq's National Best Bid and Offer (NBBO) price; moreover, if it is not posting the current NBBO, an ECN can also redirect orders to another market for being executed there. MMs are not required to match the rounded or non-displayed ECN quotes; hence, customers might be willing to execute directly on ECNs seeking a better price. The opposite may also occur: if the ECN is posting the NBBO but the ECN is not willing to match the price, orders can be redirected from MMs to ECNs.

Nowadays, financial markets see an increasing role played by high-frequency trading (HFT), which cannot be ignored when addressing any issue in the realm of market infrastructure. With reference to data available at early 2014, less than 1 trade out of 4 was of HFT type. However, orders were relatively of greater amounts vis-à-vis the other two categories: namely, "traditional" transactions carried out by investment banks and other players, as they amounted to 30% of the total. Yet, by counting every single order (i.e. any submission, modification, withdrawal, etc.), the impact of 'frequency' led HFT to represent a clear majority over the sample investigated by ESMA. Anyway, AT and HFT (which is a subset of the former)—in spite of their multiple peculiarities—are strictly linked to the structure of the platforms where they are employed. This is the reason why, here and in the following paragraphs of the chapter, we are not going to separate this issue from that of trading venues, which we shall keep referencing to.

It is not an isolated opinion, in the literature, that technological progress—driven by the broader process of globalisation, which they are inherently related to—has gone so far that the complexity of the issues regarding AT has reached a really critical level, in a way that is impossible for regulators to manage (Theodoulidis and Diaz 2012). This means that, although its relevance cannot be denied, the new wave of legislation passed as a response to the GFC could well have failed in yielding a substantial improvement vis-à-vis a disorderly, opaque, sometimes indecipherable universe. As a countermeasure to this, a possible solution—according to the same literature—consists in 'adopting the same speed and acceleration rules across markets', something which would 'reduce the complexity and improve the overall "safety" of the system': in short, auditing and compliance functions could be enhanced without harming competition. In light of this, an important tool may be found in the so-called 'circuit breakers', i.e. those mechanisms—working mainly when there is excessive price volatility and riskiness has soared to unbearable levels—designed to limit or halt trading when this is needed in order to pursue the goal of market integrity.

However, this is not the only means by which the possible negative spill-overs stemming from the use of algorithms (aimed at enhancing performance) may be prevented. In fact, some important issues arise in respect of notification of algorithms (*rectius*, of their use), which is the approach envisaged by MiFID II. In particular, in Article 17[D], par. 2., we read that *an investment firm that engages in algorithmic trading in a Member State ... shall notify this to the competent authorities of its home Member State and of the trading venue at which the investment firm engages in [AT] as a member or participant of the trading venue*. This "double notification" is something quite recurrent in the European legislation regarding *pre-* and post-trading activities, as we are going to see in the next Chapter.

Nowadays, supervisory practices usually define a timespan by which algorithms have to be notified; however, these horizons (e.g., annual ones) are too long to be reliable, for an algorithm may be changed with extraordinary rapidity. The problem, however, is even more complex. In fact, addressing 'individual algorithms' and requiring them to be notified is probably an unsuccessful approach: in fact, this does not provide a comprehensive idea of market quality and, also, raises some intellectual property concerns in relation to the participants' rights. Therefore, it seems quite reasonable to argue that supervision should rather *examine the overall system characteristics* (Theodoulidis and Diaz 2012), considering algorithms as a mere support for humans—rather than standalone recipients of supervision because of their potentially negative spill-overs at a systemic level—and, thus, requiring *testing and monitoring mechanisms for the system (human trader plus computer plus algorithm) as a whole*, i.e. *as a black-box* (Theodoulidis and Diaz 2012). Furthermore, the availability of data is not only a regulatory issue, but something which is likely to change the business model of market-infrastructure firms: from a supervisory-only practice, it is gradually becoming a service that addresses multiple stakeholders. In particular, the intervention of third-parties is required under two innovative models: 'crowd-monitoring', whereby they are in charge of plain surveillance, and 'monitoring-as-a-service', whereby they are also allowed to check additional aspects of trading, such as *latency, data package trip and storage (...) for the network and communication infrastructure of market, trading desks, brokers and, perhaps more importantly, cross-market interactions* (Theodoulidis and Diaz 2012).

However, these concerns apply to trading in general, regardless of algorithmic or high-frequency specificities. This is true notwithstanding that, for instance, latency—i.e., basically, the time delay in order execution—is a key issue for HFT much more than for ordinary-speed trading). As far as monitoring the behaviour of trading systems and network infrastructure, HFT raises peculiar concerns, because of *additional manipulation scenarios that need to be considered in relation to misuse or stress-testing of the trading platforms*, which challenge their 'performance and resilience' and address issues like the network's delay and load capacity (Theodoulidis and Diaz 2012). In order to face these concerns—that is, in order to prevent market abuse from arising, without furtherly hardening the existing laws—, important resources have to be mobilised. In 2012, a survey conducted by the British Government's Department for Business, Energy and Industrial Strategy found that *the difficulty in detecting market abuse leads (...) to conclude that it will be even more difficult for regulators to adequately monitor and detect manipulative strategies*. In fact, a share of nearly 90% of respondents—the sample being made of both "traditional" and "alternative" investors—*[did] not believe that regulators have sufficient data, technology or expertise to effectively detect market abuse*. Addressing the possible lack of regulatory effectiveness is no simple task, a fortiori if these needs have to be transposed into concrete policy recommendations, possibly spanning on all the realms that are somehow linked to the issues raised by HFT: e.g., in respect of market operators, their CG structure and practices.

4.4 The Self-Assessment of Trading Venues

AT and HFT are hugely regulated not only in the Package but, also, in market-abuse legislation. With regard to MiFID II, *effective systems and risk controls suitable to the business* operated by the investment firm are required to be put in place (Article 17^{D}, par. 1). Then, a notification to the home-country competent authorities—in relation to the Member State of both the investment firm and the trading venue—is charged onto the former, which also has to specify whether it is has full membership of the venue or is just one of its participants (Article 17^{D}, par. 2). In the provisions that follow, a large number of communication and information obligations are charged upon investment firms, which have to (inter alia): adequately store and keep their records; set out proper parameters and limits; take into account multiple features of the traded instruments in the case they pursue a 'market making' strategy, as well as *the liquidity, scale and nature* of the specific market; and, still, continuously monitor the 'suitability' of clients to the trades that are carried out.

ESMA is endowed with a pivotal role in relation to AT, for it has to issue both regulatory and implementing standards which—thanks to the Authority's supranational configuration and harmonising role—are primarily devoted to creating a set of common rules to discipline the conditions and characteristics of actions undertaken by investment firms in order to comply with the EU regulatory framework. In Annex I to its *Regulatory technical and implementing standards* to the Package, ESMA has set out a list of 'elements that have to be considered in a trading venue's self-assessment', that is, in the internal process of checking whether certain conditions are met or not and, in the case of a positive response, asking competent authorities to receive a nulla osta to HFT activities. Said list shows the criteria of 'nature', 'scale' and 'complexity', the first two directly resembling those envisaged by the Directive.

As far as 'nature' is concerned, trading venues must self-assess the *types and regulatory status of the instruments traded* (e.g., whether there are 'liquid instruments subject to mandatory trading' or not) and the eventuality that those instruments be 'traded elsewhere', something which directly deals with 'the trading venue's role in the financial system'. 'Scale' items are much greater in number. They involve quantitative information such as amounts ('the number of algorithms operating', as well as that of 'its members and participants'; but also of remote members—and their percentage, *co-location or proximity hosting sites provided, countries and regions in which the trading venue is undertaking business activity*), volumes (both in terms of 'capacities' and 'trading executed'), proportions (*the percentage of AT over the total trading activity and the total turnover traded on the venue*, as well as analogous ratios in relation to HFT). Finally, the self-assessment must regard 'the operating conditions to manage volatility'. In addition to this, the trading venue has to assess whether 'dynamic or static trading limits' are applied in order to achieve 'halts or rejection of orders', this being a really critical issue from a systemic stability standpoint.

'Complexity' is the category that most closely deals with the business model of investment firms operating the venues. In fact, they are required to ascertain *the classes of financial instruments* traded, the *trading models available* (among which the ESMA lists the auction, the continuous auction and hybrid ones), the recourse to *pre-trade transparency waivers in combination with the trading models operated, the diversity of trading systems employed* and—most importantly—the venue's ability to exercise a control over *setting, adjusting, testing, and reviewing its trading systems*. Various information about the facilities used to trading have to be collected, as well as that on *the level of outsourcing*, with particular reference to key operations, and also *the frequency of changes in terms of trading models, IT systems and membership*.

4.5 CCPs, Trading Venues, and Access to Information in MiFIR

As widely remarked, arbitrarily discriminating between entities holding the same right to access *pre-* or post-trade services is strictly forbidden by the EU legislation. Of course, MiFIR abides by this principle and clearly enforces it. In Article 35^{R}—the opening one of Title VI^{R}—is stated that non-discriminatory and transparent admission to trading must occur without prejudice to what is provided for by EMIR. At the same time, however, the principle is enforced in a wider way, stating that venues willing to be granted access to the CCP must not be discriminated regarding *collateral requirements and fees relating to access* too: that is, CCPs could not arbitrarily, a priori decide which venues will be admitted and which ones rejected. In particular, the right to *non-discriminatory treatment of contracts traded on that trading venue* applies to:

(a) *collateral requirements and netting of economically equivalent contracts*, provided that, if insolvency laws constitute a basis for this kind of contracts, their applicability does not get hurt by *the inclusion of such contracts in the close-out and other netting procedures*;
(b) *cross-margining with correlated contracts*, provided that clearing is done by the same CCP under an EMIR-compliant risk model (Article 35^R, par. 1).

An official response to the admission request—either positive or negative—must be provided by the CCP within specific deadlines. However, a denial may be issued only if some given conditions—specified by ESMA on 24 June 2016, pursuant to Article 35^R, par. 6—are met; anyway, it must be fully detailed and explained. Moreover, the CCP is required to thoroughly inform its competent authority and—in the case the two be established in different States—that of the trading venue, too. Yet, the legislation appears to be much more stringent than it could appear at first sight. On the one hand, it is true that the response is positive by default and a rejection must be precisely justified, because of its "exceptional" nature; yet, on the other, there exist two supreme, unbetrayable criteria governing the access to central clearing of derivatives transactions (par. 4), which the Delegated Regulation issued by the EU Commission upon the ESMA proposal has clearly taken into account. The access:

(a) must not require an 'interoperability arrangement, in the case of derivatives that are not OTC derivatives pursuant to EMIR (in particular, Article 2, par. 7);
(b) moreover, still from an efficiency standpoint, it must not 'threaten the smooth and orderly functioning of the markets', where the greatest concerns are 'liquidity fragmentation' and 'systemic risk'.

There are also other cases in which the issue of free access is particularly important. For instance, Article 37^R, par. 1, deals with the situation where *the value of a financial instrument is calculated by reference to a benchmark*: in such case, 'the person with proprietary rights to the benchmark' is mandated to allow CCPs and trading venues to access—on a non-discriminatory basis, of course, and 'for the purposes of trading and clearing'—both:

(a) prices, data feeds, various pieces of information, also on methodology and pricing;
(b) licences, to be *granted on a fair, reasonable and non-discriminatory basis* within three months from the request being submitted.

In addition to this, 'reasonability' must be applied in relation to both the price set in exchange for the access de quo and the intellectual property laws governing the use of the licence: this is related to a broader principle of "fairness", such that different prices may plainly be applied to different trading venues, depending upon factors explicitly acknowledged by MiFIR: inter alia, 'the quantity, scope or field of use demanded'. The obligation to licence is also delayed by 30 days in the case a pre-existing benchmark be significantly reformed after 3 January 2017, that was originally intended as the date when the Package would have started being enforced (Article 37^{R}, par. 2). Finally, there is an explicit prohibition for CCPs and trading venues to 'enter into an agreement with any provider of a benchmark' with the effect of hurting the access to information, the rights related to it, or a licence being obtained. As could be easily envisioned, there are wide margins for ESMA detailing standards and conditions in relation to the cases whereby the abovementioned free access must be deployed.

Article 38^{R} is one of those which will be under heavy supervisory spotlight after Brexit (given the saliency of London as a financial hub), as it governs the *access for third-country CCPs and trading venues*. This may be granted only if the extra-EEA jurisdiction undergoes recognition—through a decision released by the EU Commission—pursuant to Article 38^{R}, par. 4; moreover, the CCP may also have to be recognised, though under Article 25 of EMIR. Furthermore, the Commission is required to assess the existence of 'an effective equivalent system' in order to grant the access to third-country CCPs and trading venues. In order for equivalence to be acknowledged, in Article 38^{R} itself (par. 2) is explicitly stated that access must be provided *on a fair and non-discriminatory basis* to both 'relevant prices and data feeds', along with every other element underlying the use of benchmarks 'for the purposes of trading and clearing', and licences.

However, these "technical" requirements might not suffice: in addition to them, the 'legal and supervisory framework' of the third country, which the authorisation of a CCP descends from, must not only be comparable to the twofold criterion above but also put in place 'effective supervision and enforcement'. Par. 3 provides a sketch of what has to be evaluated when assessing the equivalence of the juridical framework:

(a) whether *trading venues in that third country are subject to authorisation and to effective supervision and enforcement on an ongoing basis*, i.e. neither occasionally nor only in "pathological" or extra-ordinary situations;
(b) whether the access to CCPs and trading venues 'established in that third country' occurs through an *effective equivalent system*;
(c) whether the access to benchmark information and licences is allowed *on a fair, reasonable and non-discriminatory basis* by persons holding proprietary rights in that third country, this provision being in perfect accordance with the rules applying to EEA countries.

Title VI^{R} is another part of the Regulation which would be hard for the United Kingdom to repeal without replacement, or even to substitute with different rules. In fact, London should absolutely keep the system which is already in place with regard to access to CCPs and trading venues, in order to be deemed to be equivalent by the Commission once the divorce becomes official. Will there be an interest, for British trading venues and CCPs, to remain accessible for EU-27 counterparties and also to have themselves free access to benchmark information and licences held by non-British persons? Yes, indeed. Nowadays, the degree of interconnection that shapes the financial system at a global level would not allow for different solutions where data be ringfenced inside a national realm.

There is mutual interest, for CCPs and trading venues located everywhere, to be able to communicate and exchange information with their peer entities worldwide. Of course, the extreme hypothesis of the UK leaving the EEA while remaining a member of the EFTA—combined with MiFIR provisions being terminated—would still be compatible with these rules being kept in force, if a UK–EU agreement encompassed provisions in such direction. Anyway, apart from specific issues, it is clear that the ruling on post-Brexit issues will necessarily pay significant attention to the concerns arising in respect of the circulation of data and the exchange of information, which is undoubtedly one of the most relevant *macro-* themes of our world.

4.6 The Role of Supervision in MiFIR

Title VII^{R}—*Supervisory measures on product intervention and positions*—opens with Article 39^{R} (a very standard one), which repeats the powers held by ESMA (par. 1), EBA (par. 2), and competent authorities (par. 3), in relation to markets for 'financial instruments' in the Union, 'structured deposits' in the Union and both categories in single Member States, respectively. Much more significant are the provisions that follow. First of all, Article 40^{R} encompasses a list of 'ESMA temporary intervention powers', which are nowadays fully in place and would become no more enforceable toward British persons in any scenario, including the UK retaining its membership of the Single Market through the EEA. They mainly consist of the temporary prohibition or restriction (Article 40^{R}, par. 1) of:

(a) *the marketing, distribution or sale of certain financial instruments or financial instruments with certain specified features*;
(b) *a type of financial activity or practice*.

Multiple conditions must be fulfilled in order for an ESMA intervention to be legitimate (Article 40^{R}, par. 2), there must be:

(a) *a significant investor protection concern or a threat to the orderly functioning and integrity* of either segment of the financial system (commodity markets are explicitly mentioned), including its partial or comprehensive stability, with a significant detailing role attributed to the Commission (Article 40^{R}, par. 8);
(b) no regulatory requirements 'under Union law' are able to 'address the threat';
(c) no competent authorities have efficaciously acted against such menace.

In particular, as regards point *a*, the features of financial instruments to be regarded by the Commission are the following:

- the degree of complexity of the instrument;
- the size or the notional value of the issuance;
- the degree of innovation brought;
- the leverage provided.

As one would notice, such scheme has somehow become a standard for circumscribing the cases in which an authority is allowed to exercise its powers, as it closely resembles the framework envisaged in the BRRD in relation to the cases whereby a resolution procedure may be commenced. For a useful comparison, we might suggest looking at Article 32 BRRD (Directive No. 2014/59/EU), where the Conditions for resolution are laid down. Public interest residing in the preservation of market stability, along with greater threats coming from a potential inaction, are among the concerns whose rationale is more widely reflected into the abovementioned MiFIR provisions.

ESMA cannot act arbitrarily and without envisioning the consequences to its actions (Article 40^{R}, par. 3). Said authority has to ensure:

(a) not to have a *detrimental effect on the efficiency of financial markets* in a way which is not counteracted by the benefits to investors stemming from the intervention;
(b) not to create *a risk of regulatory arbitrage*;
(c) to have consulted the other competent public bodies in charge of overseeing agricultural markets, as far as commodity derivatives are concerned.

This principle is reprised and widened in par. 4, where we can read that *before deciding to take any action … ESMA shall notify competent authorities of the action it proposes*, and this is an "essential" condition—in juridical jargon—for the intervention to be carried out (it cannot be undertaken without prior notification). This is a call to collegiality that we shall hear afterwards in Title VII^{R}, where cooperation between authorities is strongly advocated for. Anyway, the actions undertaken by ESMA—though subject to some obligations in terms of their schedule, review and disclosure (paragraphs 5–6)—always 'prevail over any previous action taken by a competent authority' (par. 7).

Article 41^{R} is dedicated to the *EBA temporary intervention powers*. First of all, the scope of such intervention is defined in the same way as in respect of ESMA in Article 40^{R}, with 'structured deposits' in place of 'financial instruments' (Article 41^{R}, par. 1). The same substitution works in the following paragraphs, which—apart from their object—exactly resemble those dedicated to ESMA. The prevalence of EBA *decisa* over any other source of regulation is confirmed, as well as the Commission being endowed with the power of detailing the features of what is subjected to the oversight of said authority. The scheme used by the European legislator in order to empower the competent authorities of Member States with some intervention tools is slightly different, mainly because of the "lower level" at which it deploys. In fact, while their powers encompass the realms of both ESMA and EBA, those attributed to the micro-prudential EU-wide supervisors are actually prevalent. The duty to consult other national authorities is here the main concern of the legislator, which is willing to avoid that a unilateral intervention by a single Member State ends up hurting the financial system of another EU country.

Notwithstanding the different wording, only a couple of elements is worth underlining. First, Article 41^{R}, par. 2 explicitly mentions derivatives as an object of the authority's intervention, in the case it threatens to have *a detrimental effect on the price formation mechanism in the underlying market*. This clearly seems to be part of the legacy of post-crisis legislation, especially if sparked from the G20 Pittsburgh summit in 2009. As underlined in the *Securities Markets Risk Outlook 2013–2014*, the G20 commitment was associated with the EU concern *to bring all organised trading venues within the regulatory net and to extend transparency requirements from equity to [non-equity instruments]*. Moreover, the 'proportionality' of the action vis-à-vis the threat must be assessed by taking into account *the nature of the risks identified, the level of sophistication of investors or market participants concerned and the likely effect of the action on investors and market participants who may hold, use or benefit from the financial instrument, structured deposit or activity or practice*, which is a very wide-ranging provision, shaped by an extremely cautious approach to supervision. Finally, if the issue to be addressed is particularly urgent (such that the standard notification period, equal to 30 days, would be inappropriate), national competent authorities are allowed to act themselves—'on a provisional basis'—rather than waiting for ESMA or EBA interventions, provided that the micro-prudential body concerned gets notified of this with a 24-hour prior alert.

In relation to derivatives, we should not avoid mentioning the fact that, during the second half of 2016, their markets have shown some changes in the degree of competition which is worth investigating. In order to do this, we are going to look at a concentration index such as the Herfindahl-Hirschman one (HHI). Across time, from mid-2009 to end-2016, the decrease in concentration of OTC derivatives markets is undoubtedly appreciable in respect of every major currency—US dollar, euro, pound sterling, yen—in which transactions are denominated. Moreover, interest-rate derivatives have shown far better results in terms of improved competition vis-à-vis foreign-exchange ones. However, we may also notice the remarkable effect of the UK referendum in yielding relevant changes, comparing GBP to other currencies which instruments are denominated in: from June to December 2016, concentration has kept substantially stable regardless of currencies and type of underlying assets.

The change recorded in respect of GBP-denominated forex derivatives, traded OTC, is not particularly relevant (+3.47%), but the HHI for analogous transactions in interest-rate derivatives has actually plummeted (−12.65%). Hence, these markets have become significantly more competitive in just half a year. This might be attributed to a sort of "crowding-out" effect on the largest players, as a market upheaval generated by exogenous factors—such as an election—may well create, in the short-term, a disorder which curbs dominant positions and yields a sort of "realignment" in players' positions. If such guess were correct, other variations should be regarded as "frictional" and absolutely contingent. Further data—to be published as time flows—will tell us whether OTC markets for GBP-denominated derivatives, which interest rates underlie, have "structurally" become less competitive. Although the overall outlook of interest rates had not changed in the second half of 2016, as they kept generally at very low levels, the Bank of England (BoE) actually tried to counteract the post-referendum turmoil by halving short-term interest rates, carried from 0.50 to 0.25% in early August (fully in line with investors' expectations). This might have sparked the abovementioned realignment, yet seems to be too a weak change in respect of the dramatic fall in the pound sterling's value.

To conclude, in Article 43^{R}, EBA and ESMA are explicitly called to cooperate. This is particularly true in relation to the cases where an intervention is carried out by national authorities and, thus, the two ESAs must ascertain whether it has been 'justified and proportionate' (Article 43^{R}, par. 1). When the ordinary 30-day notification procedure is followed, ESMA or EBA—depending upon whether financial instruments or structured deposits are concerned—will issue an opinion stating whether it deems the prohibition or restriction to be the right choice for competent authorities (par. 2). Such opinion is not formally binding for the recipients, which are nonetheless required to fully detail the reasons behind acting differently in the case they did not abide by the micro-prudential recommendation.

Chapter 2 of MiFIR opens by dealing with the issue of position management. The scheme does not differ from the one that we have previously analysed, for ESMA is endowed with significant powers also in relation to this. Article 45^{R}, par. 1, directly refers to the Regulation No. 1095/2010, which represents the legal basis of the ESFS (in particular, its Article 9, par. 5): thanks to it, if the abovementioned conditions for an intervention are satisfied, ESMA is allowed to act by (a) requesting *from any person all relevant information regarding the size and purpose of a position or exposure entered into via a derivative*; (b) requiring to perform a specified action on the position, such as reducing or eliminating it; or even (c) limiting *the ability of a person from entering into a commodity derivative*. Other provisions are very similar to those that we have encountered so far in Title VII^{R}.

What is much more significant in relation to a post-Brexit environment is undoubtedly Title VIII of MiFIR, where several issues regarding the cross-border provision (performance) of investment services (activities) are explicitly addressed, including those related to passporting. Its relevance may be understood by looking at its header: *Provision of services and performance of activities by third-country firms following an equivalence decision with or without branch*. Hence, the cases under its scope are those in which the equivalence has already been declared; and is extremely likely that such a situation will be that of the UK once formally exited the EU, for only an abrupt, hostile, rancorous ending of talks could undermine the certainty that the major part of the British juridical framework will be deemed to be 'equivalent' to the EU-27 one.

First of all, the *General provisions* encompassed by Article 46^{R} are opened by the statement that, consistently with the suggestion inside the heading, there is no need for a third-country person, which is willing to provide (perform) investment services (activities)—including ancillary ones or not—in an EU Member State, to establish a branch *where it is registered in the register of third-country firms kept by ESMA* (Article 47^R, par. 1). However, this provision does not apply in every case, as it is limited to 'eligible counterparties' or 'professional clients'. In the case the establishment of a branch be the path anyway chosen, ESMA may accept the applicant into the abovementioned register only if some basic conditions are met (par. 2), namely:

(a) an equivalence decision covering the relations toward entities registered in that third-country;
(b) the firm having been granted an authorisation to operate in its home country and, still, 'effective supervision and enforcement ensuring a full compliance with the requirements applicable in that third country' being in place;
(c) 'cooperation arrangements' with the relevant competent authorities of that third-country having been settled.

Letters *a* and *c*, along with the abovementioned registration at ESMA, all refer to specific provisions contained in Article 47^R, which we are going to discuss.

In par. 3 we may read that, in the case a registration process has been successfully undergone, the Member State cannot *impose any additional requirements on the third-country firms* in respect of matters covered by the Package. This could seem a standard statement, fully in line with the European legislator's esprit of not increasing the regulatory burden already charged to supervised entities (e.g., by forbidding to duplicate information requirements), or to the recipients of a legislation (e.g., by the prohibition of gold-plating). However, it should be immediate to understand how the wording of Article 46^R, par. 3, could well be used by British financial companies in supporting their claim that EU-27 Member States do not pursue any "regulatory retaliation" against them. Pursuant to this provision, once the equivalence between the EU-27 jurisdiction and the UK will have made the registration *de quo* be accepted, any arbitrary limitation imposed by NCAs in the former to entities subjected to the latter will be unlawful if it trespassed the scope of existing rules.

Nevertheless, the extent of such provision is strongly diminished by its applicability to non-retail clients only, thus addressing a minority of transactions. In par. 5 is stated that the authorised providers must *inform clients established in the Union, before the provision of any investment services, that they are not allowed to provide services to clients other than eligible counterparties and professional clients ... and that they are not subject to supervision in the Union* (moreover, they are required to *indicate the name and the address of the competent authority ... in the third country*). To be precise, Article 46 is unidirectional: if a professional client or an eligible counterparty starts providing an investment service or performing an investment activity at its own initiative, rather than on the third-country firm's one, the Article does not apply. Moreover, *an initiative by such clients shall not entitle the third-country firm to market new categories of investment product or investment service to that individual.* Anyway, in light of the considerable financial and legal relevance of these transactions, we might bet on this principle being frequently invoked after Brexit becomes official: e.g., as far as interbank markets are concerned, whose realm suffers from some of the greatest practical concerns arisen with the British decision to leave the EU.

As we have anticipated, Article 47^R is the main source of law as far as equivalence decisions are concerned. What must be ensured, in order for such a decision to be taken—pursuant to the procedure laid down in Article 51^R, par. 2—is that *firms authorised in that third country comply with legally binding prudential and business conduct requirements which have equivalent effects* as those set out in the Package *plus* CRD IV (given the fact that, as we are going to see, also capital requirements are taken into account) *plus* every Package-related implementing measure. Moreover, it must be acknowledged that *the legal framework of that third country provides for an effective equivalent system for the recognition of investment firms authorised under third-country legal regimes*. In relation to this, five "pillars"—identifying what third-country firms must show to possess in order to be recognised as equivalent—are drawn in Article 47^R, par. 1:

(a) authorisation and *effective supervision and enforcement on an ongoing basis*;
(b) *sufficient capital requirements and appropriate requirements applicable to shareholders and members of their management body*;
(c) *adequate organisational requirements in the area of internal control functions*;
(d) *appropriate conduct of business rules*;
(e) *market transparency and integrity*, ensured *by preventing market abuse in the form of insider dealing and market manipulation*.

Since they are the same requirements as those charged upon EU firms, the rationale of levelling the playing field seems to be reinforced by these provisions. Moreover, the need for the five pillars to be abided by third-country firms providing (performing) investment services (activities) is also rooted in their peculiar features, as it is extremely likely that, if the recipients are professional clients or eligible counterparties, the providers are of the same kind. Hence, we should be talking about banks, insurance companies, asset managers and other intermediaries whose stability and efficiency cannot prescind from those pillars. One might be tempted to establish a sort of ranking between the pillars, but this would not have much sense. In spite of this, let us remark how the 'three pillars' of the Basel II Accords—namely, 'capital adequacy', 'supervisory control' and 'market discipline'—somehow synthesise the five above.

The other side of the coin is that the EU Commission may withdraw an equivalence decision (Article 47^R, par. 4), of course if the necessary conditions are no longer met, with the result that *a third-country firm may no longer use the rights* conferred pursuant to Article 46^R, par. 1. Besides, even ESMA is allowed to take a step backwards and erase a third-country firm from the register containing the entities allowed to provide investment services or perform investment activities in the Union (Article 49^R, par. 1, referring to Article 48^R). This may occur in two cases: that is, if—according to *well-founded reasons based on documented evidence*— ESMA believes that (a) *the third-country firm is acting in a manner which is clearly prejudicial to the interests of investors or the orderly functioning of markets*; or (b) *the third-country firm has seriously infringed the provisions applicable to it in the third country*, on whose basis the Commission had released its Decision. In addition to this, two other formal conditions are laid down: (c) the third-country competent authority has managed neither to take 'the appropriate measures' nor to demonstrate the firm's compliance with its home-country requirements; and (d) the intention to withdraw the firm's registration has been communicated to the third-country competent authority at least 30 days before.

Theoretically, the changes brought to the British financial legislation by the exit from the European Union, if too deregulation-oriented, could even prompt the EU Commission to deny its equivalence decision in certain cases; or, if such equivalence were anyway granted in the immediate aftermath of the formal divorce, a review might still end up with the Decision being withdrawn in the following years. Clearly, everything depends upon the parties' goodwill: the UK should avoid abruptly cutting its ties with the Brussels-derived legislation, as well as the EU should renounce to any temptations of revenge against a move so distant from the European spirit such as Brexit. If a balanced deal is ultimately reached, there is no reason to be afraid of equivalence decisions being neither denied nor initially agreed and withdrawn afterwards.

References

Allen, F., & Gale, D. (1997). Financial markets, intermediaries, and intertemporal smoothing. *Journal of Political Economy, 105*(3), 523–546.

Allen, F., & Santomero, A. M. (2001). What do financial intermediaries do? *Journal of Banking & Finance, 25*(2), 271–294.

Barclay, M., Christian, W., Harris, J., Kandel, E., & Schultz, P. (1999). The effects of market reform on the trading costs and depths of Nasdaq stocks. *Journal of Finance, 54,* 1–34.

Barclay, M. J., Hendershott, T., & McCormick, D. T. (2003). Competition among trading venues: Information and trading on electronic communications networks. *The Journal of Finance, 58* (6), 2637–2665.

Clausen, N. J., & Sørensen, K. E. (2012). Reforming the regulation of trading venues in the EU under the proposed MiFID II—Levelling the playing field and overcoming market fragmentation? *European Company and Financial Law Review, 9*(3), 275–306.

Committee of European Securities Regulators. (2010). *CESR equity market technical advice*, No. 129.

Di Noia, C. (2000). *Customer controlled firms: The case of stock exchanges*. SSRN, Working Paper.

Di Noia, C. (2001). Competition and integration among stock exchanges in Europe: Network effects, implicit mergers and remote access. *European Financial Management, 7*(1), 39–72.

Domowitz, I. (1995). Electronic derivatives exchanges: Implicit mergers, network externalities, and standardization. *The Quarterly Review of Economics and Finance, 35*(2), 163–175.

Domowitz, I. (1996). An exchange is a many-splendored thing: The classification and regulation of automated trading systems. In A. W. Lo (Ed.), *The industrial organization and regulation of the securities industry* (pp. 93–124). Chicago, IL: University of Chicago Press.

Economides, N. (1993). Network economics with application to finance. *Financial Markets, Institutions & Instruments, 2*(5), 89–97.
Economides, N. (1996). The economics of networks. *International Journal of Industrial Organization, 14*(6), 673–699.
Huang, R. D. (2002). The quality of ECN and Nasdaq market maker quotes. *The Journal of Finance, 57*(3), 1285–1319.
Katz, M. L., & Shapiro, C. (1986a). Technology adoption in the presence of network externalities. *Journal of Political Economy, 94*(4), 822–841.
Katz, M. L., & Shapiro, C. (1986b). Product compatibility choice in a market with technological progress. *Oxford Economic Papers, 38,* 146–165.
Lucantoni, P. (2017). Il mercato dei derivati: note preliminari ad uno studio sistematico. *Banca Borsa Titoli di Credito: rivista di dottrina e giurisprudenza, 70*(2), 182–206.
Moloney, N. (2014). *EU securities and financial markets regulation*. Oxford: Oxford University Press.
Pagano, M., & Steil, B. (1996). Equity trading I: The evolution of European trading systems. In B. Steil (Ed.), *The European equity markets*. London: The Royal Institute for International Affairs.
Theodoulidis, B., & Diaz, D. (2012). *Financial markets and high frequency trading: An information management perspective*. SSRN, Working Paper.

Chapter 5
Market Infrastructure and Transparency Obligations

Abstract The chapter discusses the wide and complex regulatory framework regarding *pre-* and post-trade transparency obligations, aimed at reducing information asymmetry and contributing to the overall 'market infrastructure'. First, we provide an overview of the most salient provisions encompassed by the *European Market Infrastructure Regulation* (EMIR, No. 648/2012), as the latter—though focused on derivatives—constitutes the basis upon which the transparency framework has been drawn up in the Package. Then, we move onto the details of the discipline, which actually informs each section of both the Directive and the Regulation: inter alia, we present the different types of 'data reporting service providers' (DRSPs), which are intermediaries entitled to collect, store, and convey exchange-related information, ensuring their integrity and security. In particular, we devote a special attention to waivers and deferrals, which are critical in order to assess the likely impact of the new rules. Coming back to the content of EMIR, the chapter ends by directly facing the issue of derivatives trading, which is going to be increasingly disputed between trading venues and OTC markets, raising relevant transparency concerns.

5.1 The Role of EMIR as a Precursor of the Package

Pre- and post-trading issues—i.e. those regarding the execution of orders and their subsequent clearing—have to be dealt with regard to the different types of the market to which they refer. In fact, there is a striking asymmetry between 'public' and 'private' markets: while the former are heavily regulated (the main sources of law being EMIR and the Package), as well as subjected to strict transparency requirements, the latter ones bear a much smaller *onus* and are more likely to raise systemic stability concerns. At present-day, as we have already discussed, not the whole universe of trading in the EU has endeavoured to escape the "opaqueness" exposed by the crisis. For instance, certain types falling under the 'dark pool' category—namely, the so-called 'broker-crossing networks' or 'systems' (BCNs or BCS)—are left completely uncovered in the regulatory framework established

M. Comana et al., *The MiFID II Framework*,
https://doi.org/10.1007/978-3-030-12504-2_5

through the Package. Some have proposed to restrict the scope of OTC platforms and—symmetrically—widen that of OTFs, thus including BCNs into the latter ones (Ferrarini and Saguato 2013).

As far as the features of different markets are concerned, we may label an exchange as 'public'—thus, included among the "typical" trading venues set out in the Package—if it is formal, multilateral, non-discretionary and 'lit', this last property implying that it is subject to *pre*- and post-trade disclosure obligations. Vice versa, 'private' markets—generally consisting of investment firms operating OTC—are informal, bilateral, discretionary and 'dark', i.e. exempted from officially disclosing orders and interests to the public. The latter results in *a complex bilateral network whose opaqueness copes with—in the realm of the single intermediary, but also of national and transnational controlling authorities—an actual comprehension of the exposure to counterparty risk for single entities and to market risk for the system as a whole, the so-called systemic risk* (Ferrarini and Saguato 2013). As we may easily spot, transparency issues are addressed in two radically different ways by the two categories, especially because of the role of disclosure in price formation, which is an essential characteristic of public exchanges but not of private ones.

As for pre-trade transparency, MTFs are less exposed to the risk of disclosure influencing the subsequent transactions: in fact, they do not take any position, but only enhance the interaction between different bid and ask orders. Conversely, bilateral systems—such as OTC markets and, most importantly, SIs—take a greater risk because of their direct involvement in the negotiation, for they perform proprietary trading and, thus, are exposed to potential losses. This could eventually result in dealers being reluctant to undertake transactions, thus yielding a contraction in liquidity.

However, a tertium genus might also be identified: in the case of listed securities that are traded OTC in private markets, transparency requirements still apply. This gives rise to the category of 'semi-private' exchanges that are subject to EMIR rules, including the mandatory clearing of transactions. It is probably worth spending a few words on 'clearing', described as the mechanisms that allow:

- to limit the claims of each side of the transaction by offsetting its positions vis-à-vis the counterparty—either long or short ones—that existed when the contract was settled (so-called 'close-out netting');
- to post collateral in monies or securities, though subject to a haircut depending upon the issuer's rating, against the counterparty's insolvency risk.

The major concerns are about derivatives, given how complex and opaque they might be and, most importantly, the fact that they were loosely regulated at the moment of the GFC outbreak. Therefore, as we have witnessed, the uncontrolled spread of these instruments has yielded negative spill-overs at a systemic level; hence, they have become *the battlefields of post-crisis international regulatory intervention* (Ferrarini and Saguato 2013). However, we are not going to focus on derivatives here; instead, we take them as an exemplum of how *pre*- and post-trade legislation has changed in more recent years, in particular through the reforms introduced by the Package. Addressing the concerns raised in the G-20 summit held in Pittsburgh, the FSB (2009) has identified four 'pillars' of the new shaping of derivative markets:

- promoting the standardisation of OTC derivatives;
- enhancing transparency through trade reporting;
- establishing a central clearing system;
- trading on exchanges and electronic platforms.

Both EMIR and the Package constitute a response to these concerns, as they are aimed at strengthening the market infrastructure by devoting remarkable attention to transparency issues. In particular, EMIR establishes new reporting obligations—charged to 'counterparties and CCPs'—for every derivative transaction, whether it be 'concluded, modified or terminated'. This has to be fulfilled at a registered trade repository (TR) pursuant to Article 55 EMIR, or recognised pursuant to Article 77 of said Regulation, *no later than one working day following the conclusion, modification, or termination* (Article 9 EMIR, par. 1). In light of this, it is completely invariant whether the counterparty be a financial or a non-financial entity, for which purpose the transaction has been conducted—e.g., whether for hedging purposes or treasury finance activities—, and whether it has been centrally cleared or not.

Moreover, since the rationale of the entire post-trade legislation is that duplication of information must be avoided (still Article 9 EMIR, par. 1), the parties are allowed to agree that only one of them complete the reporting; alternatively, this last might even be delegated to a third subject. If the TR is not available for reporting, the obligation must be fulfilled by communicating data to ESMA (Article 9 EMIR, par. 3). Pursuant to Article 9 EMIR, par. 4, any reporting—whether it be addressed to a TR or ESMA—*shall not be considered in breach of any restriction on disclosure of information imposed by that contract or by any legislative, regulatory or administrative provision*.

TRs are subject to different provisions, stemming either from first-level legislation (like EMIR) or even by second-level one, such as ESMA guidelines. For instance, they are required to aggregate data on a threefold basis 'per derivative classes': namely, volumes, positions, and value. Six classes have been identified by the Authority: commodities, credit, foreign exchange, equity, interest rate and 'other'. Furthermore, as far as OTC derivatives are concerned, a precise clearing obligation is set out in Article 4 EMIR, if two conditions are met: one regarding the counterparties involved, the other about the contract being 'entered or novated'. The first requirement is that, in the contract, at least one party must be either a financial entity or a non-financial undertaking which fulfils what is laid down in Article 10 of said Regulation, par. 2, or an entity 'established in a third country' (which, anyway, *would be subject to the clearing obligation if it were established in the Union*). If the two parties are both of the latter kind, the contract must have *a direct, substantial and foreseeable effect within the Union or where such an obligation is necessary or appropriate to prevent the evasion of any provisions* encompassed by EMIR.

ESMA is mandated to identify the classes of OTC derivatives eligible to such clearing obligation, for the ultimate purpose of reducing systemic risk (Recital 21 of EMIR). It is worth noting that such identification must be done for every single OTC derivative within six months from the date when the CCP was authorised by the NCA—at the end of a 'bottom-down' procedure triggered by the CCP itself—to centrally clear a specific type of derivative. In this procedure, the NCA autonomously decides on the request; however, it is mandated to communicate its decision to ESMA, which—in turn—must launch a public consultation and hear the ESRB's opinion, too, in order to assess whether the NCA's decision may be confirmed and subsequently harmonised at a European level. Most importantly, classes do not necessarily coincide with those which are subject to mandatory clearing (we are going to detail this later), but rather describe a subset of them. Conversely, a 'top-down' approach is also envisaged in the case ESMA assessed that a certain type of derivative should be centrally cleared, while no CCP has submitted a related request. The microprudential body should assess *the level of contractual and operational standardisation of contracts, the volume and the liquidity of the relevant class of OTC derivative contracts as well as the availability of fair, reliable and generally accepted pricing information in the relevant class of OTC derivative contract* (Lucantoni 2017).

Given the importance of this kind of information, it is probably self-evident how clearing is a seminal issue in light of limiting the negative spill-overs of transacting in opaque instruments such as those in question. The more a contract is a stand-alone one, with little knowledge of it, scarce liquidity and narrow trading, the more clearing becomes necessary. By offsetting the exposures between parties, clearing offers much more reliable information—via reduced asymmetry—and prevents domino effects from arising if the settlement of a single transaction fails. This is a fortiori true if it is carried out in a centralised manner, where a 'central counterparty' (CCP), acting as a purchaser toward all bidders and as a bidder toward all purchasers, clears the positions of its 'members' and, thus, extends the benefits of clearing to the whole market. In addition to this, given the significant contribution that clearing per se offers to the reduction of counterparty risk, a CCP is also able to avoid the disruption of exchanges in the case of a member defaulting, for it will ultimately bear the whole of the counterparty risk arising in the market. It is worth noting that the idea of a CCP, though debated by the literature, has been transposed into binding legislation only a few years ago, by giving effect to the wishes of a central clearing for derivatives expressed at the Pittsburgh G20 summit in 2009.

As far as the clearing obligation is concerned, ESMA—by exercising the powers that has been endowed with by EMIR—has set out a couple of criteria that must be used to assess whether or not a non-financial counterparty is subject to the abovementioned obligation: a quantitative condition, i.e. the exceedance of a determined 'clearing threshold', calculated on the basis of the notional amount of all the positions in OTC derivatives; and a qualitative one, checked by excluding from the previous computation the derivatives held for hedging purposes. To this last goal, the so-called 'hedging test' is performed (Lucantoni 2017).

How such test must be performed is envisaged in Regulation No. 149/2013, supplementing EMIR with specific provisions on issues related to clearing. In Article 10 of said piece of legislation—referring to Article 10 EMIR, par. 4—is specified that the hedging test must be conducted by checking whether or not at least one of the following conditions is met. This means that the instrument—*by itself or in combination with other derivative contracts*—is actually held for hedging purposes: if the test gets failed, the notional amount of related positions must be included in the computation of the clearing threshold). Conditions are:

- *it covers the risks arising from the potential change in the value* of the widest range of items (assets, services, processes, etc.) that the non-financial counterparty deals with *in the normal course of its business*;
- *it covers the risks arising from the potential indirect impact* on the value of the abovementioned items, *resulting from fluctuation of interest rates, inflation rates, foreign exchange rates or credit risk*;
- *it qualifies as a hedging contract pursuant to International Financial Reporting Standards* [IFRS], whose adoption is recalled having been triggered by a European Regulation (No. 1606/2002).

Besides, risk-mitigation techniques are envisaged in EMIR with regard to those transactions which are not subject to mandatory clearing. In Article 11 is well specified that the counterparties of such exchanges, by *exercising due diligence*, must ensure that *appropriate procedures and arrangements are in place to measure, monitor and mitigate operational risk and counterparty credit risk*, among which two specific items cannot be neglected: the *timely confirmation ... of the terms of the relevant OTC derivative contract*, and also *formalised processes which are robust, resilient and auditable*. The latter, in particular, has multiple purposes: 'reconcile portfolios', 'manage the associated risk', identify and solve possible arising disputes and—"last but not least"—'monitor the value of outstanding contracts'. Although price formation is not properly a feature of OTC transactions, a wider 'rule of law' principle imposes to give certainty to transactions in order for no party to be impaired because of information asymmetry, in the case sudden price changes occurred. Still, portfolio reconciliation is substantially envisaged in Article 11 EMIR, par. 2, where is provided that all counterparties, either financial or non-financial, *shall mark-to-market on a daily basis the value of outstanding contracts*, though with a noticeable exemption: *where market conditions prevent marking-to-market, reliable and prudent marking-to model shall be used.*

Between 2009 and 2010, when the debate about amending MiFID I had not officially started yet, the Committee of European Securities Regulators (CESR 2010) advanced some proposals about *pre-* and post-trade transparency. In particular, it highlighted the need for a strong transparency framework able to contain the systemic unrest generated by the operations carried out in dark pools, whose number was significantly growing in those years (as clearly shown in Fig. 5.1). Moreover, it urged ESMA to exercise a more effective supervisory role on that issue, hoping for the release of dedicated RTS with a clarifying effect on such an "opaque" environment.

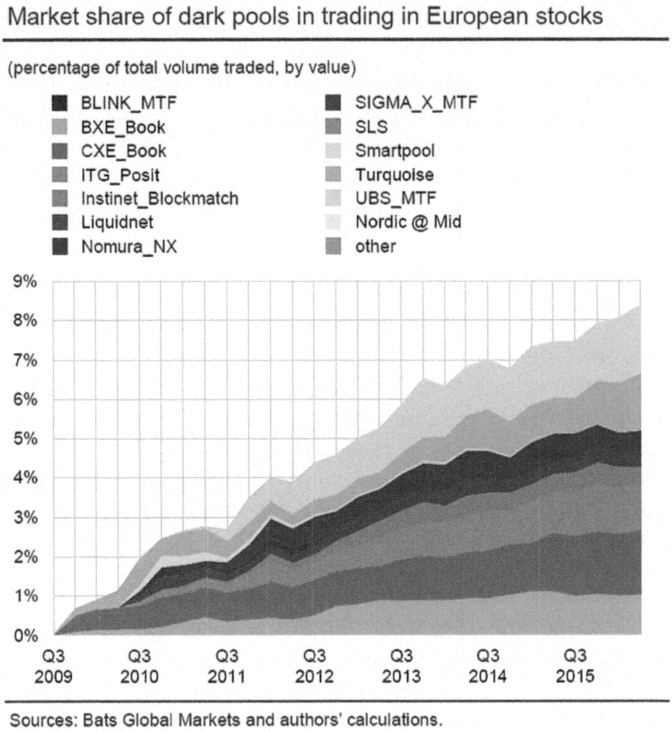

Fig. 5.1 Market share of dark pools in trading in European stocks (percentage of total volume traded, by value). *Source* Bats Global Markets, as analysed and discussed in Petrescu and Wedow (2017)

An alignment between the set of rules disciplining RMs and MTFs was also upheld, with the latter proposedly converging to the former's stricter requirements. Finally, CESR pushed for introducing 'approved publication arrangements' (APAs), whose requirements are mainly set forth in Article 64^{D}, where post-trade information should have been published. Another seminal issue was the one related to 'broker-crossing systems' (BCS): that is, *internal electronic systems operated by an investment firm that executes orders against other client orders* (Recital 7 of EMIR), whereby order execution is strongly automatised, such that it is difficult to discern them from multilateral, non-discretional systems. CESR proposed that such operations be notified, a list of these schemes be published and properly flagged, in order to obtain reliable data on OTC trading. Ferrarini and Saguato (ibidem) argue that BCS may also trade against 'house accounts orders'.

In summer 2010, the European Parliament caught these needs and issued a resolution explicitly designing the path—especially in relation to derivatives—that somehow laid the basis for the forthcoming Package. In this document (namely, the *Resolution of 15 June 2010 on derivatives markets: future policy actions*), transparency was still widely addressed, but the goal of avoiding negative spill-overs on liquidity and efficiency was also clearly underlined. In the following December, the EU Commission consulted on the first ideas about a MiFID reform, mainly concerning market infrastructure and the characteristics of trading venues: it dealt with RMs and MTFs for the purpose of aligning the two regimes and, thus, extending the transparency framework of RMs to equity-like instruments (among these, depositary receipts, ETFs and certificates). It also addressed the need for new venues and the rules which they would have been subjected to, as well as the requirements charged to BCS, and so on.

However, multiple responses were not particularly enthusiastic of proposed novelties. In fact, at that time it was immediately clear that this new financial legislation was endowed with the responsibility of healing many of those inefficiencies that had burst during the crisis. Hence, it would have substantially reduced the scope of OTC markets; besides, turning out to be disproportionate vis-à-vis the actual needs of the financial industry, it could have impaired the flexibility of markets. Nowadays, this is (with few variations) the argument shared by many critics of the current framework established by the Package: that is, the failure of 'one size fits all' approaches. In fact, although financial markets are intrinsically complex and various, there are many cases in which the legislator has tried to prescribe the same rules to radically different intermediaries. Despite the Package having actually preserved—for instance—the variety of trading venues, this concern still keeps its validity nowadays.

Before moving to MiFID II, however, we should recall the amendments to EMIR brought by the Package's directly-applicable component. This is done in Article 53^R, where the most relevant changes are about Article 7 EMIR. Its par. 1 has been rewritten by detailing the provisions stating that CCPs must clear contracts *on a non-discriminatory and transparent basis (...) regardless of the trading venue*: nowadays we may read that this obligation also applies *as regards collateral requirements and fees related to access*.

In particular, in the new environment shaped by the Package, the forbiddance of a discriminatory treatment is substantiated by a specific right held by the trading venue, and such right is in relation to:

(a) *collateral requirements and netting of economically equivalent contracts*, provided that *the inclusion of such contracts in the close-out and other netting procedures of a CCP based on the applicable insolvency law would not endanger the smooth and orderly functioning, the validity or enforceability of such procedures*;
(b) *cross margining with correlated contracts cleared by the same CCP*, provided that a 'risk model' such as that envisaged in Article 41 MiFIR is put in place. Finally, thanks to an addition to Article 81 EMIR, par. 3, TRs are subjected to MiFIR rules—those laid down in Article 26^R—in respect of the transmission of data to competent authorities.

5.2 The MiFID II Rules Regarding Information

When discussing the innovations brought by the Package, first we should underline to which extent it has been so important in the realm of legislation on trading and clearing. In short, we might say that the focus of the Package is on transparency, which had been well addressed by EMIR but had probably faded in the larger context of disciplining *pre-* and post-trading operations. However, in addition to the transparency regime, OTC derivatives are considered by the Package's legislator also for the purpose of defining the SIs, whose *dealing on own account when executing client orders* must occur on an '*organised, frequent, systematic and substantial basis*'. In particular, 'frequency' is defined in respect of the contracts de quo.

In Article 17[D], devoted to algorithmic trading, par. 5 provides valuable prescriptions in terms of 'direct electronic access' (DEA). The allowance of DEA must be notified by the investment firm *to its own Member State*, along with the country *of the trading venue at which the investment firm provides direct electronic access accordingly*. In particular, a trading venue is prohibited from implementing DEA without putting in place the appropriate controls, i.e. those making the system 'effective' and ensuring *a proper assessment and review of the suitability of clients using the service*. Moreover, this must be mandatorily reviewed, as well as *exceeding appropriate pre-set trading and credit thresholds* must be avoided. Besides, proper monitoring and risk controls must be applied, such that risky trading with potentially damaging effects on the market is denied. A periodic reporting—either regular or an ad hoc basis—may also be required by the NCA of the investment firm (which operates the market). The monitoring activity is also performed in order to detect any misconduct, which could even be classified as 'market abuse'. Anyway, infringements must be reported to the competent authority.

Furthermore, still pursuant to par. 5, *the investment firm shall ensure that there is a binding written agreement between the investment firm and the client regarding the essential rights and obligations arising from the provision of the service*. In this case, it is explicitly envisaged that the investment firm retains responsibility under the provisions of the Directive, which every member of the venue is required to comply with. Information received by the investment firm must be communicated 'without undue delay' to the NCA.

Most importantly, *the investment firm shall arrange for records to be kept in relation to the matters referred to in this paragraph and shall ensure that those records be sufficient to enable its competent authority to monitor compliance* with the requirements set forth by the Directive. In fact, in absence of such basic provision, the data set in which compliance can be checked would be insufficient or not existing; thus, any effort aimed at reducing information asymmetry, ensuring an efficient supervision on inherently sensitive operations and avoiding negative spill-overs onto the market could be vanished, as if every safety measure were implemented with regard to a foundation-lacking building.

Finally, *an investment firm that acts as a general clearing member for other persons shall have in place effective systems and controls to ensure clearing services are only applied to persons who are suitable and meet clear criteria*; moreover, *appropriate requirements are imposed on those persons to reduce risks to the investment firm and to the market*, these obligations being set out in a 'binding written agreement' between the entity and the persons de quo.

Other fundamental issues related to market infrastructure are dealt with in Articles 48^{D}–50^{D}, whereas admission to and removal from trading are disciplined in the subsequent articles. In Article 48^{D}—meaningfully headed *System resilience, circuit breakers and electronic trading*—general principles are stated. With regard to RMs, systems must be 'resilient' in order to adequately bear 'peak order and message volumes' in scenarios of 'severe market stress', with the supreme goal of ensuring the 'continuity' of services in case of 'failure' of the trading system. We have dealt with the other requirements set out in that Article in the previous chapter, devoted to trading venues.

However, Article 49^{D} is equally important, for it disciplines trading on a RM under a technical, quantitative point of view. Headed *Tick sizes*, it encompasses the seminal provision of RMs being required to adopt such regimes *in shares, depositary receipts, exchange-traded funds* (par. 1), in order to:

(a) *reflect the liquidity profile of the financial instrument* in respect of different markets (and, as far as the bid-ask spread is concerned, by considering its average value), because *enabling reasonably stable prices without unduly constraining further narrowing of spreads* is deemed to be a desirable thing (provided that it occurs "spontaneously", something which would signal a high degree of liquidity);
(b) *adapt the tick size for each financial instrument appropriately*, in accordance with the provisions set forth by ESMA in RTSs, ultimately implemented by the EU Commission via Delegated Regulation No. 2017/588 of 14 July 2016.

Besides, in relation to second-level regulation, ESMA should issue its prescriptions by adequately keeping into account *the price, spreads and depth of liquidity of the financial instruments* (par. 3). Finally, although it might seem a naïve provision, in Article 50^{D} is stated that *all trading venues and their members or participants synchronise the business clocks* with the purpose of correctly reporting 'date and time' of exchange-related events.

With regard to rules disciplining the post-trade infrastructure, Article 55^{D} is really critical, for it encompasses *provisions regarding CCP and clearing and settlement arrangements*. First of all, the establishment of 'appropriate' agreements between CCPs (or clearing houses) 'and a settlement system of another Member State' is completely liberalised and not subject to any restrictions. The is that the goal of ensuring a properly-working, efficient settlement of trades is clearly superior (par. 1). In fact, these reasons are the only that—when potentially endangered—may allow for a restriction in the cross-border participation into a settlement system, i.e. in the case such a prohibition be necessary *in order to maintain the orderly function* of the RM (par. 2). This "liberal" tone is also kept when dealing with supervisory issues, as 'duplication of control'—with regard to 'clearing and settlement systems'—must be absolutely avoided (par. 3).

As far as commodity derivatives are concerned, 'position limits and position management controls' are very widely envisaged in the lengthy Article 57^{D}. After stating that *the limits shall be set on the basis of the positions held by a person* or on its behalf, and that this computation must be performed 'at an aggregate group level', the EU legislator defines the realm of this second-level regulation. Delegated to ESMA, it is aimed at preventing market abuse and supporting 'orderly pricing and settlement conditions', i.e. favouring a convergence between the price of the derivative and that of its underlying commodity, 'without prejudice' to the latter's price discovery. Consistently with the rationale—which actually informs the whole of the Package—that hedging strategies must be taken into account when dealing with risky exposures, limits do not apply to those positions *which are objectively measurable as reducing risks directly relating to the commercial activity*, despite this provision being circumscribed to non-financial entities (par. 1).

The content of ESMA's RTS is also envisaged, ranging from the maturity of the derivative contract to the 'deliverable supply' of the commodity; from the open interest of both the derivative and the commodity to the 'volatility of relevant markets'; from the 'number and size of market participants' to the features of the commodity market and the 'development of new contracts' (par. 3).

Adopting the methodology for calculating position limits set by ESMA, competent authorities take official decisions on position limits *for each contract in commodity derivatives traded on trading venues*, applying to 'economically equivalent OTC contracts', too. This follows a procedure envisaging the publicly-disclosed opinion of ESMA on the limits that national supervisors are willing to set (paragraphs 4–5). In the case 'the same commodity derivative' be traded in large amounts on different venues subject to different jurisdictions, the authority in charge of the venue where the largest trade occurs is allowed to mandate the extension of those limits to the other identical derivatives (par. 6).

Position management controls are another important issue, their implementation being charged to investment firms or market operators 'operating a trading venue which trades commodity derivatives'. These measures range from the monitoring of positions to the access to information; from termination or reduction of a position (*on a temporary or permanent basis*) to the obligation to *provide liquidity back into the market at an agreed price*. The competent authority must clearly be notified of the measures undertaken by the operator of the trading venue; in turn, it has to communicate them to ESMA (par. 8). The latter has been endowed with the mandate to propose RTS on a number of detail issues (par. 12), representing a sort of "cap on toughness" for regulation, which cannot be hardened by NCAs unless such measures be strongly required by the goal of preserving liquidity and ensuring the 'orderly functioning' of the market. Otherwise, if this occurred under the provisions of domestic laws, concerns related to gold-plating might be raised. However, precise limits to the automatic renewal of such more restrictive ones are laid down, too.

Finally, Member States are also entitled to allow competent authorities to impose sanctions in case of infringements of position limits, regarding breaches either committed at home by foreign persons or abroad by persons authorised by the competent authority in the Member State de quo (par. 14).

5.3 Transparency in MiFID II

It is no doubt that MiFID II legislation has put a remarkable focus on the enhancement of transparency: other than being a tópos in the literature concerning the Package, this goal has been underlined multiple times by legislators and regulators. Whichever consultation or discussion paper or technical document dealing with the innovations brought by the Directive we take, it is often mentioned as one of the fundamental targets laid down in the new legislation (in an investor-protective framework, of course).

In abidance by a broader principle of proportionality, transparency requirements may substantially differ depending upon the infrastructure concerned. Nevertheless, the whole of the Package is informed by the necessity of ensuring a greater degree of transparency. For instance, despite this might seem contradictory or at least counter-intuitive, the extent to which transparency requirements may be applied also to OTC markets is thoroughly debated. In fact, despite these 'private markets' being —by definition—'informal and opaque', we can legitimately ask ourselves a set of important questions: whether or not a larger set of transactions should be affected by transparency legislation; whether or not 'a wider range of trading venues' should be pulled 'into the regulatory net'; and, finally, in light of considerations rooted in the purpose of favouring those exchanges which are mandated to be transparent, whether OTC markets should be narrowed or not (Ferrarini and Saguato 2013).

The first question moves from the assessment that, due to the upheavals succeeded in financial markets over time, some transactions have actually gone away from certain types of venues—in particular, RMs—and reached the alternative ones, where the regulatory *onus* is doubtlessly lower. In addition to this, even without performing OTC exchanges, transactions may be more "tailored" upon the mutual needs of counterparties. Yet, such "migration" has even affected OTC trades, a significant portion of which is nowadays executed on MiFID-compliant trading venues.

However, notwithstanding that one could be tempted not to make any distinction among instruments, the issue has been dealt variously depending upon the object, either equity or non-equity trades. A fundamental change occurred in the wake of the GFC. Before it broke out, it was common opinion—among legislators and regulators worldwide—that transparency requirements should have not been applied to transactions in non-equity instruments. Nevertheless, once the dismal consequences of the contagion were evident, the abovementioned approach incurred a radical change. The standard provision is that, regardless of the type of instrument which is traded, transparency requirements must be abided by.

Of course, the significant move from OTC "alternative" markets to "ordinary" ones did not give rise to merely regulatory issues. In fact, there were important considerations to be done in respect of transaction costs and the efficiency of venues. Nowadays, the Package's provisions apply, also, to those categories of exchanges that were previously excluded from the extent of similar MiFID-compliant venues. This was the case of BCNs, which could be defined neither as MTFs (because of their discretionary nature) nor as SIs (for they do not act as dealers toward their clients). Such inconsistency of MiFID I provisions with certain "modern" types of exchanges was, thus, one of the main drivers of the recognition of OTFs as a new category of venues, with relevant effects on the treatment of information and market data. As a result of this, the scope of OTC markets turned out to be narrowed, in line with the "wishful thinking" expressed at the Pittsburgh G20 summit. Altogether, the support for introducing OTFs outweighed the opposition to it. Nevertheless, as recalled by Ferrarini and Saguato (2013), a deep divide was between (part of) the 'exchange industry', on the one hand, and 'investment intermediaries', on the other. The iter of the reform at a European level was propelled by the favourable view expressed by the International Swaps and Derivatives Association (ISDA), which nowadays is mainly in charge of setting the standard 'Master Agreement' on whose model such contracts are drafted.

Anyway, the move of a relevant number of transactions from "opaque" to "transparent" markets would have not been effective if some significant discretional choices had been left to Member States in implementing MiFID II. In fact, this last may be regarded to be of 'maximal harmonisation', as highlighted by the legislator itself in respect of the whole of the Directive, clearly including transparency and information-related issues. Moreover, in the *Explanatory Memorandum* to MiFID II, we may read that *the EU has committed to minimise, where appropriate, discretions available to Member States across EU financial services directives*, with the purposes of—inter alia—*establishing a single rulebook for financial markets* and creating a more levelled playing field.

Such commitment is so wide and important that its pursuit has been not limited to EEA countries, but rather extended to the broader context of the Single Market. Hence, *pre-* and post-trade transparency requirements are thoroughly laid down also in extra-EU legislations, such as the Swiss one. Anyway, the information subjected to reporting obligations are detailed in MiFIR: as far as non-equity instruments are concerned ('bonds, structured finance products, emission allowances and derivatives'), Article 8^{R}, par. 1—devoted to pre-trade—lists *current bid and offer prices and the depth of trading interests at those prices which are advertised through their systems* as the elements to be disclosed by market operators and investment firms, whereas Article 10^{R}, par. 1—devoted to post-trade—refers to the obligation to *make public the price, volume and time of the transactions* in non-equity instruments *as close to real time as is technically possible*. Similar provisions are laid down with regard to equity-like instruments in Articles 3^{R} and 6^{R}, for pre- and post-trade transparency respectively.

In addition to this, the USA are also currently committed to enhancing transparency with regard to HFT transactions, where the issue of 'spoofing'—i.e., in general, the falsification of the identity of the user of IT services—is extremely relevant and worth addressing, despite a very recent surge. In fact, the first case of spoofing was decided upon by an American court—in accordance with the Dodd-Frank Act provisions—only in 2015, when it was assessed that the 'spoofer', thanks to the 'interconnectedness' of markets, had placed 'non bona fide orders on one exchange' and, then, had executed transactions involving the spoofed securities 'at artificial prices on other exchanges (Jaccard 2015). It has been noticed that, apart from the technical tools which de facto enable the wrongdoing, the essential element without which no spoofing would be possible is undoubtedly the speed of execution or—more precisely—the 'frequency' at which trading occurs (Jaccard 2015). In a case, the court observed that the investor, who had apparently changed its mind with astonishing rapidity in order to act accordingly with market movements, could not have done it 'so quickly, so often, and with such precision', if a spoofing scheme had not been put in place. Nevertheless, since this is per se a risky activity which might well end up with the wrongdoer being uncovered and prosecuted, the transaction withdrawn and any unduly gained wealth being subjected to recovery, improving the quality of data may well help markets in provisioning against such occurrences.

Anyway, the so-called 'dark pools', which are generally chosen by wholesale traders, are still subject to lower transparency requirements. Yet, this does not exempt from putting in place every provision aimed at reinforcing the stability of the infrastructure and, thus, minimising the probability of error in the management of orders: this means, for instance, preventing the sending of erroneous ones (Jaccard 2015). This is a fortiori true as long as those aspects of systemic stability that deal with the "physical" execution of transactions have at least the same relevance as the accountability of order-executers. Actually, this is gradually losing centrality, in a context where the universe of venues is also populated by bilateral ones. Moreover, 'flash crashes' are not as rare as they should be, if we just think of those occurred on 6 May 2010 and 6–7 October 2016. Moreover, if the safeguards put in place by dark pools were deemed to be insufficient from an investor protection standpoint, we would not be able to explain why an increasing number of 'institutional players' (e.g., pension funds), bound by a substantive regulatory *onus* in order not to undertake hazardous investments, actually trade on dark pools or (at most) OTFs. In particular, these latter—vis-à-vis the former—present the disadvantage of less "tailored" transactions but the advantage to have the venue itself—which is allowed to trade against its proprietary capital—as a counterparty of exchanges, despite the flows of information being multilateral. In short, given their characteristics, OTFs and dark pools highlight a trade-off between liquidity and transparency, as they are —generally speaking—more liquid and less transparent than RMs and MTFs.

Anyway, the rationale underlying the substantive strengthening of transaction reporting standards vis-à-vis MiFID I should be found in the comprehensive reshaping of market infrastructure in the aftermath of the GFC: on this topic, someone has noted that the centralisation of clearing, with the rise of CCPs, has somehow weakened the 'external control' exercised upon trades, thus raising the necessity of stricter transparency rules (Berti De Marinis 2016).

Within MiFID II, there is not much variability in how transparency is intended, apart from the fact that is always tied to non-discrimination, a principle which resembles the broader features of the European financial legislation. Anyway, some relevant provisions are encompassed by Article 90^D (*Reports and review*), where ESMA is entrusted with the duty to 'present a report to the European Parliament' within 3 March 2019 on multiple subjects. In addition to a comprehensive review of the functioning of trading venues, the Authority has been endowed with the duty of monitoring AT, including the high-frequency segment, as well as the treatment of certain 'products or practices', the application of criminal sanctions (with a view, in particular, to pursue the harmonisation of national rules). Finally, under a provision which directly affects transparency, it has to check the application of:

- position limits and position management on liquidity, market abuse and orderly pricing and settlement conditions in commodity derivatives markets; *the development in prices for pre- and post-trade transparency data from regulated markets*;
- MTFs, OTFs and APAs (we are going to detail what APAs are);
- the impact of benefits—either monetary or of other nature, in the form of fees or different income—*in connection with the provision of an investment service or an ancillary service to the client*, aimed at assessing *the proper functioning of the internal market on cross-border investment advice*.

In Article 90^D, par. 2, is furtherly specified what these ESMA reports should be made of. Two main elements explicitly envisaged: that is, the *availability and timeliness of post-trade information*, under a 'consolidated' format which should ensure that:

(a) all transactions be included, *irrespective of whether they are carried out on trading venues or not*;
(b) *the availability and timeliness of full and partial post-trade information that is of a high quality*, with the purpose of securing their accessibility to market participants and—with a more general phrase—their availability 'on a reasonable commercial basis'.

As laid down in par. 3, the entity which is by default in charge of such data collection is a 'consolidated tape provider' (CTP), whose role we are going to furtherly detail. Nevertheless, in the case of failure (i.e. if the CTP turned out not to fulfil the *criteria* above), the Commission would require ESMA to launch a procedure in order to choose the entity to which these duties will be delegated.

5.4 Categories and Functions of Data Reporting Services Providers

Pursuant to Article 59^D, the so-called 'data reporting services' (DRSs) represent an authorised macro-category of entities encompassing three different reserved activities: 'consolidated tape providers' (CTPs), 'approved publication arrangements'

(APAs) and 'approved reporting mechanisms' (ARMs), which are presented in Annex 1, Section D of the Directive. If it is committed to providing one or more of the abovementioned services, a firm is labelled as 'data reporting services provider' (DRSP). Of course, albeit a specified iter has to be undertaken in order for an ad hoc authorisation to be released, investment firms and market operators are allowed to exercise such activities, too; in this case, however, competent authorities are endowed with the duty to perform some stringent checks aimed at verifying the compliance with MiFID II provisions (in particular, with Title V^D, devoted to DRSs).

As far as CTPs are concerned, a greater integration—i.e. lower fragmentation—of the market, which is generally associated with rising liquidity, is the main goal pursued by the European legislator by envisaging such 'consolidation' of trade data. Of course, as clearly stated in Article 65^D, par. 1, the CTP must implement adequate policies and arrangements in order to perform, first, the collection of data. Then, such information has to be 'consolidated into a continuous electronic data stream' and, finally, it must be disclosed to the public 'as close to real time as is technically possible' (again, 'on a reasonable commercial basis'). In practice, the information must be 'made available free of charges' within 15 minutes since its publication; dissemination is mandated to occur 'efficiently and consistently'; and the non-discrimination principle must clearly be abided by. In order for this to be achieved, the legislator has explicitly mentioned the possibility of arising conflicts of interest, stating that 'effective administrative arrangements', aimed at preventing them, must be required from the CTP by its home Member State (Article 65^D, par. 4). Actually, with regard to non-equity transaction, the consolidating obligations are scheduled not to apply before 3 September 2019 (originally the same date in 2018, as envisaged in Article 93^D, par. 1, with the one-year-ahead shift reflecting that in the Package as a whole).

Anyway, one could legitimately ask whence the information collected, consolidated and disclosed by CTPs come. The answer is: from APAs. In fact, this reporting service finds its raison d'être in the provision encompassed by Article 20^R, where is stated that *investment firms which, either on own account or on behalf of clients, conclude transactions in shares, depositary receipts, ETFs, certificates and other similar financial instruments traded on a trading venue, shall make public the volume and price of those transactions and the time at which they were concluded*, by seminally adding that such information 'shall be made public through an APA'. This category—a fortiori, given its "institutional" tasks which cannot be renounced and are essential for the whole of the transparency architecture—is mandated to put in place those arrangements (in terms of efficiency, non-discrimination, etc.) that we have discussed in respect of CTPs. We just add that the definition of a 'reasonable commercial basis' is left to the Commission's delegated acts. Moreover, an entity authorised as APA must design some organisational tools aimed at separating different business functions.

As far as ARMs are concerned, they find their source in Article 26^R and, like APAs, are much more clearly defined than CTPs. Pursuant to Recital 54^D, they are entrusted with *reporting details of transactions to domestic competent authorities or ESMA*. Their discipline does not significantly differ from that of the previous two, such that we may actually identify a comprehensive, consistent MiFID II reporting universe whereby the so-called 'grandfathering'—i.e. the automatism in authorising those service-providing entities that had already being authorised pursuant to older rules—is denied. The result is that, for instance, DRSPs existing under the British law, like 'trade data monitors' (TDMs) and "local" ARMs, have needed to initiate a different iter—compliant with Title V^D of MiFID II—in order to keep working.

5.5 Transparency Waivers and Deferrals

Waivers and deferrals are recognised to transactions in both equity and non-equity instruments. With regard to the former (Article 4^R, par. 1), waivers are exactly of the same kind as those available to trading venues for shares admitted to trading on an RM: that is, the following conditions are met:

(a) systems that match orders whose price is derived from the trading venue where the financial instrument was first admitted to trading, or from the most relevant market in terms of liquidity;
(b) systems that formalise negotiated transactions;
(c) orders that are large in scale compared to normal market size;
(d) orders held in an order management facility pending disclosure. The use of these waivers may be disciplined through Delegated Regulations adopted by the Commission upon the basis of RTS drafted by ESMA.

As far as *non*-equity transactions are concerned (Article 9^R, par. 1), cases (c) and (d) are kept, whereas the other two are replaced by a couple of conditions that are clearly specific of these instruments, in respect of which liquidity issues are far more relevant vis-à-vis the equity ones:

- actionable indications of interest in request-for-quote and voice trading systems that are above a size specific to the instrument, which would expose liquidity providers to undue risk;
- derivatives that are not subject to the trading obligation under Article 28^R and other financial instruments for which there is not a liquid market.

National regulators are entrusted with the duty of notifying both the competent authority and ESMA of the intended use of a waiver, along with an explanation of its functioning. This submission must be made at least four months before the intended use of the waiver; within two months after notification, ESMA will issue a non-binding opinion. Moreover, said authority may act as a conciliator in the case competent authorities disagreed over the waiver's legitimacy.

The rationale followed by the legislator, who acknowledges the trade-off between liquidity and transparency, is that instruments whose exchange suffers from an insufficient liquidity might be helped by relaxing the transparency requirements charged to them, up to total exemption. Such configuration, whereby price-formation and investor-protection sensibilities are somehow subjected to the greater goal of securing systemic stability via an efficient market, is not so common in the Package, but is undoubtedly part of the most visible juridical heritage of the financial crisis.

As far as deferrals are concerned, since they deal with post-trade transparency which is deemed to have 'a wider scope than *pre*-trade' one, OTC markets are widely affected. MiFID II allows investment firms, provided that they meet certain requirements, to defer the publication of post-trade information about shares admitted to trading on an RM. As for equity transactions, in order for the deferral to apply, a given size must be trespassed, and the exchange must be between an investment firm dealing on own account and a counterparty (however, matched-principal transactions are excluded). The term to which the publication may be deferred depends upon the asset class—i.e. shares, ETFs or depositary receipts—which is concerned. Anyway, it cannot be longer than one trading day or, in the case of transactions concluded late in their day of execution, the maximal deadline for publication is set at noon of the second trading day after.

With regard to *non*-equity instruments, deferral rules are much more complex. Conditions that must be met in order for a deferral to be extended are somehow similar to those for obtaining a waiver (Article 11^{R}, par. 1):

(a) they have to be 'large in scale' vis-à-vis 'normal market size';
(b) a 'liquid market' must be lacking;
(c) the threshold set by the 'size specific to the instrument' must be trespassed in exchanges other than matched-principal ones;
(d) particular requirements are laid down in the case of 'package transactions'.

For non-equity instruments, the standard deferral consists of two trading days rather than only one; however, supervisors are deeply concerned about the deferral possibly hurting market participants, such that their authorising powers—aimed at ensuring that the deferral actually 'benefits' all the parties interested by it—take great relevance and apply to both trading venues and investment firms.

Let us take a look back to the situation under MiFID I, in years from 2008 to 2013. Across Europe, as we may spot by trivial calculations from data in Figs. 5.2 and 5.3, financial instruments different from shares that are 'large in scale' vis-à-vis normal market size are a small number compared to equities (the sum of the two categories gives the 'Total n. FIs' figure).

The number of instruments that—because of size—must abide by transparency requirements has remarkably declined from 2008 to 2013 (−16.6%). In contrast, the story is quite different regarding orders with an average daily turnover (ADT) lower than € 100,000: shares belonging to such category, i.e. the most illiquid ones, have witnessed their information obligations shift from before trade to after its execution. This suggests us that waivers have been effectively used in fulfilling the purpose they had been conceived for: the overall *onus* on equity transactions has decreased over

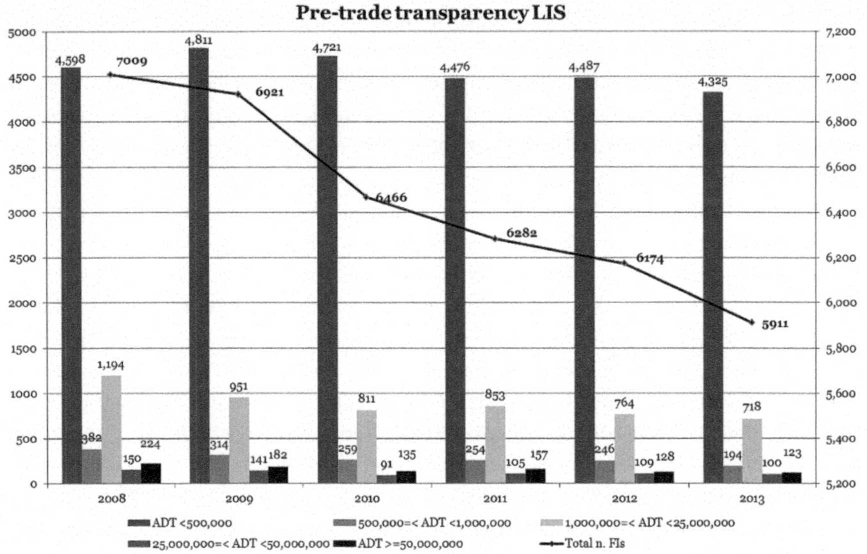

Fig. 5.2 Number of shares subject to pre-trade transparency requirements for large-in-scale transactions, grouped into average daily turnover (ADT) classes. *Source* ESMA MiFID database

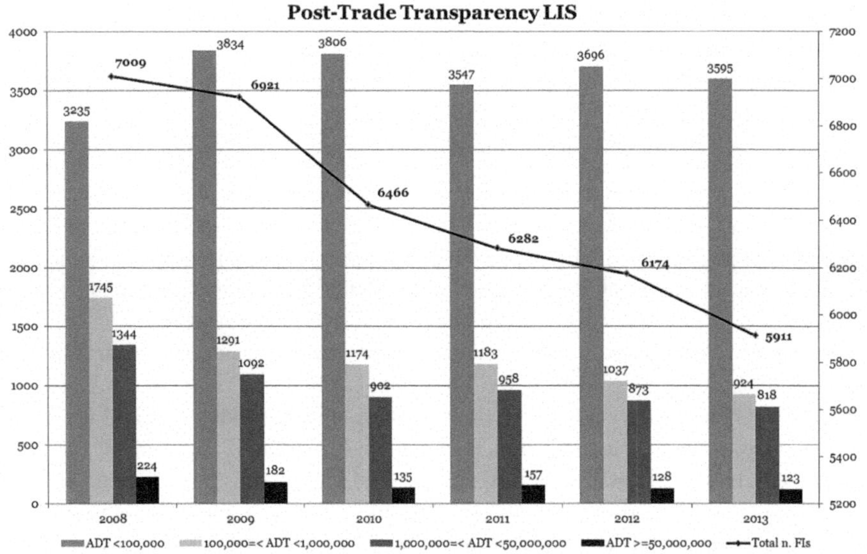

Fig. 5.3 Number of shares subject to post-trade transparency requirements for large-in-scale transactions, grouped into average daily turnover (ADT) classes. *Source* ESMA MiFID database

time, and illiquid shares have been discharged of some burdens that could have furtherly harmed them. Hence, given the appreciable performance under the previous Directive, the EU legislator has wisely opted for continuing on the existing path.

Specific deferrals are also allowed in Article 11^R, par. 3, where the possibility to 'calibrate' them is attributed to (both kinds of) operators: implementing such principle means that:

(a) certain trades can be reported prior to the expiration of the deferral period;
(b) others may be deferred for a longer time than the standard one, either with no regard to volume, or
(c) in an aggregate form, whereas
(d) sovereign bonds (exclusively) may have their publication obligations indefinitely postponed.

The abovementioned rule entrusts competent authorities with the power to require that certain duties be honoured by operators.

5.6 Transparency Provisions of Direct Applicability

The language used by the MiFIR legislator, though very closely resembling the one of MiFID II, is generally more direct and concise. This is clearly referable to the intrinsic peculiarity of a Regulation vis-à-vis a Directive, as the former is provided with direct applicability. Hence, though informed by the same principles as the other piece of legislation, MiFIR shows less generic parts and enforces clearer rules in relevant situations, which investment firms and other players have already started dealing with. The direct applicability of Directives—so-called 'self-execution'—has always been widely debated, since the European Community was established. Even if no consensus has been reached yet, the most credited opinion is that, under certain conditions that somehow make possible to apply a general provision to a particular case, Directives may be directly enforced in respect of their fundamental principles (this should anyway be recognised by a ruling and has no general validity).

We could easily imagine that transparency issues for trading venues are very widely addressed by what is endowed with immediate execution. As previously underlined, in a specific provision contained in the Regulation (Article 3^R) is stated that current bid and 'offer' (ask) prices of exchanged securities must be made public by market operators and investment firms, which are also mandated to do that—toward the 'public' of investors—*on a continuous basis during normal trading hours*, in the case they operate a trading venue (par. 1). Such obligation does not depend upon the functioning of the trading systems (par. 2); in fact, any market operator must provide non-discriminatory access to *investment firms which are obliged to publish their quotes* (par. 3). These are the most general rules, derogated by "particular" provisions defining waivers and exemptions for both equity and non-equity instruments.

In light of direct applicability, a particular relevance is taken by Article 5^{R}, which deals with specific 'volume caps' not to be exceeded: as some waivers, if actually exploited, might theoretically 'unduly harm price formation', there are additional 'restrictions' applying to 'trading under those waivers'. First of all, (a) waived trades cannot represent a proportion higher than 4% *of the total volume of trading in that financial instrument on all trading venues across the Union over the previous 12 months*; moreover, (b) keeping such basis as a reference for calculation, *overall Union trading in a financial instrument carried out under those waivers shall be limited to 8%.*

The following rules detail the procedures disciplining the cases in which the thresholds are trespassed, with the most significant provision being that, within two days dating from the occurrence of the breach, the competent authority—i.e. the one which had released its authorisation to employ the waiver—must suspend the *use on that venue in that financial instrument*, if limit (a) is broken (par. 2). Analogously, the abovementioned body must block '*the use of those waivers across the Union for a period of six months*' if limit (b) is not abided by (par. 3). In order to assess whether one of those rules have been disregarded, the competent authority must rely upon data periodically published by ESMA and relative to the previous year (par. 4), also in the case the proportions referred to in (a) and (b) reach the "alert levels" of 3.75% and 7.75%, respectively (par. 5-6). Par. 7 is also strongly relevant, as it sets forth the principle that trades executed under those waivers must ensure the possibility to identify the traders using them and, clearly, secure compliance with thresholds (a) and (b).

Chapter 3 of Title II^{R} introduces two provisions that we have already mentioned, whose relevance shapes the whole of the transparency framework in the Regulation: namely, the twofold obligation to make pre- and post-trade data available 'separately' (Article 12^{R}) and 'on a reasonable commercial basis' (Article 13^{R}). The former is substantially delegated to ESMA: this authority proposed RTS 14 regarding 'data disaggregation', which also carried amendments to EMIR and eventually ended with the Commission Delegated Regulation of 2 June 2016. In accordance with MiFIR provisions, the core issue has been identified with the 'level' of such disaggregation in the information released by trading venues to the public, something which is extremely important—as underlined by the Commission—because it *will reduce market data costs for market participants by allowing them to acquire only the very specific pre-trade or post-trade data they need.* In order for the disaggregation level to be decided upon, different aspects have to be taken into account: namely (Recital 1 of said Delegated Regulation) the asset class, the country of issue, the currency 'in which a financial instrument is traded'. However, the subject operating the trading venue must clearly specify the criteria to be met by a 'financial instrument or type of data', whenever the disaggregation rationale appears to be ambiguous (Recital 3).

Paragraph 1 of the single article of said Delegated Regulation does the following: (a) identifies the different asset classes; (b)–(c) underlines the other two main criteria, i.e. the country and the currency associated with the instrument; (d) introduces a separation based upon discerning between 'scheduled daily auctions' and 'continuous trading'. Paragraph 2 provides a breakdown of the generic item 'derivatives' referred to in (a); the following one repeats the above-mentioned principle of "disambiguation". The last two are more technical, as they clarify that the criteria may be applied in any -combination of them (par. 4) and that market operators and investment firms are allowed to bundle the data they provide (par. 5).

Title III^{R} deals with transparency issues regarding SIs and 'investment firms trading OTC': that is, subject to these rules are entities different from trading venues stricto sensu, because of either the role exercised in the context of exchanges or how trades are executed. Notice that these entities are somehow left aside in the Directive, which explicitly submits their discipline to what is stated in MiFIR or MAR (Regulation No. 596/2014), establishing a framework of directly applicable rules in relation to some entities whose operations, inherently cross-border and continuously ongoing, could not be artificially segmented by national provisions amended throughout time. This is the reason why Regulations are much fitter than Directives in harmonising the discipline on both systematic internalisation and OTC trading, albeit this has not prevented the Member States from introducing domestic provisions on this matter.

Articles 14^{R} introduces some remarkable principles. First of all, in the case an instrument be not liquid enough, disclosure by SIs may be provided at the client's request; moreover, this approach is also valid if the size involved is lower than the 'standard market' one (par. 1). In particular, SIs can decide the sizes in correspondence of which they will post the quotes, and this volume cannot be lower than 10% of the standard size (par. 3). Moreover, the competent authority for the most relevant market where the instrument is traded has to decide—with annual frequency—the class in which it has to be included (par. 6). Another important principle is the one affirmed in par. 7, where an 'efficient valuation' of instruments is envisaged, along with the objective to *maximise the possibility of investment firms to obtain the best deal for their clients*.

Also, extremely significant is Article 15^{R}, too, centred on the 'execution of client orders'. Par. 1 mandates SIs to publish their quotes *on a regular and continuous basis during normal trading hours*, in order to make data *easily accessible to other market participants on a reasonable commercial basis*. It is worth noting that the wording of legislation remarks that SIs are not a trading venue nor an operator of it, but rather play some role which is closer to that of 'other participants' rather than of the infrastructure itself (which they nonetheless give a seminal contribution to). Paragraph 3 clarifies that these subjects may execute transactions even at a price different from the quoted one, if multiple instruments are involved in the same operation or, still, *orders are subject to conditions other than the current market price*. Since these provisions are quite "liberal" and do not charge excessive burdens on a (small) category of entities which nowadays could not lack in a developed financial market, even in this case we should suppose that post-Brexit legislation will not bring relevant changes.

This *spirit*, which fully acknowledges and valorises the role of SIs, is also consistent with the provisions laid down in Article 17^R, one of the few examples of rules protecting the supply side of the industry, rather than the demand one. In fact, it envisages some clear limits to the non-discriminatory approach of the whole of the Package: consistently with a truly Anglo-Saxon way of conceiving fairness, is attributed to SIs the faculty to decide which clients will be given free access to quotes, still avoiding any arbitrary discrimination—that is, two identical situations must be treated equally—but also 'on the basis of their commercial policy'. This means that SIs are allowed to *refuse to enter into or discontinue business relationships with clients on the basis of commercial considerations such as the client credit status, the counterparty risk and the final settlement of the transaction* (par. 1). Moreover, they can *limit the total number of transactions from different clients at the same time*, with the *caveat* that, in order for such a measure to be implementable, the 'number and/or volume of orders sought by clients' must be 'considerably' above the 'norm'.

Anyway, the objective of enhancing liquidity in non-equity markets—which, by their inner nature, are exposed to these risks more than equity ones—is somehow taken into greater consideration by the EU legislator. In Article 18^R we may read that *investment firms shall make public firm quotes in respect of bonds, structured finance products, emission allowances and derivatives traded on a trading venue* where they operate as SIs, even if the degree of liquidity should suffice. However, the following provisions clarify that the abovementioned one is not binding at all but ultimately depends upon the counterparties' will. In fact, a couple of conditions has to be met in order for this stricter requirement to apply: (a) a client of the SI asks for a quote to be provided; (b) the internaliser agrees to satisfy such request (par. 1). Quotes may be updated at any time or even withdrawn 'under exceptional market conditions' (par. 3).

Articles 20^R and 21^R—regarding transactions in equity and non-equity instruments, respectively—discipline 'post-trade disclosure by investment firms', SIs included. First of all, 'volume and price of the transactions, along with 'the time at which they were concluded', are mentioned in par. 1—of both articles—because they are deemed to be essential, thus setting a common basis for data publication all across the EU, even in respect of transactions concluded outside of trading venues (that is, OTC), as stated in Article 20^R, par. 2, and Article 21^R, par. 4. Conversely, the discipline of deferrals is not exactly the same between the two categories, as competent authorities are allowed to authorise them only in respect of transactions in non-equity instruments. Moreover, since the relevance of reporting is (generally) regarded as positively associated with riskiness, in Article 20^R, par. 2, is clearly stated that *each individual transaction shall be made public once through a single APA*, in order to avoid any duplication or redundancy (which could have as negative effects as lacking information).

It is clear, thus, how MiFIR does not depart from the provisions encompassed by the Directive; yet, given the Regulation's immediate enforcement, its approach is more prudent and soft-handed *vis-à-vis* that of MiFID II. Such "caution" is reinforced by the subsequent rules (Articles 22^R and 23^R), where no distinction is made between trading venues, APAs and CTPs. In fact, a competent authority may ask information to any of them, in order to perform calculations *for determining the requirements for the pre-trade and post-trade transparency and the trading obligation regimes*, as well as in order to assess *whether an investment firm is a systematic internaliser* (Article 22^{R}, par. 1). Still, RMs, MTFs and SIs, alongside foreign venues deemed to be equivalent, are the only "places" where listed shares—i.e. admitted to trading venues—can be exchanged (Article 23^{R}, par. 1), unless (a) trades are *non-systematic, ad hoc, irregular and infrequent*, or (b) at least one counterparty is an 'eligible' or 'professional' one and, hence, does not contribute to the 'price discovery process'. As for point (a), the use of *and* probably marks a 'hendiadys', because the four adjectives—though not completely overlapping and each one giving a particular nuance—in fact identify the same features of a trade. Probably, ad hoc would have encompassed the other three meanings. Anyway, clarity probably is the MiFIR legislator's supreme goal, and its pursuit therein is much more convincing vis-à-vis the Directive.

5.7 Transaction Reporting in MiFIR

Article 24^{R} is quite an unicum in the Package, as it opens a Title (IV^{R}) by immediately stating that—'without prejudice' to MAR provisions—NCAs have to cooperate, under the coordination of ESMA, in monitoring *the activities of investment firms to ensure that they act honestly, fairly and professionally in a manner which promotes the integrity of the market*. The following provisions (Article 25^{R}) do not differ too much from those set out in the Directive, as they substantially mandate to keep records, which may be accessed by ESMA and competent authorities, too. They must also contain 'the relevant data that constitute the characteristics of the order, including those that link an order with the executed transaction(s) that stem from that order' (par. 2). A further requirement is encompassed by Article 26^{R}, where we find the provision that 'complete and accurate details' of transactions be submitted *as quickly as possible, and no later than the close of the following working day* (par. 1).

There are, still, more precise requirements: among others, *details of the names and numbers of the financial instruments bought or sold, the quantity, the dates and times of execution, the transaction prices* and also the identification of natural persons such as the clients *on whose behalf the firm has executed the transaction*, the employees at the investment firm responsible for the investment decision, the algorithms used, and 'a designation to identify a short sale' in the case of shares and sovereign debt being exchanged. For the abovementioned purposes, 'short sales' are defined in Article 2, par. 1, letter *b* of Regulation No. 236/2012, whereas the provisions regarding shares and sovereign debt are consistent with what is laid down in Articles 12, 13 and 17 of that piece of legislation. With regard to commodity derivatives, a peculiar attention to the reduction of risk 'in an objectively measurable way', pursuant to the provisions of the Directive, is also invoked

(Article 57^{D}). Specific provisions are laid down regarding transmission of orders, which may be electively treated by investment firms—in relation to details to be included in what is reported to the competent authority—as if they were transactions, thus being subject to different requirements (par. 4).

A significant pattern regarding the way in which information is reported is also envisaged in the same Article, with an approach aimed at charging investment firms with significant responsibility but, at the same time, discarding them from being held liable for violations not attributable to them. On the one hand, in par. 7, we may read that they are responsible for *the completeness, accuracy and timely submission of the reports which are submitted to the competent authority*, whereas the subsequent provision is explicitly intended as a 'derogation' and states that, *where an investment firm reports details of those transactions through an ARM which is acting on its behalf or a trading venue*, it will not be held liable for failures whereby deficiencies in checking for the above-mentioned features 'are attributable to the ARM or trading venue'. However, investment firms must not interpret this as a waiver from exercising any due control regarding *the completeness, accuracy and timeliness of the transaction reports which were submitted on their behalf.* For these purposes, the European legislator has envisaged the possibility to widen the subjectivity of ARMs, because trade-matching and reporting systems, as well as TRs (complying with EMIR), may be authorised as ARMs by their national competent authority.

Par. 7 details the effort to be sustained by investment firms. First of all, 'sound security mechanisms' are required by the home Member State for various purposes, clearly oriented toward the same objectives: *to guarantee the security and authentication of the means of transfer of information, to minimise the risk of data corruption and unauthorised access and to prevent information leakage maintaining the confidentiality of the data at all times*; in addition to this, another requirement deals with the maintenance of 'adequate resources' and 'back-up facilities'. Both 'errors' and 'omissions' may be corrected with a new submission, too. Finally, in the case of data transmissions to the host competent authority because of a specific obligation to do so (the Regulation references to those envisaged in Article 35^{D}, par. 8.), that piece of information must be reported by the recipient to the home authority, unless this last has declared itself unwilling to receive it.

Article 27^{R}—in particular, par. 1—concludes Title IV^{R} by highlighting the importance of 'identifying reference data' being provided by trading venues to competent authorities in relation to the instruments that are traded, in order for the obligations under Article 26^{R} to be matched. Of course, 'an electronic and standardised format' is required and—most importantly—the supply of such data must occur 'before trading commences in the financial instrument that it refers to'. This Article (as well as the preceding others) encompasses a large number of provisions detailing the content of ESMA second-level technical regulation to be issued or proposed, which is widely referred to in that Title. Such an approach is quite common in Regulations, whose highest-possible level of harmonisation de facto works as a constraint against a too heavy intervention on more specific issues.

Nevertheless, the whole of Title IV^{R} seems to be designed in order to empower that micro-prudential authority in a way whose ultimate goal is creating a common technical framework which works in such an efficient, standardised, replicable way that national jurisdictions would have really narrow margins to act differently. This is consistent with higher-level rules being clear, but rather minimalistic, also because of the lengthy and rough path undertaken by the 28 Member States—each one with its own legitimate interests relating to its own structure, size, and functioning of financial markets—, which requires diverging positions to be conciliated.

5.8 The Greatest Concern: Derivatives Trading

The second half of 2016 saw a large contraction in the volumes of exchanged derivatives, measured with the open-interest method. Open interest expresses the net evolution in outstanding derivative contracts: for instance, with regard to options, it increases whenever new ones are created and long positions are taken; conversely, decreases whenever positions are closed or rights exercised. Therefore, it is a more "refined" measure vis-à-vis the simple 'average daily turnover', which is a more "rough" way of representing traded volumes. Looking at Fig. 5.4, we may note that post EU referendum spill-overs have likely affected derivatives markets due to the global relevance of the City of London in respect of their trading, because of investors being highly concerned about the future of such a remarkable hub.

By the end of 2016, compared to six months earlier—i.e. to the monetary figure recorded just one week after the referendum, forex derivatives had shrunk by more than 20%, and interest-rate ones by nearly 30%. The former contracts have finally come back and even beyond pre-Brexit levels; the latter have not (actually, the volatility of these markets is inherently high).

Reading the header of Article 28^{R}—which opens Title V^{R}—might even suffice to doubt whether a post-Brexit UK would pursue a "conservative" stance regarding the provisions contained therein or rather show a substantive deregulatory attitude, aimed at removing those rules which could be intended as a restriction to the free exchange of securities. One of these provisions is exactly that laid down in Article 28^{R}, par. 1, applying to both financial and non-financial counterparties as defined in EMIR (Article 2, par. 8 and Article 10, par. 1, letter *b*, respectively). It sets forth the 'obligation to trade on regulated markets, MTFs or OTFs'—actually, a third allowed category being 'third-country venues' recognised to be equivalent—for those derivatives which are outside the two main definitions set out in EMIR. It attains to those being *neither intragroup transactions as defined in Article 3 (...) nor transactions covered by the transitional provisions in Article 89 (...)*, the reference being to EMIR, with the latter actually having a more detailed scope. These transactions may be 'with other such financial counterparties' or—alternatively—with 'other such non-financial counterparties' matching the conditions set out in Article 10 EMIR, par. 1, letter *b*.

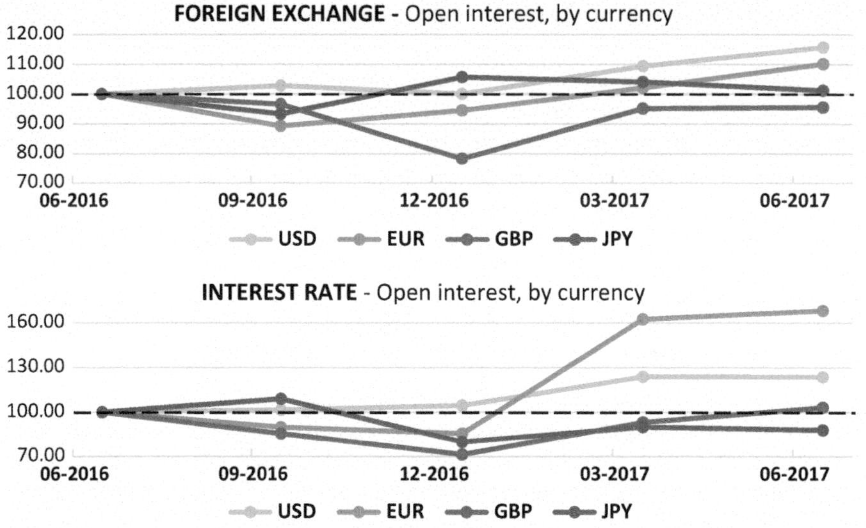

Fig. 5.4 Evolution of derivatives transactions (computed with the open interest method), by currency, from June 2016 (=100) to June 2017. Original data expressed in trillion USD. *Source* authors' elaboration on Bank for International Settlements data

However, said obligation applies only in the case the exchange consists in *derivatives pertaining to a class of derivatives that has been declared subject to the trading obligation*. MiFIR explicitly recalls *the procedure set out in Article 32*^{R} *and listed in the register referred to in Article 34*^{R}, which we are going to discuss. Anyway, every kind of trading venue—which may be freely chosen by the counterparties, within the abovementioned range—is mandated to admit derivatives to trading 'on a *non*-exclusive and non-discriminatory basis' (Article 28^R, par. 3). This stands in clear accordance with the 'prudential', non-interventionist, lean approach to regulation that shapes the European juridical framework.

In Article 28^R, par. 2, is underlined that, provided that the exchange consists in derivatives pertaining to a class which is subject to the trading obligation, this last applies also in the case of counterparties being *third-country financial institutions or other third-country entities that would be subject to the clearing obligation if they were established in the Union* or, alternatively, if *the contract has a direct, substantial, foreseeable effect within the Union*; finally, a residual condition that might enable the trading obligation is that it is *necessary or appropriate to prevent the evasion of any provision* contained in MiFIR, this being furtherly detailed in terms of 'systemic risk' and 'regulatory arbitrage', upon which ESMA is called to exercise its surveillance.

Article 28^R, par. 4, encompasses a thorough discussion about those conditions that, if met, would allow to deem a third-country venue to be equivalent for the purposes of enforcing a trading obligation. They are quite standard and—after all—extremely basic, as they encompass (a) the existence of an authorisation to operate as well as 'effective supervision and enforcement'; (b) 'clear and transparent rules' regarding the admission to trading to a 'fair, orderly and efficient manner' of exchanging instruments; from (c) 'periodic and ongoing information requirements ensuring a high level of investor protection' to (d) 'market transparency and integrity'. The equivalence decision may also be 'limited to a category or categories of trading venues', rather than to the whole of those registered in a certain country.

Other significant rules are those that discipline the clearing of transactions. First of all, pursuant to Article 29^R, every transaction in derivatives concluded on a RM must be cleared by a CCP (par. 1), which is mandated to ensure—through 'systems, procedures and arrangements'—that both the submission and the acceptance of a transaction occurs 'as quickly as technologically practicable using automated systems' (par. 2). The clearing obligation may be either "legal"—that is, pursuant to what is explicitly stated in legislation; in particular, transactions in derivatives concluded on a RM must be cleared in accordance with the abovementioned Article 29^R, par. 1, whereas other categories are dealt with by Article 5 EMIR—or "contractual", where agreed upon by the counterparties. The delicate issue of 'indirect clearing' is also addressed (Article 30^R, par. 1) with extreme caution, such that it is allowed only if no increase in counterparty risk is yielded and the 'protection' substantially remains the same—meaning that it must have an 'equivalent effect', in the MiFIR wording—as in the case of direct clearing.

Finally, portfolio compression is waived from best execution obligations; nevertheless, such provision is balanced by strong information and communication requirements: that is, the volumes of transactions interested by the compression must be made public through an APA, as well as records be kept 'complete and accurate', by investment firms and market operators providing such a service. The rationale of this should be quite clear: portfolio compression is rooted in the consent of counterparties and is conceived to yield mutual benefits, albeit is clearly possible that one party takes a greater advantage vis-à-vis the other.

Provisions on clearing obligation, indirect clearing and portfolio compression seem to be based upon common-sense considerations (especially in light of the United Kingdom being one of the few countries where there is no monopoly on central clearing, but CCPs are numerous and quite competitive). Besides, they show a moderately "liberal" face consisting in a deregulatory attitude but cum iudicio. Instead, trading obligation is a radically different story. First of all, we should consider that, nowadays, trading venues get a larger share of their income from dealing in derivatives rather than from trading in different securities. This does not mean that OTC markets have lost their appeal for uncommon, illiquid, tailor-made products: notwithstanding the introduction of OTFs, many exchanges in derivatives are still concluded over-the-counter.

As we may spot from BIS data, no single EU-27 country is by far comparable to the United Kingdom in terms of the scope of OTC derivatives markets, both in terms of places where trades are executed and of currency. Despite the Eurozone-at-large being more quantitatively relevant than the UK; nevertheless, this last still remains among the top four or even three largest players at a global level in respect of the volume of derivatives trading. However, in the second half of

2016, as shown by BIS data, it actually experienced a decrease in exchange-traded futures and options, probably as a direct effect of Brexit-related fears. Finally, though the Kingdom hugely outnumbers Japan as a country, the yen sometimes shows better figures vis-à-vis the pound sterling, mainly regarding OTC exchanges. These data show that, however derivatives markets may be blamed, their competitiveness is still a serious concern to be addressed by any open, modern, thriving economy, even in a post-GFC environment.

References

Berti De Marinis, G. M. (2016). Regolamentazione del mercato finanziario e principio di trasparenza. Responsabilitá civile e previdenza. *Rivista bimestrale di dottrina, giurisprudenza e legislazione, 81*(3), 992–1013.

Committee of European Securities Regulators. (2010). *CESR equity market technical advice*, No. 129.

Ferrarini, G., & Saguato, P. (2013). Reforming securities and derivatives trading in the EU: From EMIR to MiFIR. *Journal of Corporate Law Studies, 13*(2), 319–359.

Jaccard, G. (2015). *High frequency trading: The technological puzzle*. SSRN, Working Paper.

Lucantoni, P. (2017). Il mercato dei derivati: note preliminari ad uno studio sistematico. *Banca Borsa Titoli di Credito: rivista di dottrina e giurisprudenza, 70*(2), 182–206.

Petrescu, M., & Wedow, M. (2017). Dark pools in European equity markets: Emergence, competition and implications, *ECB Occasional Paper Series*, No. 193 (July 2017).

Chapter 6
Investor Protection

Abstract The chapter analyses the major changes occurred in investor protection, which is one of the broader aims of the whole of MiFID legislation. In particular, we focus on two disruptive novelties: first, the so-called *know your merchandise* rule, entailing that investment firms identify a 'target market of end clients'; second, the overarching principle that they must act 'in the best interest of the client', including so-called 'tied agents' when providing investment advice. The heavily-impacting rules on inducements—which independent advisors are almost completely banned from receiving—are also discussed. In addition to this, we review the criteria determining the categorisation of both products (complex vs. non-complex) and clients (retail, professional, eligible counterparties). Besides, we show the content and the purpose of the suitability and appropriateness tests, discussing which conditions allow not to administer the latter. Also, the strengthening of investor protection is read in the light of product governance and intervention, which are critical to prevent wrongly-designed investment decisions from backfiring.

6.1 The Idea of Investor Protection Over Time

The rationale of investor protection has always been found in the information asymmetries between the providers (performers) of investment services (activities)—typically banks and other financial intermediaries—and their recipients. The two phrases are often intended as synonyms, in the Package itself as well as in many implementing legislations at a domestic level. Yet, some national legislations—e.g., the Dutch one—have actually discerned between them. In fact, there are significant differences across industries: in banking and insurance, counterparties might be the least viable ones (adverse selection) or might behave in a way inconsistent with their obligations (moral hazard). As of the underwriting of units of a collective investment scheme (CIS), as well as the purchase of a security, the uncertainty yielding the asymmetry is much more on the seller's side, as this latter is often represented by an 'institutional' subject, endowed with far more awareness of that product's risk than the vast majority of clients.

M. Comana et al., *The MiFID II Framework*,
https://doi.org/10.1007/978-3-030-12504-2_6

The concept of ‘investor protection’ is probably the first that comes to mind when thinking of MiFID, either the first or the second Directive. Before it, the idea that the weakest party (i.e. buyers) in financial relationships should BE adequately protected was present but not yet very well developed. In fact, the baseline idea—rooted in the legislation inspired by the French Revolution throughout continental Europe—was that there existed no relevant difference between financial contracts, on the one hand, versus non-financial ones. With the passage of time, along with the development of finance and an increasing number of mala gestio cases harmfully affecting retail investors, that belief has been substantially revised. The 2010 Dodd-Frank Act represented a renewed legislative commitment towards constraining banking activities onto less risky ones, unlike what had been pursued in the past (so-called *Volcker Rule*). Named after the former Fed chairman Paul Volcker, it prohibited banks from engaging in proprietary trading tout court, without any discernment between different kinds of products or instruments. As a matter of fact, notable deregulation has unfolded over time; nevertheless, what cannot be established without ideological prejudices is the link between liberalised financial services, on the one hand, and the propagation of GFC effects, on the other.

Supervision had its faults, thoroughly addressed by the 2009 *De Larosière Report*. The EU legislation had its own guilts, as MiFID I was far from ensuring a perfectly levelled playing field and an improved efficiency of financial markets. Yet, much of the criticism directed at the Directive started from the ideological assumption that an insufficient degree of regulation had prompted supervisors to exert insufficient control upon overseen entities. In turn, these latter ones had been able to disregard transparency requirements, widen information asymmetries in their exclusive interest (to the detriment of clients), originate and distribute products encompassing a significant component of systemic risk.

Since globalisation has somehow “made the world smaller”, individual interactions have become increasingly closer ad, thus, the effect of a single financial decision—especially if involving relatively high amounts of money—may well either influence other people’s choices or have an impact on their financial results. If transparency—labelled as *the best of disinfectants* by US Supreme Court justice Brandeis (1914)—were not a value per se (it enhances the efficiency of price formation), a “neutral”, non-ideological legislator could not state that information improves performance in an economic environment. Throughout these last years, we have seen that many episodes of “panic” have been driven by the uncontrolled spread of information, not always consistent with the underlying reality, with self-fulfilling effects. This repeatedly occurred during the sovereign debt crisis of various European countries (mainly the so-called ‘GIIPS’) between 2011 and 2012: at that time, irresponsible deficit-oriented fiscal policies scared investors much more deeply than the actual macroeconomic conditions. In fact, with the possible exception of Greece (and perhaps of Ireland, where a severe banking crisis was taking place), they showed deteriorating yet still viable fundamentals. The waterfall effects stemming from the sudden rise in the cost of sovereign bond issuances, triggered by panic sell-offs of those securities, eventually impaired those fragile economies.

Markets convey signals and transmit incentives; they do not offer universal solutions for financial problems that differ from individual to individual. Besides, financial chronicles have worried the EU legislator with the idea that HFT is intrinsically a source of systemic risk. This belief may be true, but only if we qualify such risk as a 'tail' one: that is, very unlikely to occur, but very pernicious upon its occurrence. This correctly means that, for one time in which it triggers or magnifies turbulences, there are much many others in which HFT supports market efficiency, as well as liquidity, hence turning out being extremely beneficial not only for traders which employ it, but even from a market-wide standpoint. The EU legislator has actually failed in acknowledging this; hence, such huge innovation is still seen under great suspicion.

It is unfortunately true that *regulation often comes after disasters* (Gordon 2000), and this is exactly the reason why it struggles to deliver on its purposes: rules are designed to address "pathological" conditions rather than "physiological" ones. MiFID I partially succeeded in avoiding such negative feature, as it was the response to a more limited crisis (basically, the intertwining between the short recession following 9/11 attacks and the 'dot-com bubble'). Most importantly, it came when long-term trends were undoubtedly pointing to growth and development. At that time, the GM still promised a shining future, however approaching to end.

6.2 How Investor Protection Shapes the Package

When a person not directly involved in the financial industry thinks to the MiFID universe as an investor-protection framework, this would probably happen because of the voluminous *corpus* of documents that one is required to sign when applying for the purchase of a financial product and that find their origin in the provisions of MiFID framework. One of the most remarkable papers of this kind is undoubtedly the *Key Investor Information Document* (KIID), which was actually introduced by the UCITS V Directive and is required in the case of a person purchasing units of an investment fund. In the common parlance, however, 'MiFID' is steadily associated with the requirement of large amounts of informative documents to be explicitly approved by a retail investor—with lower knowledge and expertise vis-à-vis the "insiders" of the financial industry—for the sake of its 'protection', whenever the provision of a financial service or the sale of a financial product be concerned. In this chapter, we are going to clarify the exact rules governing this matter. In fact, Directive 2004/57/EC was the first piece of legislation to explicitly address it in a way that revolutionised the pre-existing landscape of the relationship between providers and "consumers" of financial services, albeit no investor protection mechanism can neither totally erase the information asymmetries between sellers and buyers, nor prevent investors' losses. The right equilibrium between protection and a completely free market cannot be easily reached, as it not only involves technical issues but, also, raises also questions of value and rights in terms of “what comes first”. Should clients be better informed, or should financial intermediaries avoid selling too risky financial products? How might it be possible to find a fair setting of laws to grant investors’ right to purchase what they think it best suits to their financial needs (naturally taking risks), while ensuring that the products they buy be adequate to their knowledge and risk tolerance? In fact, one of the most important aims of the MiFID framework, such as investor protection, was also one of the most delicate to address. The objective was to find a mechanism that did protect investors either from products they do not need or cannot fully understand, leaving room for an active and competitive market for investments.

As we anticipated, the rationale of protecting investors is rooted in the information asymmetries that inevitably doom the abovementioned relationship, though they significantly differ across industries. In fact, while in banking and insurance the counterparty might hide relevant information either before the contract being concluded (giving rise to ‘adverse selection’ phenomena, such that less creditworthy counterparties are actually financed or more in general a bank cannot fairly price the counterpart’s creditworthiness) or even afterwards (through a behaviour labelled as ‘moral hazard’, eventually ending with the debtor’s solvency deteriorating, the borrower defaulting or the insurer being mandated to pay), in the underwriting of units of a collective investment scheme or the purchase of a security of any kind these asymmetries are much more relevant on the seller’s side, which—in the majority of cases—is an ‘institutional’ entity, i.e. a financial company with far more awareness of the risks inherent to that specific product than many of its customers. Therefore, the latter are generally deemed to be the ‘weak’ party of the transaction and, thus, to deserve a ‘protection’, this clearly not being the case of professional counterparties who are somehow “comparable” or “similar” in term of awareness and understanding of the financial needs, type of product and risk-return profile.

Nevertheless, in spite of the high “popularity” of MiFID legislation in relation to the promotion of an investor-protective set of rules, we should not forget that the concept of defending the ‘financial order’—i.e. preventing negative systemic spill-overs from arising—by reducing asymmetries was not first addressed by MiFID I, nor was first referred to dealing in financial instruments: in fact, the *Prospectus Directive* (No. 2003/71/EC), for instance, was informed by the same principles. We should probably acknowledge that such a sensibility surged at the beginning of this century, when some goals of higher priority—this being a “positive” statement, not a “normative” one—had already been successfully pursued at a European level: inter alia, the creation of a level playing field between market participants, whose necessary condition was the liberalisation of both the ownership and the operations of financial intermediaries, widely restrained in many countries (e.g., Italy).

Generally speaking, we might say that, while the last two decades of the twentieth century witnessed the “disruptive” implementation (again, only in a “positive” sense) of a liberal approach that had never been experimented before, the

GM years brought moderation even in the legislator's attitude toward regulating markets, setting the goal of fair balance between the openness and efficiency of the financial system, on the one hand, and the protection of weaker parties, on the other, for the ultimate purpose of enhancing systemic stability.

Having said this, we may immediately spot that client categorisation (or 'classification') is an essential tool for exercising supervision upon conduct-of-business issues, despite neither affecting the release of any authorisation, nor being transposed into 'operational/prudential rules' (Moloney 2014).

The major scheme envisaged in MiFID I is still in place, despite having undergone relevant amendments. First of all, clients are divided into three classes, reflective of their knowledge, skills, and experience, but substantially categorising them in accordance with subjective characteristics. If they match the criteria laid down in Annex II[D], entities are deemed to be 'professional clients'; if they do not, they are residually classified as 'retail clients'. There is actually a third category which might be thought as a "subset" of the professional clients one; nevertheless, explicitly identified types of entities, which would otherwise encompassed by the 'professional clients' category, are allowed to opt-in their classification as 'eligible counterparties' in some specific cases: i.e., in summary, if they are the recipients to which a credit institution or an investment firm provides the services of reception and transmission of orders on behalf of clients and/or execution of such orders and/ or dealing on own account.

Anyway, the structure built by MiFID I remains in place: given the fact that retail clients and eligible counterparties are the most and the least protected respectively, and that professional clients are somehow in the middle, any subject is generally allowed to file for being classified differently vis-à-vis its standard categorisation, opting-into a category which is either more or less protected (this is sometimes referred to as the 'elevator mechanism' of the MiFID universe). As one may easily suppose, it is much more likely that professional clients ask to be treated as retail ones and potentially eligible counterparties deciding to stay in the 'professional' category, than retail clients file for becoming professional ones.

Having said this, we should focus on the three main issues that the MiFID legislation has dealt with for investor-protective purposes: that is, the principles of 'suitability' and 'appropriateness' to be regarded when providing financial services and the 'best execution' of client orders. Given the "strength" of its meaning—for it requires a certain operation to be accomplished by those subjects which are 'suitable' to perform it, suitability is not exclusively related to the provision of investment services but is widely invoked in the MiFID universe. For instance, considering the United Kingdom, in order to understand how the principle de quo is rooted in national, secondary-level legislation, in the FCA *Handbook* we may read the statement that *a firm must take reasonable care to ensure the suitability of its advice and discretionary decisions for any customer who is entitled to rely upon its judgement*. Again, in the case of providing DEA to a trading venue, the competent authority must be notified of such activity being undertaken but also given an explanation of the 'suitability' of the access, because the DEA provider—as we have previously discussed—is required to have in place adequate systems and controls in order to *prevent trading that may create risks to the investment firm itself or that could create or contribute to a disorderly market* (Article 17^D, par. 5), or breach MiFIR or even the rules governing the trading venue. Therefore, along with the obligation not to exceed 'pre-set credit and trading thresholds', aimed at fulfilling these purposes, the Directive mandates 'a proper assessment and review of the suitability of clients using the service' (ibidem). Another example is provided by the situation in which the obligation to be member of a clearing house be not directly abided by the person concerned, but occurs via an intermediary bound by a specific agreement: in this case, *the service provider must carry out appropriate due diligence to assess the suitability of the client for the service provided* before the agreement be reached, in order to *reduce the risks to both the service provider and the market'.*

Suitability is the most commonly-known principle of the MiFID universe, especially when a retail person approaches an investment. In particular, the Directive—since its first version—has required that, in the case of 'personal recommendation' or portfolio management (even toward potential investors), clients disclose their 'knowledge and experience', along with their 'financial situation' and 'investment objectives', in order to assess whether the investment is 'suitable' or not. For these purposes, a questionnaire is generally filled by the recipient of the service. This occurs in a way allowing the provider to know, apart from the investor's financial expertise, which time horizon is the preferred one (in general, maturity and the holding period are two of the most relevant characteristics of any financial instrument), for the goals pursued by investing (hedging against some kind of risk, as well as provisioning for social-security or pension reasons) is radically different from the management of the monetary amount yielded by a rent or an una tantum inflow.

Instead, 'appropriateness' refers not to the general profile of the investor, but—specifically—to him/her dealing with a specific instrument. It is aimed at assessing whether or not said instrument be 'appropriate' or not to the client: in fact, investment advice and portfolio management are not subject to this principle. Therefore, experience and knowledge must be analysed in respect of that specific product or service, rather than a wide, generic array of investment alternatives. Given the distinction—introduced by MiFID I—between 'complex' and 'non-complex' products (actually, it is much more relevant for firms rather than for consumers), an 'appropriateness test' is mandated in respect of the whole of complex products and those which cannot be sold 'execution-only', as well as in those cases other than a 'direct offer' financial promotion (for this would imply an "individual" assessment of the client's knowledge and experience, something which is quite unlikely to be done). In summary, the test has to be performed when the firm clearly plays a seminal, active role in advising or supporting the client in undertaking the investment.

Finally, 'best execution' is the principle swearing that, when executing orders, a firm *must take all reasonable steps to obtain the best possible result for its clients taking into account the execution factors* (CESR 2007), these last being all the traditional characteristics of a transaction in financial instruments: price, costs, speed of execution and settlement, size, nature, etc. Similar obligations are also charged upon the firms either placing (e.g., when providing a portfolio management service) or receiving and transmitting orders. The need for 'appropriate information' as an essential requisite for 'best executing' client orders in also stressed in the MiFID legislation. When discussing the detailed rules encompassed by MiFID II, we shall also analyse another aspect of the investor-protective "big tent": the requirements 'for the management body of a market operator', as well as the treatment of 'inducements' aimed at enhancing their efficiency and fair-acting, something whose importance has clearly got a boost from the concerns raised by the GFC.

6.3 Suitability, Appropriateness, Best Execution: What MiFID II States

For our purposes, a brief overview of MiFID II *Annexes* should be given. Annex I^{D} is divided into four sections, providing a list of:

(a) investment services and activities;
(b) ancillary services;
(c) financial instruments;
(d) data reporting services.

Therefore, it is extremely important in terms of the Package's architecture. Annex II^{D} is the one which mainly shapes the investor-protective framework of the Directive. In fact, a list of categories whose members have to be classified as 'professional clients' is laid down, and—as the legislator has explicitly acknowledged—must be intended in an "extensive" way, such that an entity performing the same activities as those mentioned must be treated—by default, subject to the exercise of the 'elevator mechanism'—as a professional client. This kind of entities may be summarised with the wording used in letter *i*: that is, 'institutional investors'; hence, credit institutions, investment firms, insurance companies, pension funds, derivative dealers are some of the persons encompassed by the definition.

The other category mentioned in Annex II^{D} has been constructed by setting three requirements, of which at least two must necessarily be met. This criterion, also in relation to the financial statements items that are concerned, is widely used in the Italian commercial legislation in order to define certain kinds of entities: after two EU-wide 'Recommendations', the definition of SMEs—actually discerned between 'medium', 'small' and 'micro' entities—has been laid down in terms of employees, turnover and total assets. It is fulfilled if at least two out of the three requirements are met. The minimum thresholds are (in million euros) 20, 40 and 2 in terms of total balance sheet, net turnover and own funds respectively. Among the other players, we encounter *national and regional governments, including public bodies that manage public debt at national or regional level, central banks, international and supranational institutions* (WB, IMF, ECB and EIB are explicitly mentioned as examples) along with other *institutional investors whose main activity is to invest in financial instruments*, here encompassing the subjects involved in securitisation processes. Investment firms must inform these categories of clients that they will be treated as professional clients, unless they ask for opting-out of that scope and—by entering a written agreement—being endowed with a higher degree of protection.

The subsequent rules specify that persons outside the scope presented above may *waive some of the protections afforded by the conduct-of-business rules*. However, this occurs not so easily, because *an adequate assessment of the expertise, experience and knowledge of the client* must be undertaken in order to give *reasonable assurance, in light of the nature of the transactions or services envisaged, that the client is capable of making investment decisions and understanding the risks involved*. These 'identification criteria'—of which two must be matched, the evaluation occurring as carefully as possible—are made of the client's remarkable activity on the relevant market 'at an average frequency of 10 per quarter over the previous four quarters', a 'financial instrument portfolio' (including cash deposits) exceeding € 500,000 and a 'professional position' in the financial industry—requiring 'knowledge' of transactions and services—having been held for at least one year. Annex II underlines the importance of internal procedures to be established by investment firms in order to properly classify clients; moreover, professional ones must inform the firm of occurred changes that could affect their categorisation.

Let us now move to investor protection per se. Article 24^{D}—regarding *General principles and information to clients*—is one of the most relevant bases of current legislation. In par. 2 is stated that *investment firms which manufacture financial instruments for sale to clients* (notice that the verb used here, 'manufacture', implicitly underlines the firm's active role and, thus, its responsibility toward clients) *shall ensure that those financial instruments are designed to meet the needs of an identified target market of end clients within the relevant category of clients*, as well as that 'the strategy for distribution of the financial instruments is compatible with the identified target market; Moreover, is mandated that *the investment firm takes reasonable steps to ensure that the financial instrument is distributed to the identified target market*. Furthermore, an investment firm holds some relevant duties in relation to instruments: it must 'understand' them, 'assess the compatibility' with the needs of clients, also in light of the 'target market'; and, most importantly, any offering or recommendation must occur 'in the interest of the client'. These provisions design a comprehensive framework inspired by the principles of suitability and appropriateness.

Such legislation moves somehow in parallel with consumer protection laws, or —at least—provisions inspired by that segment of private and commercial law. This is clearly shown in Article 24^{D}, par. 3, where is highlighted that *all information ... shall be fair, clear and not misleading*, with the obligation to explicitly label any marketing communications. In par. 4, the term 'appropriateness' is referred to the set of information provided to clients (also potential ones) 'in good time', regarding not only 'the investment firm and its services' but, also, 'proposed investment strategies, execution venues and all costs and related charges'. This provision is followed by a list showing the content of such information: first of all, it must be stated whether 'the advice is provided on an independent basis' (the alternative clearly being the advice given by a 'tied agent', acting in the interest of a specific firm); then, the 'scope' of the investment must be clarified. Finally, such disclosure has to declare whether a 'periodic assessment of the suitability of the financial instruments recommended' is scheduled.

The second category of information to be necessarily released is the one dealing with 'appropriate guidance and warnings on the risks', also including the declaration on whether that specific instrument 'is intended for professional or retail clients', still in light of the principle of identifying a 'target' for a certain investment and addressing all the advice to potential clients referrable to that target. Finally, the third kind of content to be provided is that related to 'both investment and ancillary services', in relation to "direct" costs—such as that of the instrument, the amount to be paid by the client and the disbursements to be faced by third parties (if any)—and the price for 'ancillary services', such as advisory itself.

Article 24^{D}, par. 4, also encompasses one of the most important principles followed by the legislation, i.e. the clients' right to fully and effectively understand the more technical financial aspects of what is offered to them: not only in terms of return but—most importantly—in relation to 'all costs and associated charges' linked to it, without anything kept hidden: that is, the expenses or losses—or, with more neutral wording, the 'effect on cumulative return'—yielded by something other than 'the occurrence of underlying market risk' must be carefully reported to the client; in turn, this last might require a further detail by asking for an 'itemised breakdown', which cannot be denied. Moreover, such information must be provided 'on a regular basis', i.e. 'at least annually'. This is a quite standard provision; otherwise—if no periodicity were envisaged—its enforcement would become difficult. This gets strengthened by what is stated in Article 24^{D}, par. 5, whereby to Member States is de facto suggested to implement 'comprehensible form' in order to make clients 'reasonably able' to understand what they are warned of and—even more importantly—the requirement of a 'standardised format' for such information.

A more detailed explanation of the conditions to be met for an advice to be regarded as 'independent' are laid down in Article 24^{D}, par. 7: first of all, a wide and 'diverse' range of financial instruments—instead of a narrow or too little diversified one—must be presented to the client, with the prescription of not being limited to what is offered by a single investment firm or other related entities. Moreover—this is something often intended as the true, "popular" meaning of independence—the investment firm must not accept 'fees, commissions or other monetary or non-monetary benefits' from third parties, these inducements being limited to 'minor non-monetary benefits', provided that they do not bring prejudice to the investment firm acting in the client's interest but, conversely, they enhance the 'quality of the service'. The same rules are laid down in Article 24^{D}, par. 8, in relation to portfolio management. Further provisions on these minor, legitimate benefits are encompassed by par. 9, focused on disciplining what must be disclosed to clients in these cases. Investment advice being provided on an independent basis is one of the hottest issues of the whole of the Package. These rules are not criticisable per se, as they correctly circumscribe the meaning of 'independence', something that should theoretically prompt investors to better decide when advised on a given investment. However, in light of the pre-existing structure of the investment industry, they are often regarded as disproportionately burdensome. Moreover, the Directive does not waive 'tied agents' from abiding by the supreme rule of acting in the client's best interest. The outcome is a clear paradox: on the one hand, the advisor's independence is valorised by means of an express definition; on the other, it is not significantly separated from different situations, with a definite increase in the overall regulatory charge.

Other rules are inspired by the legislation preventing conflicts of interest and market abuse (often intended, especially in the antitrust legislation at a EU level, as the prevention of 'dominant positions' from being unduly exploited. Consistently with what had been previously envisaged, Article 24^{D}, par. 10, states that the staff of firms providing investment services cannot be remunerated in a manner that copes with the investor-protective goals of the legislation, whereas par. 11 addresses the case of bundled (packaged) products, whose 'cost and charges' must be thoroughly disenfranchised, along with the firm's duty to inform clients about the possibility of having each component of the service being sold separately, with a great, specific, unavoidable focus on the risks generated by such bundling practice. As far as cross-selling is concerned, a reference to the guidelines issued by ESMA —in cooperation with EBA and EIOPA—is explicitly made. Article 24^{D}, par. 13, lists the matters on which the Commission is empowered to issue delegated acts, with some indications on the content laid down in par. 14.

Article 25^{D}, rather than stating general principles, enters more decisively into regulating assessment, suitability and 'reporting to clients'. In par. 1 is immediately appealed the 'necessary competence and knowledge' to be possessed by the investment firms, which are mandated to 'ensure and demonstrate' it to Member States. In par. 2, further prescriptions are given about how checking suitability in MiFID II: not only 'knowledge and experience in the investment field' must be assessed, but also the person's 'ability to bear losses, and his investment objectives including his risk tolerance'.

In the case of bundled services being provided, suitability must be checked in respect of the whole of the "package", as well as stated for appropriateness in par. 3 (of course, the provisions inspired by this principle refer to the 'specific product' the client is advised on). However, it is extremely significant that a clear 'warning' must be issued in the case a lack of appropriateness be retrieved (par. 3). Article 25^{D}, par. 4, provides indications on the features that allow an instrument to be regarded as 'non-complex'. This stems from the explicit acknowledgement that, if investment services *only consist of execution or reception and transmission of client orders with or without ancillary services, excluding the granting of credits or loans (...) that do not comprise of existing credit limits of loans, current accounts and overdraft facilities of clients*, they can be provided 'without the need to obtain the information or make the determination provided for in par. 3' (namely, the appropriateness test).

All these conditions must be met:

(a) the instrument (to which the service is related) fulfils the criteria laid down in the table below;
(b) *the service is provided at the initiative of the client or potential client*;
(c) this last has been 'clearly informed', even by means of a warning 'provided in a standardised format', about the lacking appropriateness test;
(d) *the investment firm complies with its obligations under Article 23^D*: that is, it abides by the rules regarding conflicts of interest.

Everything submitted to clients, or agreed with them, must be carefully recorded by the investment firm and clearly contain all the relevant information (Article 25^D, par. 5–6). Distance communications 'which prevents the prior delivery of the suitability statement' are specifically addressed (par. 6), such that the abovementioned document may also be provided 'immediately after the client is bound by any agreement', subject to a couple of conditions: (a) the client's consent and (b) the firm having granted the client the option to defer the transaction 'in order to receive the statement on suitability' in advance. An updated assessment of whether the investment meets 'the client's preferences, objectives and other characteristics of the retail client' is also mandated in the case of portfolio management.

An interesting exemption from suitability and appropriateness rules is the one addressed in Article 25^D, par. 7. We are referring to the case of the extension of a mortgage on 'residential immovable property' being subjected to the prior acceptance, by the recipient of financing, of an investment service on a mortgage bond, such that the loan is somehow collateralised and, thus, may become 'payable' and be 'refinanced or redeemed'.

The short Article 26^D addresses the situation of another investment firm intermediating between the one providing the service and the client receiving it: if this is the case, *the investment firm which mediates the instructions will remain responsible for the completeness and accuracy of the information transmitted*, as well as *for concluding the service or transaction*, also relying upon *any recommendation in respect of the service or transaction that have been provided to the client by another investment firm*.

Article 27^D deals with best execution, whose main goal is the 'best possible result' in terms of the features of the trade that we have mentioned before, once accounted for every possible income and expense (including the costs associated with a specific trading venue, in the case multiple venues compete for executing the same transaction). Yet, if the client gives specific instructions regarding the execution of an order, the firm must follow them (Article 27^D, par. 1). The same provisions preventing conflicts of interest from hurting the investor are also envisaged (par. 2). A transparency provision is laid down, too, as Member States must require that each trading venue or systematic internaliser—in relation to transactions in every financial instrument—*makes available to the public, without any charges, data relating to the quality of execution of transactions on that venue at least on an annual basis* (par. 3), including the disclosure of the 'top five execution venues in terms of trading venues' based on data from the previous year and 'the quality of execution obtained' (par. 6). Since all the arrangements needed for best-execution purposes have to be put in place via a so-called 'order execution' policy (par. 4), this last must include—'in respect of each class of financial instruments'—information regarding the different venues where the order may be executed and what drives the choice between them, of course with the 'best possible result' as a major goal (par. 5).

In addition to this, 'appropriate information' must be provided to clients, 'in a sufficient detail and in a way that can be easily understood', with regard to how execution is carried out; moreover, Member States must require the clients' explicit consent to the execution policy submitted to them. In fact, certain cases cannot be left, per se, without any explicit investor's approval, such as where orders could be executed outside of a trading venue. This consent may be given either under a general agreement or in respect to each single transaction. A careful check of whether or not the 'best possible' result has actually been achieved or not—i.e. a proper monitoring of the 'effectiveness'—must be carried out 'on a regular basis', too, and in the case of 'deficiencies' being found proper changes must be brought (par. 7). The role of the Commission and the ESMA in issuing second-level regulation is also clarified (paragraphs from 8 to 10).

Article 30^{D} is devoted to 'transactions executed with eligible counterparties. First of all, many of the provisions that we have just dealt with simply do not apply, given the much lower protection entrusted to this kind of persons. Yet, investment firms are not waived from their traditional obligations: they still have to act 'honestly, fairly and professionally' and, also, 'communicate in a way which is fair, clear and not misleading' (Article 30^{D}, par. 1). As far as the identification of eligible counterparties is concerned, 'credit institutions, insurance companies, UCITS and their management companies' may file for being classified in this way, as well as other authorised financial institutions, governments and public bodies. Member States may introduce other criteria, but clearly subject to strict (mainly quantitative) requirements.

A step backwards should be taken in order to detail the treatment of 'inducements' from an investor-protective standpoint. With regard to this, requirements 'for the management body of a market operator'—which might be obvious, but certainly not less important than other provisions—are envisaged in Article 45^{D}, par. 1, where is stated that 'good repute', as well as 'sufficient knowledge, skills and experience' must be possessed. More precisely, 'members of the management body' are required to dedicate sufficient time to their task: hence, they cannot hold directorships in too many entities. However, while in general there are no specific constraints in respect of this, quantitative limits are set out for those *market operators that are significant in terms of their size, internal organisation and the nature, the scope and the complexity of their activities* (par. 2). The thresholds not to be breached by the members of the management body are identified with one executive directorship combined with two non-executive ones or, alternatively, four of the latter kind. Clearly, the compliance with these limits must be checked at a consolidated level: that is, considering the whole group to which the market operator belongs and even those entities wherein holds a significant stake.

6.4 The Weaknesses of Investor Protection in MiFID II

Before the Package, the *Prospectus Directive* had not represented any tilt towards the "modern" idea of investor protection, albeit it was centred around admission to trading and, thus, a potential harm to the overall stability in case of too weak financials underlying the exchanged stocks. In Europe, there had been many situations in which investors suffered damage from an unfaithful representation by the companies wherein they had invested. The EU legislator viewed this in the most simple and unquestionable manner: a breach of contractual bonds.

MiFID I had amended but not rejected the approach upholding classical economic rights in an undifferentiated manner, without making any discernment between financial and non-financial contracts. Starting from the abovementioned piece of EU legislation, the regulator had thought client categorisation' as the major tool to enable investor protection without directly disrupting markets. However, the effect of some CC-based rules could be particularly pervasive: in fact, the performance of certain activities, or the provision of services related to certain instruments or products, may be prohibited to certain groups of investors, with a clear limitation of their private autonomy.

As discussed in the previous paragraph, the EU legislator envisages three main categories, reflective of investors' knowledge, skills, and experience. If a subject meets the characteristics laid down in Annex II[D], it is deemed to be a 'professional client'; otherwise, it is residually a 'retail client'. The third category—actually, a subset of the former—is that of *eligible counterparties*, made of subjects which in some specific cases may ask to be classified in that way (hence, via an opt-in mechanism). This is consistent with a more general *elevator principle*—which allows a subject to be classified differently from its default categorisation—is extended to the passage between retail and professional clients: if seeking for less protection (and, thus, more investment opportunities), the former may ask to be treated like the latter, the reverse occurring if the investor desires tighter protection. This is a surprisingly liberal provision which helps mitigating the overall rationale of investor protection in MiFID II: thanks to it, a financial player is still allowed to self-assess its profile and, thus, make its own choice regarding the trade-off between opportunities and protection. A perfect allocation within the three categories would probably occur only in a perfect world, which—as we have seen—the EU legislator sometimes seems to unrealistically assume. As a matter of fact, however, the elevator works frequently downwards and rarely upwards, for in troubled times every potentially experienced investor—e.g., high-net-worth individuals—prefers adopting a more prudent approach, abiding by the regulatory constraints not to engage in certain operations. It is a curious case whereby the recipients of supervision, instead of attempting escaping it, wants the oversight to be stricter. Of course, had the elevator mechanism been in charge during GM years and not only GFC ones, we would have witnessed the reverse trend, as low (high) volatility plainly makes riskier investments relatively more (less) financially viable.

The ‘elevator mechanism’ works under strict provisions set forth by the Directive. More specifically (Annex II, section II), *in order to waive some of the protections afforded by the conduct-of-business rules*, the EU legislator requires *an adequate assessment of the expertise, experience and knowledge of the client*, for the purpose of giving *reasonable assurance, in light of the nature of the transactions or services envisaged, that the client is capable of making investment decisions and understanding the risks involved*. This prompts us taking a little step backwards to discuss the pillars on which the whole of the investor-protective architecture is based.

We can find three of these pillars (Di Noia 2017): (a) product governance; (b) product intervention; (c) rules governing the relationship between intermediaries and their clients. The difference between product ‘governance’ and ‘intervention’ appeals to the semantic difference between the two words, which in turn reflect two major approaches used by regulators throughout history: either *prudential* (nowadays the most common), based on the idea that overseers should not distort the ‘structure’ of the market by directly ruling the business, or *structural*, advocating the latter supervisory style instead.

The third pillar of the Package—namely, rules governing the interaction between intermediaries and their clients—is the one which has faced the largest overhaul during recent years, increasingly intended in a way which we could define as a ‘cradle-to-grave’ approach. As if the client were a baby, incapable of taking care of himself/herself, the Package advocates a thorough commitment, by the provider of financial services (in particular, portfolio management), toward *the best interest of the client* (Article 24^{D}, par. 8). Another surprising element is the absence of any substantial mitigation of such principle, as we are going to see. If the ‘manufacturer’ and the ‘distributor’ of a financial product do not coincide—something which is increasingly common, given the complexity of modern financial markets, the Package mandates specific attention to be paid, the rationale being that the double layer of financial intermediation represents per se a threat to clients’ interests. In fact, reality—though after the Package being approved—has rather proven the reverse. For instance, several misconduct cases have actually occurred whenever credit institutions have placed to their depositors the products they had manufactured: e.g., subordinated debt instruments whose inherent risk had not been fully understood by such retail clients.

In addition to client categorisation, the other relevant issue concerning investor protection addressed by the Package—but, still, resembling MiFID I provisions—is about the ‘suitability’ and the ‘appropriateness’ principles, along with the ‘best execution’ of client orders. First of all, we should remark that the Directive does not show the noun *suitability* or the adjective *suitable* only in the technical meaning that we are going to clarify: actually, the legislator invokes them in different context and for different purposes. For instance, competent authorities are charged with the duty of ensuring that DEA to trading venues gets provided to market participant in a ‘suitable’ manner (Article 17^{D}, par. 5), such that risks potentially contributing to a disorderly market (Article. 17^{D}, par. 5) may be prevented from arising.

Both principles are currently enforced by means of ad hoc questionnaires ('tests') aimed at assessing various clients' characteristics. 'Suitability' takes into account the investor's general features for "profiling" reasons; 'appropriateness', instead, has a more refined purpose: once detected the investor's general profile, the regulator wants to ensure that the intermediary provide a valuable service to that single, specific investor, for that specific instrument, in that specific moment in time. In the test aimed at assessing the former (imagine dealing with a retail client who is a natural person), we may find questions about the client's household's composition, monthly revenues and expenses, financial obligations toward third parties (both in terms of periodic outflows and outstanding debt), security and real-estate holdings, his/her investment profile (risk-averse vs. risk-loving attitude), along with the preferred time horizon and the reason underlying investment choices (saving for retirement, income smoothing, etc.). As regards the latter, conversely, questionnaires must necessarily investigate more personal and contingent information: they include education, job, frequency of update on financial markets, knowledge of basic economic dynamics (e.g., risk-return association, the meaning of certain types of risk, etc.), the client's financial behaviour in terms of operations recently undertaken, their monetary amount, the products invested in, etc.).

In particular, the EU legislator seems to have somehow revived its commitment toward preserving private autonomy by envisaging that the appropriateness test may be waived if all the following conditions are met (Article 25^{D}, par. 4):

(a) the instrument to which the service is related fulfils specific criteria which allow it to be considered as non-complex (see Table 6.1);
(b) *the service is provided at the initiative of the client or potential client*;
(c) this last has been *clearly informed*, even by means of a warning *provided in a standardised format*, about the lacking appropriateness test;
(d) the investment firm complies with its obligations regarding conflicts of interest, pursuant to Article 23^{D}.

As we may see, the legislator ends up devising a heavy set of conditions. In particular, we should consider that 'non-complex' is a quite narrow label; moreover, condition (b) is not as burdensome as conducting an appropriateness test, but nonetheless accrues the ponderous number of supervisory requirements charged by the Package upon intermediaries. In a world which moves at increasing speed, opportunity costs associated with compliance should not be underestimated. Furthermore, we shall see how the 'conflicts of interest' issue has been very inefficiently addressed by the EU legislator.

As of the *best interest of the client* objective, we should not think that this be pursued by means of the suitability and appropriateness tests. Instead, it is something different: in Recital 71^{D}—reprised by Article 24^{D}, par. 2—is mandated that the Member States not only ensure that investment firms act in accordance with the best interests of their clients and comply with what is provided for by the Directive but, also, that those entities *establish and review effective policies and arrangements to identify the category of clients to whom products and services are to be provided.*

Table 6.1 Necessary conditions for an instrument to be regarded as a non-complex product

Shares	if they are admitted to trading on: • a regulated market, • an equivalent third-country market, • a multilateral trading facility; • and they are shares in companies; unless they are: • shares in non-UCITS collective investment undertakings • shares that embed a derivative
Bonds or other forms of securitised debt	if they are admitted to trading on: • a regulated market, • an equivalent third-country market, • a multilateral trading facility; unless they: • embed a derivative; • incorporate a structure which makes it difficult for the client to understand the risk involved
Money-market instruments	by default, unless they: • embed a derivative or • incorporate a structure which makes it difficult for the client to understand the risk involved
Shares or units in UCITS	by default, unless they: • are in structured UCITS, i.e. those which—pursuant to Article 36, par. 1, subpar. 2 of Regulation No. 583/2010, provide investors, at certain predetermined dates, with algorithm-based payoffs that are linked to the performance, or to the realisation of price changes or other conditions, of financial assets, indices or reference portfolios or UCITS with similar features
Structured deposits	by default, unless they: • incorporate a structure which makes it difficult for the client to understand the risk of return or the cost of exiting the product before term

Source authors' elaboration on MiFID II (Article 25^{D}, par. 4)

More in detail, the reference is to both the 'manufacturers' and the 'distributors' of the products, in a way which allows to *meet the needs of an identified target market of end clients within the relevant category of clients.* This—labelled *know your merchandise rule* by the doctrine—is the most radical version of the appropriateness principle: even before administering any test to the single investor, the intermediary is required to circumscribe its counterparties and, thus, fine-tune the provision (performance) of its service (activity) to what is most financially advantageous to the group of clients identified in that way. Once that data will have become more widely available—that is, once a good number of MiFID2-compliant questionnaires, different from those based on MiFID I, will have been administered over a sufficiently large time horizon –, behavioural economists would tell us whether such treatment actually yields different choices by similar investors depending on whether they 'received the treatment' (namely, they answered the questionnaire). While waiting for such research be materially possible, we might discuss whether the method is a valuable one from an individual liberty standpoint.

Best execution encompasses provisions that are not directly referred to investor protection but nonetheless deemed to be relevant for the orderly functioning of exchanges: on the one hand, we have the requirements charged on market operators (in particular, on their management bodies); on the other, the discipline of inducements related to the provision of investment advice.

This prompts us considering, more in detail, how 'information' is dealt with by the Package. It is easily understandable that, while too few information is a problem, the same should be told in case it be overwhelming. Although with reference to the online-available knowledge, some even posit that an information overload equals the absence of it, and may eventually lead to manipulating decision-making (Persson 2018). In respect of this issue, the parallel between the Package and consumer-oriented legislation is particularly striking: in Article 24^{D}, par. 3, we may read that *all information ... shall be fair, clear and not misleading* with the obligation to explicitly label any marketing communications. In par. 4, the term 'appropriateness' is referred to the set of information provided to clients or potential ones *in good time* (that is, by allowing the recipients to carefully read and analyse them), regarding not only *the investment firm and its services* but also *proposed investment strategies, execution venues and all costs and related charges*. This provision is followed by a list showing the content of such information: first of all, it must be stated whether the advice *is provided on an independent basis* or, alternatively, is given by a 'tied agent' acting on behalf of a specific firm; then, the 'scope' of the investment must be clarified; finally, such disclosure has to declare whether a *periodic assessment of the suitability of the financial instruments recommended* is scheduled.

Moreover, the second category of information to be necessarily released is the one dealing with *appropriate guidance and warnings on the risks*, also including the declaration on whether that specific instrument *is intended for professional or retail clients*, still in light of the principle of identifying a 'target' for any product and addressing all the advice to potential clients referrable to that target. Finally, "direct" costs to be disclosed are related to *both investment and ancillary services*: hence, they encompass the amount to be paid by the client, the disbursements to be faced by third parties (if any), and the cost of advisory itself.

The wording above plainly shows that investor protection—declined in terms of suitability and appropriateness—is not intended under a "static" point of view, but rather a "dynamic" one: the outcome of those tests has to be compulsorily reviewed over time, as previous conditions might rapidly change in an evolving economic environment. In this way, the whole of the uncertainty incorporated in any financial contract turns out being significantly reduced, and the contract itself converges towards non-financial types, at the cost of a remarkable compliance burden to be borne by intermediaries. Moreover, such MiFID II provisions seem not to consider the importance of legal certainty, for the review of suitability and appropriateness may well end up terminating the contract well in advance of what could have been rationally expected. Even more harmfully, this might happen because of changes not in market conditions but in the investor's personal situation.

6.5 Implications of the New Investor Protection Framework

Investor protection is one of the pillars of the Package, and it does show the same weaknesses of said legislation as a whole. In particular, the EU legislator seems to have achieved—by means of the overlap between different rules, even of different rank—what has been defined as a "legislative flooding". The overall effect is a deplorable one: since the financial industry is "crowded out" by the frequency and the content of the multiple layers of regulation to which it is subjected, investors end up being "paralysed" in their activity and, thus, either renounce to undertake certain operations or have to recur to suboptimal choices. The equivalence between too much information and its absence is, unfortunately, a matter of fact. Since retail clients do not form a monolithic category, many of the least experienced and least informed investors tend to restrain themselves from entering any financial contracts, especially in the wake of the alleged scandals reported in the financial realm. Coupled with the intermediary's policy of recommending quite hazardous instruments—e.g., subordinated debt—to clients with a very prudent risk/return profile, this has yielded a substantive, alarming capital misallocation in the industry as a whole. It is undoubtedly too early to openly judge the financial consequences of the Package, yet one thing is clear: uncertainty—rectius, volatility—is surging. The new "moderation" of interest rates, achieved by means of the ECB's direct market intervention—which we are not going to discuss, for it would clearly deserve a separate analysis—has slightly receded starting from 2016. No one could foresee what the future will look like: we can only reasonably argue that, since the 'quantitative easing' (QE) programme was definitely terminated in December 2018, interest rates will come back to their remarkably fluctuating path. This will occur not only due to the ECB's retreat but—at least in the medium-to-long term—because of the structural change in financial markets that will likely be triggered by the evolution of investors' behaviour, in turn adjusting to the new regulatory framework.

Such perspective prompts us facing that old, unescapable question: are investors really different from the 'consumers' of goods and non-financial services? Or, conversely, consumer laws could be reasonably applied—mutatis mutandis—to the provision (performance) of investment services (activities)? Given the reasoning that we have developed, the answer should be clear. At least theoretically, there is no reason to opt for a differentiated treatment, as this is likely to have several contraindications and might eventually turn out yielding results opposite to the legislator's intent. What seems to have been forgotten in the Package is that financial contracts do involve an uncertainty which is often absent in other kinds of agreement but—in general—belongs to both parties. Which actually bears a higher share of risk is hard to determine: in fact, the difference between types of risk is much wider than the reasons why one might fail to fulfil its contractual obligations in other industries. The party holding the higher bargaining power—i.e., usually but not necessarily, the intermediary—will be able to shift most of the uncertainty onto the other. Yet, this occurs in financial markets as well as in other ones. Moreover, one of such common reasons is actually the same in the two worlds: namely, the unaffordability of some payment duty, in a way which had not been known ex ante. Therefore, a person which enters a plain-vanilla contract with a large financial conglomerate would not deserve any reinforced protection vis-à-vis that afforded to clients of a great supermarket chain: lest, the regulator would make an arbitrary value judgement. Anyway, direct regulatory intervention—inherently distortive of decision-making—is something further than public authorities exerting legitimate control upon intermediaries. Unfortunately, the Package—and, even more, secondary legislation derived from it—follows the latter approach instead of the former, and much more vigorously than MiFID I.

Therefore, this would imply rethinking how asset categorisation is applied, repealing the ideological statement—made several times throughout the Package—that intermediaries must act in the client's best interest (for instance, to step back on those burdensome rules on inducements), ensuring that product governance and intervention do not make markets shrink (in terms of thickness, width, and elasticity), as well as avoiding any counter-productive information overload spurred by the suitability and appropriateness tests, should be the moves that the EU legislator should make before good intentions end up backfiring.

References

Brandeis, L. D. (1914). *Other people's money and how the bankers use it*. New York: Frederick A. Stokes.

Committee of European Securities Regulators. (2007). *Best execution under MiFID questions and answers*. Ref. CESR/07-320.

Di Noia, C. (2017, June 15). *Hearing at the Finance Committee of the Italian House of Deputies*, Rome.

Gordon, J. S. (2000). *The great game: The emergence of wall street as a world power: 1653–2000*. New York: Scribner.

Moloney, N. (2014). *EU securities and financial markets regulation*. Oxford: Oxford University Press.

Persson, P. (2018). Attention manipulation and information overload. *Behavioural Public Policy, 2* (1), 78–106.

Taleb, N. N. (2007). *The black swan: The impact of the highly improbable* (Vol. 2). Random House, New York.

Chapter 7
Transposing the Package: A Cross-Country View

Abstract The chapter compares the implementation of MiFID II, along with the enactment of MiFIR, across the largest EU economies (Germany, Spain, France, Italy) *plus* the United Kingdom, whose exit—almost surely effective on 29 March 2019—raises several concerns over the destiny of Europe's financial hub, especially in terms of its accessibility for EU-based investment firms. Before discussing each country's attitude toward implementing the Package, we draw up a short overview of its macroeconomic and financial fundamentals. We underline the connection between the different characteristics of financial markets in a given country, along with the response to the GFC, on the one hand, and the positions held in respect of Package-related issues, on the other. In fact, EU Member States have dealt with said legislation in a variety of manners: some have pursued a copy-out approach; some have hardened the discipline of certain issues, on the edge of gold-plating; some have tried to soften it by listening to many of the industry's complaints. Although maximal harmonisation is still far away, we highlight similarities to be enhanced and differences to be possibly overcome for the purpose of levelling the playing field and bettering the Single Market for investment services.

7.1 A Missed Opportunity for the Level Playing Field?

As we have already had the opportunity to discuss, MiFID II, along with all the other EU financial regulation generated as a response to the GFC, aims at moving towards one of the fundamental principles of the Capital Markets Union (CMU), which is the creation of a level playing field. This is in order to create a competitive and truly integrated Single Market for financial services. Despite this objective being repeatedly mentioned in various legislations at both European and domestic level, some Member States are still reluctant to relinquish sovereignty over various aspects of internal financial regulation in the name of national specificities. This represents an important limit to the fully achieving the objectives of the new regulation.

M. Comana et al., *The MiFID II Framework*,
https://doi.org/10.1007/978-3-030-12504-2_7

This problem also concerns MiFID II very closely. We want to give a general picture—however limited to the major European countries—of the process of implementing the Directive, which obviously still suffers from delays in adaptation and transposition. It has to be noted that as of January 2018, 12 Member States—almost half!—were called upon to rectify the transposition of the Directive as it was considered partial, or insufficient compared to the required standards. By September 2018, Spain and Croatia had still made a partial transposition, while Slovenia had not yet proceeded to a real implementation of the Directive.

It is anticipated that the content of the national rules is also very different from one country to another. For instance, the United Kingdom, despite adopting a hard-line stance on the strictness of the rules of the Package during their discussion at the European level, and then making a copy-out of the EU rules in its internal jurisdiction, has essentially positioned itself halfway between a "tough" enforcement on the edge of gold-plating (e.g., the Italian one), and a more liberal approach, protective towards the national financial industry (e.g., the French one).

7.2 Germany

Among the leading EU economies, Germany is par excellence the symbol of sustainable growth, pursued in a low-sovereign-debt, low-unemployment, low-inflation environment, in a way which apparently defies the most rooted convictions in modern macroeconomic thinking. Not surprisingly, the German economic *consensus*—though based on the so-called 'social market economy' (*Soziale Marktwirtschaft*), theoretically descending from Ordoliberalism (Röpke 1941)—has been blamed by many Keynesian economists for allegedly shaping a 'neoliberal' EU financial architecture.

Nevertheless, the Bundesbank—endowed with supervisory powers over the banking system—has recently acknowledged that some risks might be easily underestimated and, thus, could eventually reveal themselves with surprisingly great magnitude. The accrual of such risks—argues the German authority—has been possible 'over the long period of low interest rates', as they have artificially pumped many asset valuations up, not unlikely what occurred—at least in the USA—during GM years, paving the way to the GFC. Hence, *market participants, lulled into a false sense of security, might form overly expectations* underestimating the likelihood of 'high losses'. The main threat is to debt sustainability, in light of a possible sudden rise over the deterioration of *macro-* conditions, albeit even the too long persistence of such low rates is a source of concern.

The German financial system is one of the most bank-centred among relevant world economies. Nevertheless, following a trend which is actually common to all advanced countries, banking is currently shrinking, whereas the investment industry witnesses a noteworthy expansion in accordance with the broader re-intermediation trend, following the generalised loss of confidence toward credit institutions. This is not circumscribed to 'clients', intended as depositors or the recipients of investment services: interbank markets are narrowing, as they prompt banks pursuing riskier policies in order to seize higher returns.

The German market for credit is, also, strongly concentrated around housing loans: more than half of total ones extended to domestic households and non-financial companies (NFCs) for home-purchase purposes represented more than two thirds of household debt in 2017. The Bundesbank itself acknowledged this situation to resemble the American one right before the GFC outbreak: in fact, a growing demand is pushing prices up, such that real-estate assets are reported to be increasingly overvalued. Hence, an interest rate rise would drive much underlying values down, with negative spill-overs onto the whole of the financial industry.

Thus, the German regulator appears to be overly concerned with systemic stability, far in excess of what would be allowed by the actual state of the economy. The idea that a downturn might occur soon, marking one of the very few times in the post WWII history, has prompted Berlin to adopt a very interventionist stance when transposing the Package into domestic law. As a matter of fact, the implementation of MiFID II has affected dozens of German sources, both primary and secondary. However, for brevity reasons, we are going to consider only the main law on financial activities: namely, to the Second Financial Markets Amendment Act (*Zweites Finanzmarktnovellierungsgesetz*, simply abbreviated as *FiMaNoG*), whereby the 'amendment' has been carried mainly to the Banking Act and the Securities Trading Act. Moreover, Berlin has taken a tough stance in respect of the implementation of soft-law settlements into hard law provisions: for instance, *BaFin* has noted that the risk buffer charge onto 'other systemically important institutions' (O-SIIs), which equals 2%, may be too low. As for the structure of the German financial system, the Bundesbank acknowledged that, following the GFC, several credit institutions were changing their business models by stepping back from riskier international activities, mainly because of technological progress (e.g., the spread of fintech). Of course, in the regulator's view, this widens systemic risk and requires a more interventionist approach.

Conversely, according to Deutsche Bundesbank (2017), the favourable *macro*-landscape has stirred a renewed focus on credit. In particular, consistently with the (intuitive) findings by the literature on NPLs, the very low level of interest rates—though slightly resurging since 2016—has been accompanied by a steady decline in the number of insolvencies: from more than 100,000 in 2010 to less than 80,000 in 2016. Another relevant dynamic in the German economy has been the remarkable deleveraging experienced by NFCs whose percentage of equity over total liabilities has surged from less than 20% in late-Nineties to roughly 30% in 2016. The current situation is even more promising if we look at the whole of the industry: the 'financial stress indicator', which aggregates data from different sources to yield a comprehensive figure ranging between 0 and 1, had reached its peak (about 0.8) in correspondence of the sovereign debt crisis, for many German banks held bonds issued by troubled EU countries. In mid-2017, when that source of turmoil was going to an end (the Greek bail-out programme will have been terminated one year later), it approached 0.2. The breakdown of such risks highlights even more important results: at the zenith of the "fear", sovereign credit market and contagion risks were all strongly relevant; in mid-2017, the latter had become the main driver of the index, to which it contributed negatively like all the others except for the market liquidity one, alarmingly surged between the first two quarters of 2017. This has mainly occurred because German banks, facing narrowing interest margins, have increasingly relied upon maturity transformation. Moreover, the retreat from international derivatives trading—i.e. the "physiological" countermeasure taken in the wake of the GFC—, as well as the significant tightening in EU regulation represented by EMIR, might too have played a role.

Therefore, at the time of the Package's implementation, the German economic and financial system did not show any signs of immediate concern. Yet, the structural changes that had been underway over recent years might represent a reason for investors to be cautious and have already prompted a particularly interventionist attitude by supervisors—both *Bundesbank* and *BaFin*—when addressing MiFID II implementation or MiFIR application. The influence exerted by the path of interest rates over intermediaries' operations and business models—which has become highly unpredictable—is plainly common to the whole of the EU. Yet, we deem it to be even more significant in Italy and Germany, where the financial system is centred around commercial banking. It is not a case that these two countries have witnessed a heavy regulatory intervention to exploit all the possible room for discretion and legislative fine-tuning when transposing the Package into domestic rules.

The FiMaNoG was definitely passed on 28 June 2017; yet, in order to understand the rationale behind many changes, we rather take into account the draft passed by the federal government on 23 January 2017, in its version incorporating *Bundestag*'s observations. If we just look at the table of contents, we may spot the remarkable novelty of several new provisions devoted to the issues related to information, transparency, and reporting, of which some refer to the powers of regulatory authorities to enforce communication obligations. In addition to this, the implementation of position limits—particularly on derivatives—is another novelty along with the rules disciplining transaction reporting (and DRSPs, too). Finally, the overhaul of market infrastructure is complemented by reshaping the organisation of markets, whereas investor protection provisions have not played such a notable role in the German transposition of the Package.

It can be reasonably claimed that this is reflective of a country where financial literacy is at very good levels (Batsaikhan and Demertzis 2018). Also in light of the fact that there have never been relevant misconduct cases in the industry (at least—apart from some issues regarding the fair value of assets included in the regulatory capital—not in the way occurred in countries like Italy and Spain), the urgency of protecting financial consumers has never been perceived as a priority hitherto. Consistently with the difference between MiFID I and II, the scope of application of financial rules has undergone significant changes, even involving the specification of the content of certain classes of instruments, mainly because of the novelties brought by financial engineering (e.g., structured deposits, emission allowances, and so on). Of course, Berlin has not carried salient amendments to the definition of investment services and ancillary activities, apart from specifying the content of some functions and techniques—e.g., HFT and systematic internalisation—or describing the *related services* in respect of safekeeping and custody (which are ancillary activities, pursuant to the Package).

Reading the amendments to FiMaNoG, the first striking difference is represented by scrapping the possibility, allowed to the foreign issuers of securities traded on OTC markets, to have them admitted on a domestic (i.e. German) MTF, as this opportunity is now subjected to the condition that those instruments be traded solely on German MTFs, not elsewhere (the plural wording is consistent with MiFID I's repeal of the 'concentration rule', for today a single security may be traded on multiple venues). The same rationale is applied to foreign issuers willing to offer their securities on German OTFs. Of course, similar provisions are addressed to German subjects, which, before applying for the admission of their securities to a domestic market, had them traded on different EEA countries (but not outside of the Area). This is nothing particularly surprising, as it defines MTF/OTF issuers in a way which is compliant with the fundamental freedoms (to provide services, make capital circulate, and so on) enshrined in the Treaties. Yet, scrapping OTC platforms marks a relevant change, signalling the legislator's intent of moving onto trading venues as much of the "external" transactions as possible.

Consistently with the rationale of MiFIR, the provisions on the federal financial supervisory authority (Sect. 2) have been completely rewritten. Inter alia, in addition to reinforcing the provisions allowing for the trading in a certain instrument being suspended or prohibited by NCAs—under the product intervention framework—, the German law envisages a detailed list of information that supervisors may request from the entities under their oversight: changes in the portfolio of financial holdings, exposures to the corporate sector, positions in commodity derivatives (and data about the underlying assets). The new kind of 'informational supervision' is now exerted in respect of AT, on which—pursuant to MiFID II—the FiMaNoG requires market participants to disclose as widely and truthfully and possible.

In particular, BaFin is endowed with the possibility to conduct very severe inspections, envisaging the seizure of any object which might have some probative value. This is not a provision directly stemming from the Package, yet it was already encompassed by the German law. In fact, the subject has inherently to be disciplined at a national level, for supervisory styles have historically differed across countries. This extremely tough approach by Berlin is shown, also, by the provisions which mandate the maximum transparency in disclosing the identity of the suspects of any wrongdoing, or even makes somehow an attempt to allow whistleblowing without explicitly disciplining it. We shall see how this practice, whose idea should be found in the Sarbanes-Oxley Act (2002)—enacted in the USA in the wake of the Enron scandal—, has been addressed by the Italian legislator, which has transposed the Package by inserting explicit whistleblowing provisions.

Still, the FiMaNoG has encompassed all the EU novelties regarding position limits, which were not considered by the pre-existing German law. They are designed in a way which theoretically prevents 'market abuse' pursuant to the MAR definition, benefits the 'orderly pricing' as well as the establishment of fair and efficient 'settlement conditions'. The aim is to stir convergence between prices of derivatives and those of spot markets for underlying commodities. 'Open contract' items have to be carefully monitored, with relevant duties charged upon national authorities (pursuant to MiFIR): these requirements are those of informational kind, i.e. those to set up a framework where relevant transactions cannot be missing.

Reinforced obligations regarding the communication of positions is set forth with respect to derivatives traded throughout Europe, whereby multiple competent authorities are involved. Of course, BaFin can impose position limits only if it is the competent authority. Relationships between it and other NCAs are specifically addressed, for the sake of information circulating broadly and efficiently, in abidance of the Package's esprit of strengthened collaboration between national supervisors. Waivers to the application of position limits are envisaged—again, in a copy-out approach to EU legislation—for those non-financial entities which enter derivative contracts for hedging purposes. Conversely, reporting positions is strictly required from the operators of trading venues, which clearly have direct knowledge of the contracts concluded therein, especially for those categories subject to heavier regulatory scrutiny (commodity derivatives, emission allowances, or derivatives thereof), also discerning based on the type of position-holders: namely, investment service providers and credit institutions, investment funds, or other enterprises (both in the financial industry and outside). The standard time for disclosure may be fastened in its frequency under deteriorating market conditions, and the content of the information required may be widened.

Also, FiMaNoG sets forth DRSPs' obligations, still in a copy-out approach to implementation. The informational obligations charged upon them have been rewritten vis-à-vis the pre-existing legislation, but they directly stem from the Package and—above all—detail the requirement that every player act in the clients' best interest, which should be allowed to make 'an informed decision' regarding investment services or ancillary ones. Yet, the provisions against the (mis)use of inducements are laid down in a way which significantly impairs the possibility to have a 'management by objectives' in the financial industry, as its discipline—mirroring MiFID II—extends to each intermediary-client relationship. Other relevant bounds created by the Package have been copied out, too; hence, we are not going to reiterate them. We can just note that in a healthy macroeconomic environment, in a country which is the main financial hub of continental Europe, and with an appreciable degree of financial literacy, EU rules have been transposed by adopting a (partially) surprising hard-line approach.

German-specific rules are set forth in respect of pension plans, mainly in terms of information being provided upon request, as if it were an investment service like others. In such realm, additional obligations may be imposed by the federal Ministry of Finance, in agreement with that of Justice. As for the provision of investment services, rules envisaging the intermediary's duties, along with the features of 'independent advice', have remained unchanged vis-à-vis the Package.

With respect to this, the former Ministry is entitled to issue secondary provisions which do not require *Bundestag*'s approval but rather take the form of 'ordinances'. In accordance with what is allowed in the Package, the latter Ministry is entitled to detail how information has to be disclosed to clients when providing investment advice. Berlin has, also, introduced specific provisions aimed at preventing excesses in both concentration and exposure in a client's investments: in particular, one cannot hold assets from the same issuer for an amount larger than € 10,000, provided that his/her overall holdings (to be precise, 'free assets in the form of bank deposits and financial instruments'), are worth at least € 100,000, or twice his/her monthly net income. A little spark of the old liberal view may still be retrieved: in fact, if the client has provided the abovementioned information by him/herself, the intermediary is not responsible for the incorrectness or incompleteness (which must otherwise be ensured).

The role of 'third parties' in investment advice is, also, widely disciplined by the FiMaNoG, especially as far as grants are concerned (which must thoroughly be disclosed to clients, even on a continuous basis if the intermediary receives benefits more times in a year). Hence, particularly salient is the provision designed to implement the requirements laid down in the Commission's Delegated Directive No. 2017/593 of 7 April 2016, as long as it mandates the separation between fees charged to cover research costs, on the one hand, and investment services stricto sensu, on the other, 'in a recognisable manner'. Also in this field, the federal Ministry of Finance is allowed to issue ordinances even without parliamentary consent.

As for trading venues and market infrastructure (e.g., central clearing), Berlin has copied-out the provisions entailed by the Package, with no significant shifts from it. Of course, the Ministry of Finance claims all the powers attributed to it by the EU legislator to national authorities, though keeping the door open to transferring them onto *BaFin*. As regards the prevention of conflicts of interest, the issue of tied agents—whom have to be pushed to act in the client's interest—and the use of AT for market-making purposes, as well as the need to identify a target market of end clients to which financial instruments be offered, the German legislator mainly follows the Package, though transposing it into particularly severe provisions. This is especially true as regards secondary provisions mandating a regular review of such "pre-emptive" evaluation of suitability in relation to groups of clients, which is probably the pillar of the whole investor-protective framework. Like in the Package, these rules are complemented by provisions requiring investment firms to check the ability of their staff (in terms of skills, knowledge, and experience), along with charging the management with direct supervisory tasks over the processes and policies undertaken by these firms.

As for the provision of investment services per se—that is, how the intermediary-client relationships actually occur: e.g., with respect to contracts concluded by distance, like those by means of telephone conversations—, Berlin's approach is again an almost-exact transposition of the Package. Instead, what is really salient—and, also, meaningful of the German regulatory approach—is the attention devoted to auditing, whose legal basis must be found in the Banking Act.

In particular, the novelty consists in envisaging a form that auditing cooperatives, or the auditors of savings banks or giro associations (another kind of mutualistic credit institutions) have to submit to Bundesbank and BaFin, which summarise the results. The form is envisaged regardless of whether proper auditing report is requested or not. As for the authorisations to which third-country investment firms are subjected, Berlin has plainly transposed MiFIR provisions with an inevitable copy-out approach. The FiMaNoG also encompasses some of the MAR provisions: regarding the dissemination of untrue or inaccurate insider information, the general principle is that, if it negatively affects a third party, this latter must be compensated.

A peculiar feature of the German law is the severity of criminal sanctions for violating rules about the auctioning of greenhouse gas emission allowances: not only they may entail detention up to five years but, also, given the large category of negative effects considered as evidence of wrongdoing, they apply to a very wide range of subjects and cases of misconduct. As a result, almost the whole of the industry is covered, and rules are enforced in a very strict way. This is probably a reflection of the special sensibility not only to environmental issues, as the German legislation has always represented the European avant-garde in the field, but in relation to the social despicability of market players being deceptive as far as pollution is concerned, which is a plain consequence of the Volkswagen's Dieselgate scandal.

As for the sanctions related to the infringement of various transparency provisions, the FiMaNoG makes reference to different EU pieces of legislation: Regulation No. 2365/2015 *on the transparency of security financing operations and re-use*, which amended EMIR, and Regulation No. 1011/2016 *on indices applicable to financial instruments and financial contracts*, which amended Directives No. 2008/48/EC and 2014/17/EU, as well as Regulation No. 596/2014. The cases of misconduct envisaged by the FiMaNoG are mainly referred to subjects which either show negligence (e.g., with respect to conflicts of interest, internal control, and so on), or acts in contravention to the abovementioned pieces of legislation (e.g., without honesty or the required independence), or—again—exhibit some flaws in abiding by their informational duties, or simply get involved in mala gestio cases (e.g., fail to hire independent auditors, outsource tasks which they should directly deal with, and so on). The impressively wide array of possible infringements is, again, a clear evidence of the legislator's intent not to allow any case of misconduct to escape sanctions. In addition to board members, people sitting in the supervisory board are charged with criminal offences, too, if they fail to exert adequate control, do not ensure any integer and reliable CG (and, thus, implementation of strategies), as well as they do not guarantee that the firm complies with communication requirements. It even entails sanctions for issuers—whose securities have been admitted to trading—which are not compliant with the *Prospectus* discipline. Subjects involved in the execution of orders, as well as in clearing transactions—i.e. market operators, investment firms which may have also established OTC platforms, CCPs, etc., also in abidance by rules stemming from different pieces of legislation: inter alia, Regulations No. 1033/2016 and 236/2012—, are not waived from this discipline, but even subjected to similar rules.

Fines and other administrative sanctions are also envisaged, making the German enforcement of the wide transparency framework one of the most effective ones all over the EU. Discussing all these cases in detail would clearly be outside the scope of our work; yet, we would like to underline the strengthening of intervention powers which *BaFin* has been endowed with pursuant to MiFIR, its derived secondary legislation, and FiMaNoG itself (with some exemptions: in particular, for 'decisions imposing investigative measures' and decisions whose publication is supervisors is charged to supervisors of stock exchanges). Yet, some caution is exerted in the case of likely systemic drawbacks from the disclosure of such decisions: if a threat is deemed to exist, disclosure may be delayed until risk has been annihilated, or the communication to the public may occur in an automated way, as well as concealing those details useful to identify the recipient. If these countermeasures turn out being insufficient, given the prevalence of systemic stability over any others, the sanction may be either diminished in its strength or even avoided at all. Close cooperation with ESMA and thorough data protection rules are also laid down.

An additional discipline is set forth with the holding of stocks admitted to trading, in a manner which allows the owner—also, by means of different securities, which nonetheless incorporate, or might potentially incorporate, claims on the company's capital—to exceed certain thresholds (5, 10%, etc.). This is something which does not directly relate to the Package and would also require a deeper analysis of German laws on the property of firms, in a juridical environment traditionally shaped by 'institutionalist' views.

7.3 Spain

Like Germany, Spain could count on good economic fundamentals and a positive attitude upon the Package's implementation. As commonly known, however, the situation had not been so favourable over the last years: in fact, it had suffered turbulences on its sovereign debt during the 2011–2012 crisis, after which it embarked on a path leading to financial soundness and sustainability. Despite some remarkable cases of mala gestio in the banking system—mainly related to the wrong design of compensation policies for managers in small cooperative institutions: namely, the so-called *cajas* (Martín-Oliver et al. 2017)—, the country has started been perceived as a reliable place for investing, as it represents a noteworthy "success story" on how to escape trouble and regain viability.

Nevertheless, if read alone, some figures might still be alarming. For instance, according to Banco de España (2018), credit to resident private sector fell by almost 2% between 2016 and 2017, though consumer credit continued growing and a decreasing trend in NPLs—contained in absolute terms, yet significant given the industry's structure and recent history—was also observed. In particular, looking at resident private sector only, NPLs peaked at more than € 180 bn in 2013, accounting for more than 13% of total loans, having steadily grown from an almost-null level in 2007; afterwards, they have started plummeting to eventually reach a level slightly higher than € 100 bn in 2017, with a ratio hovering around 8%. The comprehensive figure of the NPL ratio—accounting for the whole of the banking activity—has always been at lower levels: 4.7% in 2017 (down from 5.6% in 2016), slightly above the EU Figure (4.4%). If we look at assets in general, the ratio of impaired over total ones has significantly reduced between 2016 (4.1%) and 2017 (3.3%). In short, the reprise of lending—including the mortgage segment—has not occurred detrimentally to the soundness of credit: as additional evidence of this, the overall coverage ratio has steadily hovered around 40%, which is remarkably good, from 2014 onwards.

Banks' capital requirements remained in their positive trend, at a time in which EU-derived resolution procedures started being applied for the first time (e.g., to the Banco Popular Español in early-2017). Of course, the intrinsic fragility of that economy has not been completely overcome yet. In fact, private consumption has never managed to recover from the GFC-related fall (ECB *Economic Bulletin*, No. 5/2018), whereas two major threats for the financial industry are still in place:

- a downward pressure on banks' profitability, especially in their domestic business, due not only to low interest rates but, also, to some *hysteresis* of the GFC effects, given by the heinous conjunction between credit crunch and declining asset quality;
- a potential "crowding out" of asset prices because of growing uncertainty and, thus, the real possibility that monetary policy shifts come as largely unexpected, along with a surge in volatility associated with soaring international turbulences.

In fact, the increase in consumer credit may be explained as the possible consequence of Spanish banks seeking investments with a more aggressive risk/return profile. This raises some concern over the possibility to continue reducing NPLs over time, as they are more likely recorded in the consumer segment. Housing prices in the Spanish economy followed a path which is extremely similar to the American one: steadily growing during GM years, they peaked between 2007 and 2008; then, upon the GFC outbreak, they severely shrank; finally, they showed a slow but convincing reprise between 2014 and 2015 which is set to continue in the next future. The path of household wealth—driven by real-estate holdings—is strikingly similar. Except for housing prices, the major indicators of credit and financial indebtedness in the Spanish economy have come back to the 2005–2006 levels. This "born-again soundness" has a clear counterpart in the strong improvement in government deficit and both the capital and the trade balances, which testify the regained trust and sustainability of the Spanish financial industry as a whole. In 2017, this trend has been accompanied by shrinking balance sheets (−1.7% vis-à-vis 2016), though with a small increase in assets held abroad.

As for systemic risk, the new "moderation" started approximately in 2013 is clearly reflected. After two peaks between late-2007 and the entire 2009 (namely, the GFC outbreak) and between mid-2011 and mid-2012 (when Draghi's *Whatever*

It Takes provided troubled countries, including Spain, with a reliable backstop), and notwithstanding a small reprise in the first half of 2016—mainly attributable to Spanish idiosyncratic political uncertainty—, the comprehensive level of systemic risk has stayed very low without showing any hardening signs. Upon the Package's implementation, it hovered around 0.1. Looking at the breakdown of such figure, a negative contribution—yet, shrinking in magnitude over time—comes from the correlation between the various segments of the financial industry, whereas the first source of risk—though narrow in absolute terms—is represented by bank funding, which suffers from the narrowness of its traded volumes due to the excess liquidity stirred by loose monetary policy. Moreover, by looking at the CoVar indicator—which measures the contribution of a single country to the Euro Area overall systemic risk—, we may spot how the safety of the Spanish economy has slightly decreased in absolute terms, yet it has improved in relative ones (that is, compared to its EU peers).

As for investment funds, their assets have experienced an upward trend started in 2012 and continuing still in 2017, with a surprising hike between late-2017 and early-2018. Like in many other advanced economies, the Spanish shadow banking system is expanding: in 2017, it accounted for 6% of financial institutions' total assets. If we look at these ones' return, we may spot growing trends in terms of both net interest income (given the low-rate environment, both revenues and costs decreased, the latter ones with larger magnitude) and net commissions. Relative to average total assets, gains on financial assets/liabilities and operating expenses decreased, though very slightly (3 bps); however, a much more relevant signal is undoubtedly given by asset quality, which mirrored the positive trend in banking. These good figures, however, are greatly contributed by the growing profitability of foreign stability, which actually offset quite a stagnation in domestic business. Spanish banks are—perhaps surprisingly—able to rely on better-quality capital, on average, vis-à-vis many of their European peers: as of 2017, 82% of Total Capital was represented by CET1, 14% by AT1, and only 4% by Tier 2. Regarding liquidity, Spanish banks' LCR has been at very good levels over recent years: in 2018, it hovered around the EU average (151% vs. 148%), well above the requirement (100%). Signalling more prudent credit policies, the loan-to-deposit ratio has slightly decreased from the 2006–2007 peak, when it had reached 100%, up to barely exceeding 50% in 2017. This has been possible, inter alia, thanks to the fact that Spanish banks' funding relies upon equity and deposits more heavily than their EU peers, which have extensively used different types of liabilities, including those related to derivatives.

Drawing a comprehensive picture, we may see that Spanish credit indicators historically showed some early warnings at end-2006, when the GM was coming to an end: yet, they were the first ones to come back to normalcy (between 2015 and 2016), whereas macroeconomic imbalances—which, also, started being detected at that time, and had already receded at end-2012, once the sovereign debt crisis was substantially over—actually did not manage to become irrelevant until end-2017. Banco de España (2018) acknowledged that the expectations were of this situation to continue over next quarters, 'reflecting stability as regards the absence of warning signs or cyclical vulnerabilities', with no need to activate any macroprudential policy tools. In fact, the countercyclical capital buffer (CCyB) has been steadily set by the central bank at 0% since 2016, considering that no credit overflow has been detected: the credit-to-GDP gap—namely, the surplus credit, in terms of output, relative to its long-term trend—was negative (−50.3 bps) in September 2017. However, this is due not only to output growth but, also, to a decline in credit to households and NPLs.

In other terms, after a severe crisis yielded by multiple cases of mala gestio in the financial industry, Spain is coming to a new internal moderation which is posed to counteract the external sources of potential instability. Consistently with this, Madrid has opted for a very soft stance to implementing the Package, aimed at avoiding any disruptive regulatory tightening vis-à-vis the previous, light approach. In fact, this last can hardly be blamed for past turbulence, given the structural deficiencies which that economy has always suffered from. As we are going to see, the Spanish legislator has wisely acknowledged that a rigorous but unobtrusive approach to financial regulation is best ally in ensuring growth in the post GFC environment.

As we have already underlined, Madrid's approach to transposing the Package into Spanish legislation has been a very soft one. Softness is so pronounced that, on 25 January 2018, the EU Commission even issued a statement declaring that some Member States, including Spain, had not fully implemented MiFID II yet. In fact, Madrid had arranged a significant squeeze of the provisions to be 'implemented' (that is, interpreted within the passage from EU to domestic), an extensive reference to directly applicable rules, and a decisive tilt towards secondary legislation rather than primary one. Such configuration carries more flexibility in enforcing the new provisions, denoting a regulation more well-disposed to the industry's concerns. In a *Statement on the Implementation of MiFID II* released on 2 January 2018—i.e. the day before the Directive came into force—, the *Comisión Nacional del Mercado de Valores* (CNMV), which is the Spanish NCA competent for stock exchanges and investment services in general, claimed that it would have interpreted 'the current national regulations in a manner consistent with the Directive'. It is a clear statement of a 'copy-out' approach without any pretences of charging an additional burden onto supervised entities.

Nevertheless, there are certain areas whereby the Spanish regulator shows no less devotion than its European peers: we mainly refer to transaction reporting and —more in general—transparency requirements designed to strengthen market infrastructure. In August 2017, CNMV published an *Operational Guide* based on Article 26^R and compliant to ESMA guidelines on some technical details (e.g., the format in which the transmission should occur). Previously, the authority de quo had envisaged a platform named *System for Collecting Operations Reported from Entities* (SCORE), aimed at ensuring the timeliness and efficiency of transaction reporting, as well as its own encryption system (CIFRADOC). While some of its peers are still yet to arrange specific systems—exclusively dedicated to that purpose —like SCORE, the Spanish regulator seems to have shifted its resources from direct regulatory actions to a remarkable technological effort, pursued within the framework designed at a EU level, in a way which does not end up aggravating firms' compliance costs, but rather attempts to ease them.

In particular, Spanish recipients of MiFID2-compliant transparency requirements have been involved in the drafting of a *Test Plan*—parallelly to a similar one conducted by ESMA—aimed at assessing the functioning of SCORE. Such programme—which, of course, worked as a training to the new system, in advance of its official implementation—was addressed to *entities reporting through their own means* as well as those operating a trading venue and ARMs, albeit they were not forced to carry out the test.

In other fields, Madrid even forced the copy-out approach by rejecting some amendments proposed by the industry. For instance, as regards the vexata quaestio of inducements, on the table was the possibility to allow them in a scenario described as 'advised selling', consisting not just in advice being provided to clients but encompassing the sale of investment products (mainly funds), the investment firm also providing some guidance on it. Including such scenario would have preserved the practice of receiving rebates as compensation for distributing funds, which in the Spanish financial environment are much more common vis-à-vis more complex products. Given its factual salience, such potential amendment to the Package's original content might have represented an undue departure from the EU law. Hence, though generally concerned of avoiding disruptive novelties, the prudent Spanish legislator decided not to proceed with it.

Conversely, Madrid has welcomed the industry's concerns in respect of the unbundling of research from investment services/activities stricto sensu, which is often regarded as the most controversial and impacting provision entailed by the Package (*rectius*, by its EU-level secondary legislation, though research is considered as an ancillary service within MiFID II). In fact, this point is the one which triggered the abovementioned EU Commission's warning, as long as Madrid—along with 11 other countries—had hitherto been very reluctant to properly implement Delegated Directive 7 April 2017, No. 2017/593. Instead of keeping the universal, tout court applicability envisaged by the EU legislation, Spain has decided to waive fund management, for its pre-existing domestic rules did not mandate any separation of research costs from execution ones, provided that (inter alia) the prospectus warned on the possible bundling, research was 'original'—that is, not based on public-domain material—and, most importantly, the client's investment decision benefitted from bundling. Pursuant to this principle—that is, not considering research as a different service unless there is some good reason, for clients' sake, to do so—, the Spanish law prohibits research costs being directly linked to the volume of transactions executed.

As for investor protection, the multiple cases of misconduct occurred in recent times have given rise to a very strict Spanish domestic regulation (the same can be said of Italy, as we shall see), much in advance of the tightening occurred at EU level by means of the Package. Moreover, jurisprudence has widely followed a pro-consumer stance over recent years. For instance, Spain had charged intermediaries with the obligation to provide clients with detailed information assessing the suitability of recommended investment products (CNMV Circular No. 3/2013).

Nevertheless, some new obligations have still being set forth: inter alia, a cost/benefit analysis must be performed as of the provision of investment advice or portfolio management, the latter in case of switching investments being allowed. Yet, the Spanish regulator had already intervened to contrast the 'malpractice' of selling complex products to investors that were not able to fully understand the real implications of their decisions: in particular, as regards fund units, the CNMV's mandate to distributors was, first, to check the 'accessibility' to the 'relevant client'; then, to offer only the most beneficial to clients 'from an economic standpoint' (that is, either the cheapest or the simplest classes), the same principles applying to discretionary portfolio management and investment advice. Hence, the Package's implementation has probably sharpened pre-existing provisions; however, thanks to the regulator's soft-handed but effective commitment, they have not come in a disruptive manner as far as the business of investment funds is concerned.

Notwithstanding the light approach followed in Madrid, the implementation of the Package's transparency framework has raised some concerns in the Spanish industry, too. For instance, a salient technical novelty is the Financial Industry Reference Data System (FIRDS), which has been blamed for charging certain subjects—first of all, APAs—with burdensome additional obligations, something which *does not contribute to legal certainty*. The CNMV remarked that such source of information could have not been considered as "full" and, thus, even in case it did not encompass any information on certain types of instruments, this would not have exempted firms from complying with the transparency obligations entailed by the Package, in a renewed statement of the primacy of EU law, which some other jurisdictions still fail to acknowledge. The delay in setting forth how to calculate the 'double volume caps', divergences between the interpretative criteria adopted across different jurisdictions, and the complexity of the reports on the quality of execution envisaged by some secondary EU legislation (Commission's Delegated Regulations No. 575/2017 and 576/2017, adopting RTS 27 and 28 respectively) contributes to uncertainty. Besides, the CNMV "confirmed" the openness shown by the EU legislator in dealing with third-country entities, with particular reference to tick sizes. In general, the Spanish regulator widely submitted to ESMA decisions: inter alia, it renounced to set some domestic thresholds—in respect of different classes of financial instruments—for the purpose of assessing whether a firm 'systematically' internalises trades.

We stop here, as the Spanish law does not bring other substantive innovations. The Royal Decree-Law No. 21 of 29 December 2017, which amended the *Stock Market and Financial Instruments Act* (originally enacted in 1988), contains almost exclusively provisions with an explicit reference to the Package. As far as the provision (performance) of investment services (activities) is concerned, Spain has shown to be one of the most faithfully "pro-European" jurisdictions.

7.4 France

France has a complex history as far as the development and regulation of financial industry is concerned. The mixture between political liberalism stemmed from the Revolution and enshrined in the Napoleonic Era legislation, on the one hand, and a fundamentally rural economy with a solid commercial tradition—which early embraced the Industrial Revolution, too—, on the other, had created a relatively early concern for financial regulation (whose main object were, of course, commodity derivatives).

During the twentieth century, instead, a decisive tilt toward State interventionism occurred in the whole of the French economy, and finance was not spared at all. From the recession of the Thirties to late Seventies, despite a noteworthy spread of financial services among retail investors during the Fifties (like other European countries experiencing a post-war recovery boom), the Paris stock exchange did not manage to become the international hub for which it had undeniable potential. The liberalising wave of the Eighties tried to reverse the situation, relying upon the worldwide trends of State-owned enterprises getting privatised and large companies expanding themselves at an international level. The 2003 merger between pre-existing regulators to form the *Autorité des Marchés Financiers* (AMF), which is competent for the conduct of business, helped making the supervisory architecture simpler and more effective. Yet, the delay accumulated by France over the critical years for the development of European financial markets prevented Paris from becoming the standard-setter in the regulatory field, this role being taken by the United Kingdom. We shall discuss the very legitimate *what comes next?* question when addressing post Brexit scenarios.

At the time of implementing the Package, the AMF was particularly concerned with the extent of shadow banking. In fact, alternative credit markets represented a share sizeably larger than other leading economies in the EU (9.3%). In terms of total assets, roughly two-thirds of this universe was represented by investment funds, which participate to both maturity transformation and liquidity creation by purchasing debt securities or acquiring capital interests. More in general, the state of the French economy and financial markets was not much different from the kind of situation that we have discussed with respect to Germany, albeit it was comprehensively was growing at a slower pace, and, symmetrically, faced less market risk. The Banque de France (2018a) acknowledged that, as of 2017, *the French economy appear[ed] on the whole able to withstand future macro-financial shock*; yet, there were *concerns about levels of non-financial sector debt* because of its relatively fast rise, compared to the Euro Area average. As a percentage of GDP, NFCs' indebtedness—steadily higher than those of households, with the gap narrowing only in GFC years—rose from less than 50% in 1996 to more than 70% in 2016 (beginning-of-the-year data). Overall, private debt is significantly higher than sovereign one, as it accounted for nearly 130% of GDP in mid-2017.

As a reflection of improving economic fundamentals, credit is starting to rise again in France. At the end of 2017 (Banque de France 2018b), credit to households had increased by 5.2% vis-à-vis the previous year (+5.3% in terms of outstanding loans, with a 5.6% peak in the household segment and a 6% rise as of short-term ones). Given the French economic outlook, such trend is set to continue. This is driven by the expansion of domestic demand, which over recent years—unlike Spain—has contributed to growth more significantly vis-à-vis the foreign sector, as private investments are showing a remarkable reprise, driven by low interest rates and expanding credit supply. Some encouraging signs can be detected in exports, too. Nevertheless, the federation of French credit institutions (FBF) lamented that some structural flaws were still in place as of 2017: inter alia, a clear lack of competition. In banking, concentration is strikingly high, as in 2017 there were only 364 entities in the sector. This is sensibly less than in similar EU countries, even with less bank-centred financial sectors (e.g., the United Kingdom): not only as a result of the tendency of French banks to aggregate into larger conglomerates but, also, because of larger entry barriers vis-à-vis other leading EU economies. The French financial industry represents 4.5% of total value added, 60% of which comes from banking.

However, the very "protectionist" stance shown by France with respect to banking seems to have created a very healthy environment in terms of capital requirements. The ECB-EBA stress testing and asset quality review have recently shown an average CET1 ratio exceeding 13%, far above the minimum and close to the top of EU Member States. As for the recipients of bank financing, the French environment is very close to the one which characterises Mediterranean Europe, as opposed to continental one: that is, with a noteworthy prevalence of SMEs. In March 2017, 42% of total loans from French credit institutions were extended to them, with short-term loan applications being accepted around 90% of times in the first quarter of that year. In part, this is contrasted by firms' financing decisions, which are not as bank-oriented as we could imagine (the unusually high figure of 'shadow' markets for credit is reflective of this), as *only 24% of SMEs sought an investment loan and 6% requested short-term loans at the beginning of 2017*, the FBF reported. In fact, the fundamental structure of the French financial industry is less bank-centric than in other leading EU economies: basically, the proportion between banks and other intermediaries is currently close to a 60–40 one, whereas in 2009 (end-of-year) it was something like 70–30.

In light of this, the approach followed by Paris in implementing MiFID II and MiFIR shows elements from the strategies pursued by both countries where financial markets are significantly wide, such as the United Kingdom and Germany, and the others where traditional banking is still highly predominant, such as Spain. In fact, while the former ones have chosen a very investor-protective stance, for they are much more concerned with a generalised loss of confidence toward markets, yielding heinous systemic consequences, the latter ones—with the salient exception of Italy—have exhibited a more "conservative" approach, rightly seeing their financial industry as still "nascent", in a sense, thus needing the preservation of existing rules instead of a disruptive paradigm change.

Another way to see this "double-sided" feature of the French financial industry is by noting that the 'universal bank' model is particularly developed, as even relatively small credit institutions take a significant portion of their profits from the provision (performance) of investment services (activities) to a various array of clients, from large corporations to SMEs. Extant studies acknowledge the French as one of the most financially literate people in the EU (OECD 2016). In fact, they are not used to see banks merely as extenders of credit, but rather as counterparties for the satisfaction of various and more complex financial needs. Such intrinsic consistency between clients' behaviours, the industry's structure, and the regulator's stance, is probably an unicum among leading EU economies but, also, can hardly find comparisons worldwide.

Perhaps surprisingly for the motherland of civil law, much of the French implementation of the Package deals with secondary legislation: in particular, with the General Regulation (GR) issued by the AMF, which is competent for the oversight of security exchanges. The latter engaged in a thorough process of consultation, which was generally welcomed by the industry and brought substantive novelties to Books III and V of the GR. In fact, the French legislator took upon the occasion for implementing UCITS V, too: for this purpose, it separated 'investment firms' (IFs) from 'asset management companies' (AMCs).

Moreover, Book VII was removed, as it dealt with regulated markets admitting greenhouse emission allowances to trading and was recast into GR's different sections. In particular, Book III underwent a significant overhaul, as many of its provisions were surpassed by directly-applicable EU rules, such as Commission's Delegated Regulation No. 2017/565 of 25 April 2016, or reflected MiFID1-compliant provisions which had to be replaced with new ones. Book III has experienced an update as far as the definition of 'sellers' is concerned, as the latter ones now have to comply with MiFID II's rules mandating an assessment of their knowledge and competence; furthermore, the Package's wide and detailed transparency framework has played a big role in the French implementation (in particular, with regard to post-trade requirements). This is actually common to many domestic legislations, as MiFIR endows Member States with the faculty to set forth their own waivers and deferrals in respect of that issue.

As for Book V, some novelties about transparency waivers are referred to OTC transactions entered into by SIs. Moreover, Book V encompasses all the salient innovations brought by the Package in respect of financial legislations, covering issues that MiFID I had not addressed. New rules are laid down in respect of DRSPs (in particular, regarding the authorisation process to which they are subjected), as well as the whole of the transparency framework (*pre-* and post-trade). Clearly, the envisagement of OTFs is one of the most relevant novelties in Book V; yet, the provisions regarding RMs and MTFs have undergone some noteworthy changes, too. Finally, significant amendments have been carried to Title VIII, which previously dealt with agricultural commodity derivatives: the new provisions transposed the Package's discipline regarding position limits on commodity derivatives.

After the end of the implementation process, the AMF committed itself to finding some loopholes in the EU legislation which allowed to prevent a disruption of the established practices in the industry. For instance, as regards inducements, the French regulator clarified that research produced in the context of a primary issuance can be considered as a *minor non-monetary benefit*; hence, pursuant to MiFID II—and in accordance with ESMA's (2017) Q&As on the Package—there is no problem in preserving them, along with the fact that the research provider is not subject to MiFID II. Actually, if we look at the meetings arranged between EU regulators during the drafting of the Package, we may actually have a clue on the AMF's substantial aversion to unbundling research and execution costs: in fact, Paris had supported the so-called 'commission-sharing agreements' (CSAs), used by some fund managers to compensate—with a comprehensive fee—both brokers and research providers (actually, Paris acknowledged that current provisions needed an update in order for CSAs to be fully compliant with the Package). In a consultation regarding the Package's implementation, the AMF stated its preference for a 'literal transposition' of the rules, for they represented *the result of a compromise reached following highly involved discussions and negotiations*. As we shall see, no consensus on this part was reached among European NCAs.

The main source of transposition of the Package into French legislation came by means of a decree: namely, Ordinance No. 2016-827 of 23 June 2016, which significantly amended the Monetary and Financial Code (or COMOFI): in particular, with regard to the entities different from the mutually recognised providers of investment services that are allowed to provide investment services. Moreover, it entails a strengthening of the conditions for being authorised. Among these, it is mandated that functions do not overlap and, also, that committees devoted to monitoring risk and compensation must be set up: the latter provision is somehow surprising, notwithstanding its purely Anglo-Saxon origin, it has been implemented in a country which does not rely upon any "national" governance system, but rather mixes up the two major CG approaches (the other being the 'Rhenish' one).

The very protective stance taken by the AMF toward its supervised entities is also shown regarding the scope of application of new EU rules: in fact, firms providing collective portfolio management services in relation to UCITS or AIFs have been excluded from the category of investment firms and, thus, being unbound from the Package's discipline. Although the Directive itself waives the managers of a collective investment scheme (CIS), France had to change its domestic legislation in order to allow its *Sociétés de Gestion de Portefeuille* (SGPs) to be encompassed by said categories and, thus, be exempt from MiFID II rules. Such exclusion does not apply to those entities which, other than managing a CIS, provide *discretionary* portfolio management services, a notion which entails more direct contact with clients and, therefore, strengthened investor protection requirements. However, the most striking novelties brought into domestic legislation relate with the conditions under which investment services are provided to non-professional clients in France, a field in which Paris actually showed its hard-line approach to investor protection and, more in general, a much greater sensibility to consumers' concerns rather than producers' one (in a sense, the reverse *vis-à-vis* the United Kingdom, in a way reflective of two radically different juridical traditions).

As for the noteworthy divide—across domestic legislations—between countries which do require the establishment of a local branch for allowing the provision (performance) of investment services (activities), on the one hand, and country which do not, on the other, France has used the freedom left by the Package to choose the former. This is consistent with its historical reliance upon heavy, centralised regulation of strategic industries whereby many interests are worth protecting. Since the French supervisory architecture is quite similar to a 'twin-peaks approach', the authorisation of mandatory branches has been charged upon the body competent for prudential regulation rather than the conduct of business—namely, the *Autorité de Contrôle Prudentiel et de Résolution* (ACPR), though it is not formally independent but rather encompassed by the *Banque de France*'s structure. In doing this, Paris has substantially copied-out MiFID II rules on the new instruments like structured deposits; moreover, it has envisaged a very strong discipline with respect to both CG and product governance.

In conclusion, the French implementation places itself somehow halfway between the tough German approach and the soft Spanish one. There is neither a systematic copy-out of the Package's provisions nor the adoption of an overly interventionist stance: instead, it is somehow the combination between the counterpart of Paris' obtrusiveness into private business, reflective of a "statist" view which has always driven that economy, on the one hand, and the more business-friendly attitude developed in recent years towards the financial industry, especially in the wake of Brexit. In fact, France is posed to attract many conglomerates fleeing the United Kingdom once its EU membership—and, thus, the automatic passport for firms providing (performing) financial services (activities)—will come to an end.

In order to achieve this, and in light of the relevance of investment banking within the domestic system, the AMF has shown an appreciable commitment to listening to the intermediaries' concerns, especially in relation to inducements and the big issue of research. Yet, in a country which has developed an autonomous yet remarkable consumeristic juridical tradition, the implementation of the Package has been pursued in a "neutral" manner; *rectius*, in a way which has consistently tried to temperate the needs of all the parties involved: manufacturers (i.e. issuance originators), distributors, consumers (i.e. investors), and clearly regulators as far as systemic stability is concerned.

7.5 Italy

Since the end of the sovereign bond crisis (which might be conventionally identified with Draghi's *whatever it takes* speech), Italy has been the most fragile of leading Euro Area economies. Even more clearly than Spain, structural deficiencies are to be blamed no less than the GFC itself. Such weaknesses date back very long time ago: at least following the 'economic miracle' which, in an extensive manner, may be located between late-Fifties and early-Seventies. The most overarching issue, to which all other problems may be seen as connected, is represented by productivity: starting from the Seventies, each decade has seen Total Factor

Productivity (TFP) declining vis-à-vis the previous one, with a negative spike between the Nineties and the 2000s (Università Bocconi and EIEF 2013). Therefore, when the crisis broke out, Italy had already lost 10–15 years trailing its European peers, which had grown thanks to rising productivity. Public debt is the other big issue of the Italian economy, as it currently hovers around 130% of GDP: the second highest ratio in EU-28, just behind Greece. Paradoxically, right after signing the Maastricht Treaty and, thus, committing itself to achieve the *macro*-fundamentals required for 'convergence', Italy has seen its debt-to-GDP figure skyrocketing instead of shrinking, mainly because of the lagged effect of an overly deficit spending throughout the previous decades.

In addition to this, Italy is somehow different from other leading Euro Area economies due to the peculiar shape of its financial industry. In 2013, banks represented 71.3% of the system in terms of total assets: that is, slightly more than both France and Germany (close to 67%) but well above the Euro Area average (55%). From 2001, such divergence had done nothing else than widening: nowadays, the split is going to narrow again thanks to the worldwide spread of shadow banking (which is made of players that are classified as different from credit institutions) and, hopefully, some improvement in a level of financial literacy which is incredibly low, and much more worrying for Italy than its peers (OECD 2016). However, Italy still suffers from a financial sector being visibly undersize—as for the GDP share it represents—compared to the Euro Area average (actually, Germany has a similar structural problem, though of less concern because of the considerable extent of the industry in absolute terms). Moreover, the Italian banking system is very little concentrated, despite the notable increase determined by some recent reforms aimed at a "rationalisation" of a too dispersed industry.

Coming to performance, the heinous GFC effects seem eventually over. Between 2011 and 2015, the Italian banking system had shown some first signs of recovery: CET1 ratio up from 9.3% to 12.3%, NPL coverage from 39.2% to 45.4%, RoE from 1.7% to 3.1%. Nevertheless, credit quality has remained substantially poor throughout the crisis, with an NPL ratio soaring from 6.18% to 18.11% over the said timespan. In 2017, as acknowledged by Banca d'Italia (2018), the situation turns out being significantly improved: just 7.5% of loans are impaired (with corporate exposures scoring better—on average—than household ones, as the latter show an 8.7% ratio), and the coverage ratio has climbed up to 52.7%. The Italian financial environment is, however, doomed by a much higher risk of interest rates suddenly rising, especially once the ECB's support will be terminated. In fact, Rome is perceived as a much less creditworthy borrower than many of its Euro Area peers and, thus, has steadily issued sovereign bonds with relatively higher yields (sporadically surpassed by Spain at the zenith of the crisis), with inevitable spill-overs onto the private sector. Since Treasury bonds are still extremely relevant in the balance sheets of Italian credit institutions (much more than the Eurozone average), banks and other intermediaries would not be willing to widen the spread between yields on sovereign investments, on the one hand, and lending to clients, on the other, which is already of remarkable size. With rising rates charged on loans, the asset impairment could start representing a problem again. Although the

ECB's loose and interventionist stance has been able to prevent any interest rate spike in the private sector, while also halting the yield on sovereigns from a comeback to 2011–2012 levels, the abovementioned remains a threat to be faced in the next future. However, in quantitative terms, the market risk consisting of diminishing asset values is nowadays much less frightening than in the past: *Banca d'Italia* has computed that, even if risk-free interest rates went up by 300 bps, the LCR of the domestic banking system as a whole would decrease from 172 to 143%, still far above the 100% requirement.

The path of credit is in line with the one of the other leading Eurozone economies, with a small but significant reprise over recent years, which is set to continue if interest rates did not face disruptive changes. However, the credit-to-GDP ratio is strikingly negative, ranging between −10 and −14% according to different calculation methods, and is not projected to reverse its sign even in case credit supply were actually higher than expected. To see this more in detail, we may look at the real-estate sector, which has always represented the main area in which Italian households tend to invest. In 2017, after a severe demand contraction over the GFC years, home prices have dropped again, continuing with their decreasing trend. The other side of the coin is, however, a slight yet appreciable reduction in the risks faced by banks in relation to the mortgages they issue. These positive signs, though quite contingent (thus, fragile) from a structural viewpoint, sum up to a quite viable economic outlook, provided that we ruled out any shocks of political or otherwise exogenous origin. If we look at systemic risk, we may notice that it has been steadily below 0.2 from 2016 onwards, except for a small period at the end of that year. Actually, this is the result of a very negative contribution from correlations, whereas both the public and the private segments have positively contributed to the "fever" on Italian financial markets. Conversely, the monetary segment, which had been particularly relevant during the GFC, nowadays has almost a neuter impact.

Rome's approach to transposing the Package into domestic legislation is quite peculiar, though substantially in line with the country's regulatory history. Usually, financially strong EU Member States—like Germany and the UK—have adopted a "hawkish" stance toward the industry, designing a severe investor-protective framework and constraining the operations of the entities subject to their oversight for the sake of systemic stability, whereas more fragile ones—like Spain—have been more "dovish", trying to avoid any disruptive changes. Notwithstanding this, Italy has chosen the former approach despite being one of the latter type of countries. De facto, the new architecture of product governance and intervention, along with the additional powers that NCAs have been endowed with, has allowed Rome to revamp the very interventionist attitude ignited with the 1936 banking law and ended with its liberalising reform in 1993. This occurred in the wake of some cases of mala gestio and banks getting eventually troubled, which had been highly covered by the media regardless of their actual saliency from a systemic viewpoint. As for investment services, Italy had to discount a remarkable delay over its EU peers, for no comprehensive law had been enacted before 1998 and, thus, the industry—even during the Eighties' flourishing—dealt with rules conceived with a merely "commercial" approach, ignoring the specificities of finance. Therefore, the notion of 'financial consumer' had not become common before the first 2000s, when a series of major scandals severely hit many retail investors. Since then, however, Italy has shown one of the toughest regulatory styles Europe-wide.

As far as the Package's implementation is concerned, the Italian regulator of financial markets—namely, the *Commissione nazionale per le società e la Borsa* (CONSOB)—consulted on a number of issues in respect of which it did not show any significant shift from the EU legislation regarding the issues of AT/HFT and market infrastructure. On the latter, also, it took into account several provisions laid down in EMIR and the *Central Securities Depositories Regulation* (CSDR, No. 909/2014). With respect to transparency, the implementation was first substantiated by the introduction of Article 79-bis of the Italian main financial law—namely, the Legislative Decree 24 February 1998, No. 58, best known as *Testo unico della finanza* (TUF)—stemmed from MiFID I and Regulation No. 2006/1287, connected to the former. In fact, before the Package, the Italian regulatory framework—though delegating to CONSOB the implementation of transparency provisions (as for certain instruments, subjected to hearing *Banca d'Italia*)—substantially resembled the outdated MiFID I idea of exempting the transactions in non-equity instruments. Many times, the European legislator had urged Member States to adopt rules designing a transparency framework also for the abovementioned exchanges. A sudden U-turn occurred in 2008, when the EU Commission—in its *Report on non-equities market transparency*—stated that the extension of pre- and post-trade transparency to non-equity transactions was unnecessary. Therefore, CONSOB kept its original intent by issuing Regulation No. 16191/2007, which assesses the importance of avoiding differences in the treatment of non-equity instruments but nonetheless delegates the implementation of ad hoc provisions to the recipients of supervision, from a self-regulating standpoint. Although this "liberal" approach—developed when the scope of the financial crisis was not as clear—generally has some good aspects and might effectively yield positive results, this is probably not the case. In fact, there are also other situations where a sort of "under-regulation"—that is, surprisingly lower than its theoretical optimum—seems to be underway: for instance, in relation to the large waivers allowed to SIs and those applying to RMs and MTFs even in case of equity transactions.

Conversely, the Package's discipline on investor protection has inserted over an already well-developed framework. The TUF itself had been thought in order not only to collect previous provisions into a comprehensive rulebook, but also to enhance "economic democracy" in a system still affected by several inefficiencies. The CONSOB consultation launched on 5 May 2016 addressed the investor-protective issues of MiFID II by proposing to create Article 24-bis, substantially mirroring the Directive. It envisaged that the client be informed—before the provision (performance) of the service (activity)—about whether advisory being on an independent basis or not, the breadth of market analysis conducted (including whether financial instruments be issued by related parties or not, in a way that could give rise to conflicts of interest) and, finally, whether a periodic assessment of suitability be scheduled. Moreover, still in plain accordance with the Directive, some requirements were laid down in relation to independent advisory. This would have entailed a wide range of instruments being taken into account, for the purpose of an effective diversification: i.e. including those issued or provided by entities other than the investment firm or its related parties. Finally, the Package's discipline of inducements has been substantially replicated in the Italian legislation.

As for primary legislation, Italy transposed the Package into the Legislative Decree 3 August 2017, No. 129 (henceforth, 'the Decree'). As a civil-law country, Italy has chosen to concentrate the implementation of MiFID II and the application of MiFIR in a source of law of the highest rank, from which second-level ones descend (e.g., CONSOB's *Regolamento Emittenti* on security issuances), whereas common-law countries have brought little changes to their primary legislation (e.g., in the UK, the *Financial Services and Markets Act*), heavily amending the binding documents issued by supervisors. Following the cabinet meeting on 28 July 2017, which passed the Decree, the Italian Government acknowledged that the market, becoming 'more various and complex', was worth disciplining in a renewed and more careful way, lest the juridical framework would not have retained its ability to adequately address economic and technological advancement.

Significant concerns were raised about the issue of insurance investment products: although they are addressed by the Decree, the Italian legislator has directly referred to the forthcoming implementation of a dedicated EU piece of legislation, where the definition of 'insurance products' is one of the most disputed points, especially in light of the remarkable technical changes—including, of course, the effects of a "digital disruption"—occurred in the insurance field as a whole. Of course, the principles informing the Decree—product governance and product intervention, informational transparency, independent advisory, enhancement of best execution, cooperation between supervisory authorities, etc.—are not particularly different from those envisaged in the Package; yet, some Italian specificity was nonetheless carried. This occurred in relation to the 'whistleblowing' phenomenon, i.e. when the employee of a company—irrespective of his/her own position—exposes a misconduct by the latter (in violation of either criminal law, or administrative duties, or other obligations), such that the firm's executives may be held liable for their wrongdoing. In order for the violation to be successfully uncovered and prosecuted, the 'whistleblower' should be endowed with adequate protection. Unfortunately, not unlike other cases in the realm of financial legislation, Italy was far behind its Western peers—especially Anglo-Saxon countries—with regard to disciplining such phenomenon. The provisions of the Decree are not presumed to provide a comprehensive, ultimate response to the issue; anyway, they might well be regarded as a good "first attempt" to address the issue.

In particular, the Italian legislator has "caught the opportunity" of implementing MiFID II and applying MiFIR to implement a wider reshaping of the TUF, not circumscribed to Package-related issues. Moreover, consistently with the piece of legislation de quo, the amendments take into consideration some provisions actually stemming from the interaction between the Package and other relevant EU law, such as EMIR and MAR. As a result of this, the TUF has been substantively rewritten. While the original text somehow mixed the implementation of some EU pieces of legislation of that time with authentically Italian concerns regarding the functioning of financial markets and operations (e.g., extraordinary transactions involving listed companies), the current version shows a much clearer footprint of Brussels post GFC law-making.

Unlike others, Part I of TUF has not undergone a profound reshaping: although definitions have formally been rewritten, only a few elements are worth mentioning as a substantive innovation. First, the ECB is explicitly acknowledged to have a remarkable role in overseeing financial stability, along with ESMA. This is mainly due to the noticeable change in the supervisory architecture, ended up with the ECB being put in charge of directly supervising 'significant' banks under the SSM. Nowadays, credit institutions play an increasingly relevant role in respect of the provision (performance) of investment services (activities); moreover, the once-Eurotower exerts non-neglectable powers—although, in some cases, merely formal—on 'less significant' banks. Hence, given that the ECB has become the public body responsible for the orderly and efficient exercise of banking—both commercial and, de facto, investment—, the Italian legislator has explicitly acknowledged its role in the field of investment activities, as well as already done in respect of banking stricto sensu. Whether or not such a strong delegation of powers be the result of the current Italian chairmanship in Frankfurt (until 31 October 2019), or the outcome of a progressive, EU-wide and ineluctable process of functions being transferred from NCAs to the ECB, we are not entitled to judge.

Conversely, Part II of TUF has been profoundly amended. Its new header—*General provisions and supervisory powers*—highlights a stronger focus on the oversight realm than before. In fact, CONSOB has been endowed with new and broader tools. Hence, we might even dare to say that, notwithstanding the fact that *Banca d'Italia* retains powers regarding banks and transactions in sovereign-debt securities, the Italian supervisory model is currently moving towards an architecture whose main criterion is given by the activity exercised by the supervised entity, such that CONSOB holds some responsibilities wherever the provision of investment services or the performance of investment activities be concerned. The new Article 6 TUF, par. 02, is extremely significant, as it helps legitimising some considerable deviations from the Package, not backed by provisions which explicitly allow Member States to impose additional requirements (something which would be a form of gold-plating and, thus, prohibited). In fact, regarding the requirements that investment firms must abide by, we should at least mention the duty to *safeguard the ownership rights of clients, especially in the event of the investment firm's insolvency, and to prevent the use of the financial instruments of a client on own account except with the client's express consent* (Article 16^{D}, par. 8). In addition to this, an investment firm is mandated *to prevent the use of client funds for its own account ... except in the case of credit institutions* (par. 9); moreover, it *shall not conclude title transfer financial collateral arrangements with retail clients for the purpose of securing or covering present or future, actual or contingent or prospective obligations of clients* (par. 10). In short, the Italian legislator has deemed these principles not to be adequately pursued through the provisions contained in the Package, which—inter alia—are endowed with a high degree of harmonisation, does not leave much room to Member States in departing from it. Hence, the Decree has amended the TUF by explicitly acknowledging that, in order for the principles set out in the Directive to be efficaciously pursued, Italian oversight bodies are required to cooperate. Hence, the content of the new Article 6 TUF, par. 02, acknowledges the possibility of additional requirements being imposed, yet it thoroughly circumscribes them to the *exceptional cases where these obligations are objectively justified and proportioned*, for one should take into account *the need to address specific risks in relation to investor protection or market integrity*, by adding a few but unneglectable words: the abovementioned needs must *show a peculiar relevance in respect of the structure of the Italian market*.

We shall see in a moment how the Italian legislator has delivered on its promise to let its oversight authorities impose additional requirements aimed at better responding to the investors' fears, given that "panic" situations could rapidly push an entire financial system toward the abyss. Now, let us proceed by analysing the most significant changes in Part II of TUF. There are multiple provisions highlighting the set of interventionist powers held by CONSOB and *Banca d'Italia*. First of all, the Decree endows the former, once consulted upon the latter, to identify—via a regulation—which persons be encompassed by the three traditional MiFID categories of clients (of course, consistently with the EU framework, only professional clients have to be directly defined).

The informative and inspective aspects of supervision are remarkably underlined in the new TUF (Articles 6-bis and 6-ter), as the bodies de quo may require hearings be made, documents be shown, information be communicated, having as recipients both the persons concerned (that is, their legal representatives) or those to which—either directly or to their personnel—'essential corporate functions' have been outsourced. Clearly, the Italian legislator has devoted specific attention to the cross-border operations of supervised intermediaries. Since product governance deserves an adequate level of enforcement, there should be no room for the inaction of a foreign authority: the new Article 7-quarter TUF, par. 1, endows CONSOB and *Banca d'Italia* with powers of intervention in the case of misconduct being exposed in respect of a wide array of financial firms.

If either EU or Italian laws were violated by a foreign entity, one of the two abovementioned authorities—having consulted the other, and once informed the home-country competent body—may intervene upon the recurrence of certain conditions (Article 7 TUF, par. 2):

(a) there are lacking or inadequate measures by the authority in charge where the entity is headquartered;
(b) behaviour rules are violated;
(c) misconduct may bring prejudice to the goals of 'general interest' set out in Article 5, par. 1;
(d) there is urgency in protecting investors. Further provisions are laid down in relation to collective investment schemes of any kind (UCITS and AIFs, both

EU and non-EU), which may be prevented from marketing their units or shares for a period not longer than 60 days.

Another relevant tool provided for by the TUF is the power, attributed to CONSOB by means of a decree issued by its President, to act 'with urgency where clients or markets be endangered' in order to suspend the members of the management body of a SIM (that is, one type of investment firm under the Italian law), and appoint a committee—put in charge of it—in the case of severe misconduct or violation of 'legislative, administrative or statutory provisions'. These sanctions imposed to executives are not new in the acquis communautaire, as the *Banking Resolution and Recovery Directive* (BRRD, No. 2014/59/EU) laid down similar provisions with regard to credit institutions. In addition to this, a remarkable reform has been pursued in relation to the whole of the provisions disciplining the authorisation to be released to SIMs, in terms of the conditions to be mandatorily met.

The reshaping of product governance measures entailed in the Package has led to relevant changes in the Italian financial law, too. Pursuant to the new Article 21 TUF, par. 2-bis, where financial instruments be manufactured *for sale to clients*, the providers (performers) of investment services (activities) must *ensure that these products be conceived in order to satisfy the needs of a determined reference market of end clients* and that the distribution strategy for financial instruments *be compatible with target clients*. This is probably one of the provisions that most closely resemble those contained in the Package, for it transposes into Italian law the a priori requirement charged to any investment firm when dealing with its clients. This occurs in a more overarching and comprehensive manner vis-à-vis the appropriateness and suitability tests being conducted. These last are governed by the principle set out in new par. 2-ter, where—in a way that undoubtedly strengthens what stated above—we may read that *the authorised person must know the financial instruments known or recommended, evaluate their compatibility with the needs of the clientele* from the standpoint envisaged in the previous paragraph. Finally, it must ensure that *offers and recommendations are carried out only in the client's interest*, repeating the Package's refrain.

In order for such discipline to be effective, some provisions contained in the Italian banking law—namely, the Legislative Decree 1 September 1993, No. 385, best known as *Testo unico bancario* (TUB)—are excluded from applying to:

(a) investment services and activities;
(b) the placement of financial product;
(c) the operations and services involved in Articles 25-bis and 25-*ter*: namely, *structured deposits and financial products, other than financial instruments, issued by credit institutions* and *insurance products issued by insurance companies* respectively.

This helps us clarifying the realms where certain rules are enforceable and, thus, avoiding overlaps; therefore, they represent a reasonable complement to the provisions regarding the powers and competences of overseers. In fact, given the criterion discerning credit institutions from other types of persons, banks are authorised by CONSOB—upon consulting *Banca d'Italia*—to provide (perform) investment services (activities), pursuant to the new Article 19 TUF, par. 4. This is not a novelty introduced by the Package, but nonetheless contributes to designing the "modern" supervisory architecture 'by activity'.

In relation to advisory provided on an independent basis, the new TUF closely mirrors what is established in the Directive (Recitals 72^D–75^D). Articles 26 and the following are remarkably important, for they deal with some fundamental principles such as the freedom of establishment and the mutual recognition of EU financial firms. They are closely interconnected, and domestic jurisdictions have to develop their salient legal aspects in the most consistent and harmonised way as possible. These provisions are related to SIMs and do not bring substantive innovations to pre-existing rules: like Paris, Rome has chosen a 'no-branch' approach for investment firms willing to operate in Italy, in stricter abidance by the Treaties (and, in particular, Article 56 TFEU). Nevertheless, in order for the services and activities subject to mutual recognition to be the object of these operations, either a branch or a tied agent must be employed. As usual, CONSOB—upon consulting *Banca d'Italia*—must check whether certain conditions are satisfied: that is, whether the capital and organisational structure of the applicant are adequate for the business goals to be efficaciously pursued. This requires that no negative spill-overs spread at a systemic level, along with no investors being hurt.

Some investor-protective rules are detailed in the new Article 27 TUF: par. 2 prevents tied agents put by foreign EU investment firms in charge of the provision (performance) of investment services (activities) in Italy from holding money and/or financial instruments belonging to clients or potential clients of the firm on whose behalf they operate. This means that Italy has autonomously denied tied agents a possibility which the European legislator had explicitly acknowledged (Article 29^D, par. 2). Since the other Package's provisions on foreign persons do not remarkably depart from what had been stated at an EU level, there is no other way than admitting how deep Rome has been influenced by investor-protective concerns. Furthermore, in order to have foreign entities provide (perform) investment services in Italy, effective anti-money-laundering provisions must be enforced in that country, and the host-country NCA must have settled a cooperation agreement with CONSOB. This is perfectly consistent with the list of requirements asked to extra-EU investment firms, where we may read something border-line with gold-plating. Its sole justification may be found in Article 6, par. 02: in fact, CONSOB—upon consulting *Banca d'Italia*—may authorise such entity to establish an Italian branch only if, along with other relatively standard conditions to be met, *the applicant firm has joined a compensation scheme in protection of investors*.

Pursuant to the new Article 32-*ter*, CONSOB itself—which is in charge of regulating the procedures instigated in order to reach an 'alternative dispute resolution' (ADR)—is going to establish, 'within its own balance sheet', an ad hoc fund, for the purpose of enhancing the out-of-court investor protection explicitly afforded to subjects *different from professional clients*. As well as funds established elsewhere in the financial realm (e.g., in relation to banking, those aimed at financing resolutions or insuring depositors), the fund must be contributed—mainly, but not exclusively—by players in the concerned market. Yet, its rationale is different: payments are neither voluntary nor determined a priori. They are actually more than just "compulsory": in fact, are coactively collected as a share of monetary administrative sanctions imposed to intermediaries. Apparently, this represents a remarkable detachment from previous EU-derived legislation. However, in order to assess whether this is reflective of a "punitive" attitude of the Italian legislator against intermediaries, we should note, first, that the fund has a circumscribed goal (and, thus, pecuniary amount); second, that charging only wrongdoers with a payment burden—though coactive—is probably a more pro-business and "liberal" measure than one indiscriminately requiring every person to contribute, regardless of the merits of its conduct.

Further novelties have been introduced in respect of tied agents, as they are allowed to make 'offsite offerings' on behalf of a single authorised person exclusively. In light of this, the new Article 31 TUF becomes particularly relevant, as—pursuant to it—offsite-offering tied agents are required to *immediately communicate to any clients or potential clients in what capacity they operate, and which authorised person they represent*. The same persons on whose behalf offerings or recommendations are made must ensure that tied agents possess 'adequate knowledge and skills' in order to be able to provide investment services or ancillary ones', along with accurately communicating information to the client (effective or potential); furthermore, agents entitled to make offsite offerings must be prevented from yielding negative spill-overs on MiFID-compliant activities via the exercise of activities that are not envisaged by the Directive.

Part III of TUF has received substantive amendments, for it disciplines trading venues (which, as we have seen, constitute one of the most important aspects dealt with by the Package). *Banca d'Italia* keeps its supervisory powers in respect of wholesale trading on sovereign-debt securities, in relation to which the Ministry of Treasury (once consulted both CONSOB and *Banca d'Italia*) is allowed to set out specific requirements, also in respect of the definition of a 'main operator' (Articles 62-bis). In general, trading venues are subjected to the joint supervision of the two main regulators. The central bank, however, is allowed to act upon the recurrence of both 'necessity' and 'urgency', two principles frequently invoked in the Italian administrative architecture. Such intervention may occur even in replacement of market operators, which are primarily in charge of ensuring the well-functioning of venues, in a manner which resembles the holding being regarded as a 'supervisory auxiliary' in the case of a banking group. Of course, the two main authorities are required to cooperate and there is no exception to this principle, apart from those situations in which a timely, effective solution would be threatened: hence, the two oversight bodies must exchange their information. The same prescription applies to *Autorità per l'energia elettrica, il gas e il sistema idrico* (AEEGSI), which is the body in charge of overseeing electricity, gas and water markets.

Information can be obtained in different ways (Article 62-octies, par. 1), either:

(a) the submission of documents;
(b) the hearing of whoever may know something;
(c) requests addressed to auditing companies working for trading venues.

It is also worth noting that *the acts deemed to be necessary may be carried out in respect of market operators and those to which operators themselves have outsourced essential or relevant operating functions, and their personnel* (Article 62-novies, par. 1).

Yet, this would not suffice: therefore, pursuant to Article 62-decies, CONSOB and *Banca d'Italia* are also endowed with the faculty of:

(a) publish 'warnings to the public' on their websites;
(b) urge market operators not to deal with an external person in the case this brought prejudice to *the transparency, the ordered development of exchanges, investor protection and the overall market efficiency*;
(c) remove market operators' managers, as well as—upon consulting the other authority—those of the SIM or the Italian credit institution operating an MTF or an OTF, provided that, in the case of such people remaining in charge, there would not be negative spill-overs onto the abovementioned goals;
(d) order the *temporary or permanent ending of practices or behaviours* that fail to comply with the provisions encompassed by Part III of the TUF.

Consistently with the specific attention devoted by the Italian law to the ownership structure of systemically relevant firms, the reformed TUF (Article 64-bis, par. 3) charges the operators of RMs with the duty of communicating to CONSOB—and disclosing to the public, too—information on:

(a) their ownership;
(b) any related changes, also encompassing *the identity of those parties which are able to exercise a significant influence on operating the market, along with the extent of their interests*. In this wording, 'significant' should be intended as something "lower"—in a sense—than the term 'dominant', which is more often mentioned in the Italian financial law.

The idea is that competent supervisors must be informed whenever a stake held in "sensible" firms—as market operators undoubtedly are—reaches a threshold which entails the holder being able to determine the company's strategic choices. The "corollary" to such rule is that CONSOB must be informed of any intentions of acquiring or dismissing a controlling stake held in a RM operator. Besides, within 90 days from such communication, the abovementioned authority may oppose the ownership changes if, in light of 'objective and demonstrable reasons', they would endanger the RM's sound and prudent management (Article 64-bis, paragraphs 4 and 5). The 'organisational requirements' of RMs, thoroughly laid down in the new Article 65, are quite standard ones. However, what really matters is par. 2, where is stated that, by means of an ad hoc regulation, *CONSOB may furtherly detail* said requirements, along with specifying the methodology to be used for the purpose of determining the amount of 'financial resources' that the RM is endowed with.

As far as OTFs are concerned, the new TUF specifies to which extent they are allowed to exercise a 'discretional' activity: pursuant to Article 65-quater, par. 1, these venues act in such way whenever they:

(a) *place or withdraw an order on their system*, or
(b) do not couple a specific client order with other orders available in the system at a given time, as long as this occurs in compliance with specific instructions received by the client and of the obligations envisaged pursuant to Article 6, par. 2, letter *b*.

This last provision empowers CONSOB with issuing a regulation on the good conduct of authorised person, including—in light of the amendment brought by the Decree—the cases of bundled sales. In par. 1-bis is clearly stated that the decision whether to bundle or not is a discretional one but should be agreed only in the case the interests of the clients were 'potentially compatible' and, thus, did not harm any investor. Other investor-protective rules may be found in par. 2, pursuant to which an OTF operator cannot act as a systematic internaliser, too; and in par. 3, where is stated that—in the case of market-making be outsourced, this must occur 'on an independent basis' and, hence, there must not be 'strict links to the operator itself'.

Moreover, in par. 4, we may read that orders *in direct exchange with the operator or an entity of the same group as the operator*, though sentenced not to represent (in general) a situation where conflicts of interest arise, might be prevented by some mechanisms that operators themselves are mandated to put in place. Similarly, matched-principal trading must not *give rise to conflicts of interest between the operator and the clientele* (Article 65-quinquies, par. 2). These transactions are the only kind of proprietary trading that an operator is allowed to enter '*in relation to sovereign-debt securities that are lacking a liquid market*' (Article 65-quinquies, par. 3). Finally, both the two abovementioned types of transactions are forbidden to RMs and MTFs, which in the MiFID framework have less degrees of freedom than OTFs (balanced by higher transparency).

In general, venues are required to ensure their resilience—*e.g.*, in order to properly manage a high amount of orders—and a strong provisioning against the disruption of trading systems, such that 'operating continuity' is ensured. Additional, tougher rules are imposed in respect of HFT (Article 65-sexies, paragraphs 1 and 2). This is nothing new in relation to what is entailed by the Package; nor substantially is the provision contained in Article 65-sexies, par. 3: this last, however, entails that the 'written agreements' between venue operators, on the one hand, and firms to which market-making is outsourced, on the other, must be 'binding' ones. This adjective is somehow omitted in the Package, albeit one could easily "fill in the gap" given the compulsoriness of certain requirements. Fully in line with MiFID II (Article 48, par. 2), the legislator charges the abovementioned persons with the duty of ensuring that the largest possible number of market-making firms joins those agreements and, pursuant to them, *transmit irrevocable quotes at competitive prices, with the result of providing liquidity to the market on a regular and forecastable basis, provided that this requirement be consistent with the nature and size of trading done at said venues*. Written agreements are also envisaged in the case of the outsourcing of *all or part of critical operational functions that enable algorithmic trading*.

As far as transparency measures are concerned, the vast majority of provisions contained in the new TUF mirrors those stated in the Package; yet, one might still find some Italian peculiarities. Of course, general criteria for the admission, suspension and withdrawal of financial instruments from listing and trading are carefully laid down (Article 66). However, the really important provision is the one in Article 66-bis, par. 2, where accounting transparency and the system of internal controls to be shown by extra-EU firms in order to be listed in an Italian RM are mentioned as the content of ad hoc regulations to be issued by CONSOB. Pursuant to Article 66-ter, par. 1, a withdrawal may be determined only if there is no risk of damage to either investors or the orderly functioning of the market. Furthermore, as stated in par. 3, suspension is not applied if the recipient was waived from the obligation to publish a prospectus, as well as in the case of 'additional slots of shares already admitted to trading'. In accordance with the Package's provisions, CONSOB applies to instruments traded in Italy the same measure as the one applied —by competent authorities—to the same instruments traded in another EU Member State, provided that the suspension or withdrawal is due to *alleged market abuse, public bid or to the lacking dissemination of privileged information regarding the issuer or the financial instrument in violation of Articles 7 and 17* of MAR.

The same rationale is employed in Article 68—again, in perfect compliance with the Package—with regard to position limits on derivative contracts, including equivalent ones traded OTC (par. 1), which, along with controls on the management of positions, must be 'transparent and non-discriminatory' (Article 68-ter, par. 1). However, in exceptional cases, CONSOB may impose more stringent limits than those adopted pursuant to par. 1, *by keeping into account liquidity and the orderly functioning of that specific market*. One might argue that, by pursuing such a "micro-prudential" purpose, Rome has renounced to enact wider purposes aimed at preserving systemic stability. Actually, the Italian legislator has explicitly circumscribed the regulatory response to the potentially disruptive effects of derivatives trading, despite not following the esprit of the Pittsburgh G20 summit. Anyway, this might be a merely theoretical concern, perhaps to be raised by those particularly worried by the backfiring of a loose grip on supervised entities. Anyway, the actual result of such provision is that, whenever a specific derivative market is on the brink of something negative occurring because of badly managed positions, CONSOB acts on that specific market and, thus, preserves overall stability.

With regard to *pre-* and post-trade transparency obligations, as well as the discipline of DRSPs, the Decree has closely abided by the Package's provisions. There are probably two simple reasons for such "fidelity". First, there is really little margin to mandate something different, as the balance between a "restrictive" approach and a "liberal" one seems to be really well constructed: at least from a theoretical standpoint, it would represent an appreciable compromise between a pro-business legislation consistent with the free-market foundations of the EU, on the one hand, and an effective supervision aimed at avoiding future break-ups of the financial order, as dismally occurred during the GFC, on the other. The second reason is more directly referable to the Italian context, where financial markets—in particular, equity ones—are generally less developed vis-à-vis many other advanced countries; therefore, a harmonised set of rules is a fortiori needed, for this would enable different players—investment firms as well as their clients—to have greater trust in Italy as a good place to carry out financial transactions wherein. We just mention the saliency of SME growth markets in the Italian economic environment, where smaller firms are largely prevalent. The requirements that an MTF has to match in order to be recognised as such market (Article 69, par. 2) are exactly the same as those laid down in Article 33^{D}. Inter alia, we just remark that *at least 50% of issuers whose financial instruments are admitted to trading on the system be SMEs*, something that must be fulfilled both at the registration and in every civil year.

In conclusion, the Italian approach to transposing the Package is barely based on copying out EU rules, yet with significant differences overall contributing to stricter regulation, rather than a more investor-friendly one. Even by looking at the number of consultations launched by CONSOB and *Banca d'Italia*, we may realise how committed Italy has been to enforce the new rules on investment services (activities), endeavouring to boost an industry which has not yet achieved the same development as in other leading EU economies. Given the bulk of investor-protective laws—which some argue to be at the limit of 'information overload' equivalent to no information at all (Persson 2018)—, we should legitimately expect a huge effort in spreading financial literacy. Some commendable initiatives have recently been undertaken, but time has to flow before meaningful results be observed. Without such structural change, Italy's financial markets will remain weaker, and regulators tougher, vis-à-vis their EU peers.

7.6 United Kingdom

As for the United Kingdom, we must necessarily discuss Brexit, its implications, and some first evidence on whether the referendum, held on 23 June 2016, may actually be considered as a "cutting point" associated with relevant macroeconomic changes. However, we are not going to infer any causality outside of the issues directly affected by UK–EU relationships: also, because not all fundamentals experienced a significant shift across 2016, nor even reversed their medium-to-long-term trend. For instance, the UK has not differed from other leading EU economies as far as indebtedness and credit supply are concerned, the Bank of England (2018) has found. Following a steady rise over GM years, household and corporate debt has remarkably stayed below its 2008 level; moreover, *credit growth remains broadly in line with the growth in nominal GDP and debt-servicing burdens are low*.

For instance, according to the Bank of England (2018), compared to the 8.9% average annual growth over the 1997–2006 timespan, credit has surged just by 4.9% from end-2016 to end-2017, albeit this figure should be split between much less significant reduction in terms of corporate credit (from 7.3% during those GM years to 6.2% in the last one) and a much more pronounced slowdown in lending to individuals (4.1%, compared to 10.4% GM growth). Another way of looking at this is the credit-to-GDP gap, which has been extremely negative since the GFC outbreak (up to record values around −30%) but has started rising again in 2014. The other side of the coin is the slight increase in bond and mortgage spreads occurred in 2017: this might actually signal an increase in the perception of risk following Brexit; nevertheless, by looking at a longer horizon this should not come as a surprise: along with the physiological expansion of shadow banking, the overall credit institutions' risk appetite has soared and, like Spain, consumer loans have been the main driver of such trend, sparking a buoyant reprise after the GFC years' credit crunch. Yet, credit growth might have been much higher, had the demand not been so weak as it actually was, claims the BoE.

The 1% CCyB set for one year, ending on 28 November 2018, signals the absence of immediate dangers to the UK economy, notwithstanding the (remarkable) Brexit-related uncertainty and the central bank's belief that, although there are some little signs of moderation, credit institutions will continue to fuel their risk-taking. This is the clear consequence of an environment made of low interest rates, which has not been only the one created by the ECB: instead, since the BoE has adopted similar loose policies as a reaction against the crisis, debt servicing ratios (basically, the proportion of interest expenses over after-tax nominal income) have stayed substantially constant for households—with a small increase between 2007 and 2008, as a late reaction to the deterioration in borrowers' creditworthiness —but has plummeted for corporations, from roughly 25% in 2008 to less than 10% during the recovery cycle (from 2014 onwards). If we turn to leverage in the non-financial sector, we may see that it has peaked at the acutest phase of the GFC, between 2008 and 2010; then, it has decreased over the 2010–2015 reprise; finally, it has started rising again, but still remaining sensibly lower than pre-crisis levels. In the first half of 2018, leverage has continued to soar, such that the BoE estimated a 4% growth in corporate debt, significantly up from +1.7% recorded in the previous year.

Moreover, we should take into account that much of this growth came from British credit institutions syndicating with foreign ones to extend loans. This means that the climate of uncertainty (*rectius*, volatility), sparked by the UK–EU negotiations, is a fortiori dangerous to the British financial system, increasingly reliant upon investors from abroad. This is not a fault per se: conversely, it shows how appealing has always been that country, how it has consolidated its role as a financial hub, and how globalisation—a primitive form of which, as for trade and related financial services, can be identified with the British undisputed rule over the sea from the 17th to the 19th century (Ferguson 2018)—has prompted players to become even more interconnected. Yet, there are ineluctable drawbacks: given the remarkable standing that the City of London has built over time in the financial industry—probably surpassing Wall Street's one thanks to the lighter regulatory burden, at least from the 1986 *Big Bang* onwards—, very much is also at stake with Britain exiting the European Union.

The British Parliament has definitely passed the *Great Repeal Bill* (GRB), proposed in July 2017 and slightly amended over its iter. The most overarching rationale of the GRB is that any EU-derived legislation that will be into force immediately before 'exit day' will be kept and become an integrating part of the British juridical framework; otherwise, provisions that will not be enforceable would be ultimately dropped. This has few exceptions, and they do not touch the Package's implementation. Hence, on 29 March 2019 MiFIR will be directly applicable as it has been since 3 January 2018, especially if we consider that the GRB is a serious blow to the possibility of directly enforcing Directives (something which the doctrine has harshly debated over time). After exit day, nothing would prevent the UK legislator from amending it. As for the post-Brexit scenario, which regulatory model would London choose? Will it adopt a "conservative" stance regarding the provisions contained therein, or rather show a substantive deregulatory attitude, aimed at fostering the free exchange of securities?

Moreover, there is no unique approach to be applied to every single provision of MiFIR: some rules are basically common-sense ones—thus, somehow the same across different jurisdictions and financial systems—and repealing or amending them would be quite difficult to be justified before the investor community. Anyway, many baseline provisions contained in the Package would be at stake, in case of the UK actually leaving the Single Market. If this eventually occurred, we should start envisioning London as linked to Brussels by some bond different from the EEA trade rules: for instance, by something similar to the EU-Swiss agreement, which disciplines the access of Helvetian goods and services to the Single Market. Of course, it is still possible that either no agreement be reached, or that a new, ad hoc deal be eventually settled, even if time is running out. The former is the worst scenario: if it materialised, the standard rules set out by the World Trade Organisation (WTO) would apply, de facto bringing the freedom to trade close to the lowest of any non-protectionist level.

As for the transposition of the Package into domestic law, the UK completed the process before 'exit day' (29 March 2019) and, thus, incorporated it into its legislation by means of the *Great Repeal Bill*. However, the vast majority of MiFID II and MiFIR provisions have been encompassed by secondary legislation, something which is physiological for a common-law jurisdiction. Hence, the majority of amendments can be found in the *Handbook* released by the Financial Conduct Authority (FCA), which constitutes the basis for ensuring systemic stability and de facto shapes the UK regulatory framework. Minor changes have affected the rules issued by the Prudential Regulation Authority (PRA), which—because of its functions, of course—have historically played a more active role in overseeing intermediaries and, thus, has been much less devoted to law-making and standard-setting. Finally, with regard to primary legislation, little amendments have been brought to the *Financial Services and Markets Act* (FSMA), adopted in 2000.

A major document to look at is a very wide-ranging paper released by the FCA and headed *Policy Statement II*, amending the previous one and deemed to be final (it was accompanied by a consultation on some residual issues). In its introduction, we may read how the British legislator acknowledges that *what is in the MiFID II conduct provisions is familiar in the context of existing UK regulatory framework*, yet this does not suffice, due to the remarkable delay in implementing the *Insurance Distribution Directive* (IDD, No. 2016/97/EU). Moreover, since *consumers have a clear interest in financial markets that operate fairly and transparently*, and this has shaped such recent legislative intervention in the UK (actually, it had been very uncommon in the past), London has deliberately chosen to devote remarkable attention to the issues of 'equality' and 'diversity' (to which MiFID II is not insensible, at all). In order to serve the Package's broader objectives of *consumer protection and market integrity*, along with a view to promoting competition, Britain has followed a generally cautious approach, implementing minimum requirements by copying out some essential provisions *on a wide range of firms or businesses*, in order to *achieve consistency of regulatory standards and to avoid arbitrage* (something labelled as 'intelligent copy-out'). At the same time, it entails going beyond the Directive if this helped achieving the abovementioned goals.

Something which might well be modified in the wake of the formal exit from the European Union is constituted by those thresholds—regarding transactions in equity instruments—which set out the 'volume caps' on pre-trade transparency waivers and deferrals, otherwise would be required in advance of their settlement. Pursuant to Article 5 MiFIR, waived trades cannot exceed certain given proportions. The exchange industry has repeatedly grieved about these limits; therefore, it would not be science-fiction to imagine the British legislator to intervene increasing the abovementioned thresholds after 'exit day'. In fact, price formation—which is a critical issue in relation to the orderly and efficient functioning of financial markets —is particularly sensitive to said limits; hence, they become extremely relevant from a systemic standpoint.

Of course, the British regulator hopes that *the UK remains attractive as a location for internationally active financial institutions*, thanks to the new regulatory burden be counteracted by the benefits to a wide range of stakeholders, in a "coordinated approach" hopefully consistent with the Government's policies. However, many UK players disagree with such "optimistic" view on the effects of the Package, and—especially in light of Brexit being formalised—are dramatically changing their plans for next years. In spite of this, the UK juridical framework remains one of the most business-friendly among advanced countries worldwide, and—although the process of implementing MiFID II, added on post-Brexit turbulences, has somehow constituted a step backwards on such "liberalism"—it has not completely forgotten this.

Hence, the FCA—in exercise of the faculties conferred to it by the Directive—has decided not to enact some *enhanced best execution requirements*, as suggested by the results of a cost/benefit analysis: in such cases, therefore, the old MiFID I provisions—issued by the Financial Service Authority (FSA), predecessor of the current body—are kept in force in the UK: *e.g.*, in relation to fund managers and UCITS management companies. Conversely, some strengthened rules apply to non-MiFID designated investment business in light of achieving a 'single sourcebook' to harmonise regulation on this matter, a goal which the industry strongly supports. The issues where MiFID II rules do apply outside their scope are precisely enumerated by the FCA:

- **inducements** in relation to research, something which is *consistent with the scope of application of our existing use of dealing commission rules* and, thus, makes 'discretionary investment managers' be subjected to the same rules. In fact, the goal of *ensuring value for money in spending clients' money on research* keeps its validity regardless of whether the person or the business envisaged is covered by the Directive or not;
- **client categorisation** in respect of the treatment of local authorities, for 'basic protection' should apply to them *across all of the designated investment business they undertake*;
- **disclosure requirements**, provided that they *can be inferred from the existing provisions and do not impose an additional burden*, for the purpose of creating a uniform set of information, with the result of *helping clients to compare information from different firms*;
- **independence**, in respect of *personal recommendations to retail clients in relation to non-MiFID retail investment products (such as insurance-based investments and personal pensions)*. Again, this is for harmonising purposes and in light of their positive spill-overs at a systemic level;
- **best execution**, whose standards are extended to *firms authorised under the UCITS directive*, given the saliency of such retail product; thus, they cannot be held outside the scope of application of such investor-friendly provisions. Unlike what previously declared in the *Consultation Paper* No. 16/29 (CP16/29), application to 'AIFMs, small authorised AIFMs and residual CISs' is excluded;
- **investment research**, for the FCA believes that *the production of research by non-MiFID firms raises the same regulatory risks, chiefly around conflicts of interests*, as those entities covered by MiFID;
- **product governance**, whose related provisions will be applied 'as guidance' in the case of non-MIFID designated investment businesses, because many entities actually operate both inside and outside the scope of the Directive.

Inducements are worth some additional words, as further provisions are laid down in the Policy Statement II: with a view to *managing conflicts of interest and the potential for bias in the sale of retail investment products*, the Retail Distribution Review (RDR) is maintained in respect to *adviser charging and platform rules*; moreover, *the MiFID II inducement bans for firms providing independent investment advice and portfolio management* are extended. This is a fortiori true in respect of retail clients, to which either independent or restricted advice (the latter being a personal recommendation, on a non-independent basis) cannot be provided. Moreover, firms engaged in the provision of the abovementioned services are forbidden from even accepting any commission and benefits (hence, this rule is tougher vis-à-vis the one prohibiting the retention of inducements, that actually left the intermediary free to accept and rebate them).

As far as *modifications to the minimum through policy choice* are concerned, the British regulator has decided to use its powers in order to *tailor certain obligations to the specific attributes of UK markets*. There are four main areas where the FCA has departed from the Directive:

- **client categorisation**, where the treatment of local authorities is one of the most important issues. In fact, by default they would be categorised as retail clients and, thus, enjoy the greatest level of investor protection, unless they use their eligibility as professional clients. The *Policy Statement II* encompasses some essential *criteria* with a view to *ensure that the quantitative opt-up criteria are more appropriately aligned to the structure and nature of UK local authorities, both when undertaking treasury management and pension administration activities*'. In fact, the FCA is resolved to optimise the balance between local authorities accessing financial markets, on the one hand, and the enhancement of investor protection, on the other;
- **taping**, as discretionary investment managers are charged with these rules regardless of specific situations (*an extension of scope, rather than substance*, acknowledged the FCA);
- **inducements**, where one of the critical points is that *advisory firms cannot continue to receive significant hospitality (or other inducements) from product providers* by denying any connection *with services provided to individual clients*;
- **principles for businesses** (commonly known as 'PRIN', which is the *Handbook* label for the Rules on this matter), WHICH will no more be limited to eligible counterparties in their application, unlike what the FSA had settled when implementing MiFID I.

Of course, we shall not go furtherly in detail into this: UK choices related to the rules contained in the Package are everything but definite or final, as they will likely be revised in a post-Brexit environment.

Let us now come to see how things might change after 'exit day'. Due to the astonishing development of the London Stock Exchange (even in technological terms), a salient issue when transposing the Package has been the one of AT and HFT, addressed in Section 8 of the *Handbook*. Among multiple risks, the British regulator put a particular emphasis on the fact that the messages sent by the trader to the venue generally outnumber the figure observed in case of non-algorithmic strategies. To mitigate the potential risks stemming from this, the *Handbook* has been updated with new rules regarding the market abuse regulation, with the purpose of strengthening resilience and the ability to put in place efficient controls, especially to ensure continuity in case of failing trading systems, even when large volumes are involved. Volatility, too, is extensively addressed: not only its reduction is a supreme goal, but trading venues implement some mechanisms to interrupt or terminate trading in the case of errors or some thresholds being broken. Such halting—or at least the implementation of certain restrictions—is mandatory, for an MTF or an OTF, in the case of a significant price movement. A seminal issue, related to these provisions against market disorder and instability, is represented by the 'precautionary measure' of testing algorithms. Other more detailed issues—e.g., order-to-trade ratios (OTRs), tick sizes, spread-to-tick ratio—are addressed in Sect. 8 of the *Handbook*. Although this might seem issues of minor interest from a systemic standpoint, data collected about them they are nonetheless extremely useful in order to catch the peculiarities of HFT.

In September 2016, the FCA consulted on the proposed implementation of MiFID II rules regarding—inter alia—the post-trading infrastructure. Many of the suggested amendments regarded the so-called *Conduct of Business Sourcebook* (COBS), but also the provisions in the *Handbook* about the 'recognised investment exchanges' located in the United Kingdom (UK RIEs), differentiated from 'overseas' ones (ROIEs). We may read that the former category must ensure *that satisfactory arrangements (…) are made for securing the timely discharge (…) of the rights and liabilities of the parties to transactions* on RMs operated by them, in a way mirroring Article 29^R and related EU-level secondary legislation. Transparency, non-discrimination, and investor protection are often invoked as founding principles of British rules. Some words are, also, dedicated to MiFID-compliant investment firms or CRD-compliant credit institutions, located outside the EEA, that have been regularly authorised by their NCA and operate in the UK by means of a branch: both types are endowed with the right to get *direct or remote access to or membership of any trading venue operated by the UK RIE*, and —most importantly—this must occur *on the same terms as a UK firm*. Other than being the reprise of what has been set forth in the Package, it is a clear statement that London pursues an open approach to trading venue membership by foreigners and, thus, legitimately expects the same treatment from the EU once it will have exited it, probably leaving the EEA too.

With regard to derivatives, specific provisions aimed at determining whether or not the arrangements are 'satisfactory'—are laid down pursuant to Article 29^R: first, the UK RIE must be able to demonstrate, first, the central clearing of their transactions; second, *that such transactions are submitted and accepted for clearing as quickly as technologically practicable using automated systems*. With regard to other types of transactions, the UK RIE has to disclose *the rules and practices relating to clearing and settlement*, including what is put in place with third-party persons 'for the provision of clearing and settlement services'; moreover, 'where relevant', the entity in question must highlight 'the degree of oversight' regarding the services in question. 'Arrangements' may be of really wide type: those designed for 'matching trades' and ensuring the parties' agreement 'about trade details'; those regarding 'deliveries and payments, in all relevant jurisdictions'. In fact, these systems could substantially differ from one another; yet, at a European level the TARGET2 system offers a good—though still imperfect—degree of harmonisation). Still, arrangements can be about a *procedure to detect and deal with the failure of a member to settle in accordance with its rules*, as well as the monitoring of settlement performance, or default rules and procedures.

Other prescriptions are' put in place in relation to transactions effected or cleared on the facilities of a UK RIE (without any restrictions to RMs only), including when clearing is performed by a third-party operating by such infrastructure. In these cases, 'the FCA may have regard' to the UK RIE's arrangements *for creating, maintaining and safeguarding an audit trail of transactions for at least five years* (previously, this term was in force for RMs only, being reduced to three years for different bodies) and, still, to the content of recorded information. The most important requirement, here, is that reporting occur pursuant to specific MiFIR and RTS rules. Details about the counterparties and the investment firm, as well as 'the date and manner of settlement of the transaction', must also be disclosed 'for other transactions effected on the UK recognised body's facilities'.

A fortiori in relation to the UK, which hosts the greatest European hub for their exchange, derivatives are one of the most delicate issues in the transposition of the Package and the consequences of Brexit. The second half of 2016 saw a large contraction in the volumes of exchanged derivatives, measured with the open-interest method: it seems that the referendum has noteworthy spilled over derivatives markets due to the saliency of the City of London, as a reflection of investors' concerns. By the end of 2016, compared to six months earlier—i.e. to the monetary figure recorded just one week after the referendum—, forex derivatives had shrunk by more than 20%, and interest-rate ones by nearly 30%. One year later, the former contracts had finally come back and even beyond pre-Brexit levels; the latter had not (actually, we should discount the fact that these markets are inherently volatile).

In Article 28^{R}, par. 1 (which applies to both financial and non-financial counterparties), is laid down the obligation to exchange derivatives—excluded those referred to by Articles 3 and 89 EMIR—on recognised trading venues. Anyway, every kind of platform—which may be freely chosen by the counterparties within those allowed—is mandated to admit derivatives to trading *on a non-exclusive and non-discriminatory basis* (par. 3), in clear accordance with the non-interventionist, lean approach to regulation that shapes the European juridical framework. This is a seminal part of the story: if the British regulator—once regained its law-making sovereignty—were to remove these provisions and come back to a freer exchange of derivative contracts, unbinding the market structure from said obligations, London might be able not only to retain its primacy as for such kind of trading, but to furtherly expand it by means of a notable regulatory arbitrage vis-à-vis EU-27.

Title VI^{R}—dealing with market infrastructure—is another part of the Regulation which would be hard for the UK to repeal, with or without replacement. In fact, as regards the access to CCPs and trading venues, Britain should absolutely keep the system which is already in place, in order for its 'equivalence' to be assessed by the Commission once the exit gets formalised. Indeed, there will there be an interest, for British trading venues and CCPs, to remain accessible for EU-27 counterparties and also to have themselves free access to benchmark information and licences held by non-British persons. Nowadays, the degree of interconnection shaping the financial system at a global level would not allow for different solutions, in which data be ringfenced inside a national realm. There is mutual interest, for CCPs and trading venues located everywhere, to be able to communicate and exchange information with their peer entities worldwide. Of course, the extreme hypothesis of London leaving the EEA while remaining a member of the European Free Trade Association (EFTA), combined with MiFIR provisions being terminated, would still be compatible with these rules being kept in force, if a UK–EU final deal encompassed provisions in such direction. Anyway, apart from specific issues, it is clear that post-Brexit issues will necessarily pay significant attention to the concerns arising in respect of the circulation of data and the exchange of information, which is undoubtedly one of the most relevant *macro*-themes of contemporary world.

As regards product intervention—dealt with in Title VII^{R}—, Article 40^{R} encompasses a list of *ESMA temporary intervention powers* which on 'exit day' will become no more enforceable toward British persons in any scenario, including the unlikely one of the UK retaining its membership of the Single Market via the EEA. What is much more significant in relation to a post-Brexit environment is undoubtedly Title VIII^{R}, where several issues regarding the cross-border provision (performance) of investment services (activities) are explicitly addressed, including those related to passporting. From a rational standpoint, there should be no doubt that British investment firms will be granted such passport like before 'exit day': conversely, the reverse scenario might gain likelihood only in a no-deal scenario, entailing a definite UK–EU break-up.

Theoretically, however, the changes brought to the British financial legislation post Brexit, if too deregulation-oriented, could even prompt the EU Commission to deny its equivalence decision in certain cases. Alternatively, if such equivalence were anyway granted in the immediate aftermath of the formal "divorce", a review might still end up with the Decision being withdrawn in the following years. Clearly, everything depends upon each party's determination not to cut its ties with the other side.

References

Banca d'Italia. (2018). *Relazione annuale sul 2017*, May 2018.
Banco de España. (2018). *Financial stability report*, May 2018.
Bank of England. (2018). *Financial stability report*, June 2018.
Banque de France. (2018a). *Annual report 2017*, June 2018.
Banque de France. (2018b). *Financial stability review. Non-bank finance: Trends and challenges*, April 2018.
Batsaikhan, U., & Demertzis, M. (2018). *Financial literacy and inclusive growth in the European Union* (No. 25536). Bruegel.
Deutsche Bundesbank. (2017). *2017 Financial stability review*, November 2017.

European Securities Markets Authority. (2017). *Q&As on investor protection topics*, updated over time.

Ferguson, N. (2018). *The square and the tower: Networks and power, from the Freemasons to Facebook*. London: Penguin.

Martín-Oliver, A., Ruano, S., & Salas-Fumás, V. (2017). The fall of Spanish cajas: Lessons of ownership and governance for banks. *Journal of Financial Stability, 33,* 244–260.

Organization for Economic Cooperation and Development. (2016). *OECD/INFE international survey of adult financial literacy competencies*, October 2016.

Persson, P. (2018). Attention manipulation and information overload. *Behavioural Public Policy, 2*(1), 78–106.

Röpke, W. (1941). Grundfragen rationeller Wirtschaftspolitik. *Swiss Journal of Economics and Statistics, 77*(I), 101–112.

Università Bocconi, & EIEF. (2013). By Various Authors. *Idee per la crescita. Le opzioni e le proposte per ritornare a crescere*, April 2013.

Chapter 8
Regulation Meets Business: The Effects on the Investment Industry

Abstract The chapter discusses the expected impact of the Package on the financial industry. Also, this is done in a comparison to MiFID I. While the latter was widely welcomed as a modernizing novelty, nowadays both investors and the industry tend to worry about the 'legislative flooding' witnessed during the last decade, whose capacity to fulfil its goals deserves a thorough analysis. By looking at how product governance and intervention are going to be materially enforced, we debate some of the greatest concerns for the financial intermediaries affected by the Package: from the rise of additional compliance costs—mainly with regard to best execution and transparency requirements—to the consequences of wider disclosure to clients; from the change in distribution channels up to the duty of separating research-related revenues from different ones. In particular, we discuss these issues in connection with other seminal pieces of EU legislation in the fields of insurance and asset management, highlighting that several entities are likely to have their business model completely overhauled in the near future.

8.1 The Challenges Ahead

Looking at the extent of the Package's effects onto financial intermediaries, we would reasonably ask whether the whole of the intervention undertaken by the EU legislator has revealed to be adequate or not, perhaps even turning out being counterproductive. Would things have gone better, had MiFID I been kept in place? For the moment being, there is not enough track-record, data or reported extreme events to answer such question. The way in which the Package has been shaped, along with the weight of the resulting regulatory burden, may well be questioned. Anyway, it is strikingly evident that MiFID I was very well-intentioned, yet probably too soft-handed to reduce information asymmetries in the investment industry and build the necessary "safety net" against the financial system's imbalances.

Notwithstanding that the first version of the MiFID had been in force for less than one year when the trouble came, it proved remarkably weak and, most dramatically, obsolete in relation to the main roots of the crisis. The world in which MiFID I had been conceived substantially disappeared over a few weeks.

M. Comana et al., *The MiFID II Framework*,
https://doi.org/10.1007/978-3-030-12504-2_8

As underlined in Chap. 4, market fragmentation was notably high: although it was actually the side effect of the liberalisation carried out by repealing the 'concentration rule', consequences went further than intended. In fact, the GFC drove many transactions out of trading venues in favour of dark pools and similar OTC platforms, where many securities started being exchanged as well as on RMs and MTFs (where originally listed). Commodity markets rang the most serious alarms. The EU legislator envisioned some possible solutions: position limits, circuit brokers at venue-level, a set of reporting obligation to be fulfilled in respect of NCAs, relevant powers attributed to EU-wide supervisors, and more effective rules to grant harmonisation and third-party access.

If anyone intended this as a blow to change occurring "normally" on markets, it would not be inaccurate at all. In fact, by gazing at the failures exposed by the GFC, many started thinking that technology had someway gone too far. While proposing new constraints upon investment firms and their operations, Brussels determined that the so-called "market discipline" should have been enhanced by strengthening investor rights. Hence, many entities in the financial sector appear as constrained by a twofold layer of tight regulation, both above (supervisors) and below (stakeholders and customers), much more than in the past. In some cases—as we are going to see—this entails an overhaul of business models, either indirectly rising from the new rules or explicitly pursued by legislation. Compliance costs are expected to face a substantive increase. Whether it attains to CG provisions applying to the boards of investment firms, or rather deals with reporting obligations related to the operations carried out, we expect large amounts of time, monetary resources, and human capital being mobilised in the first years of the Package's enforcement. New subjects have been created within the realm of market infrastructure, and the pursuit of greater transparency has been the major rationale inspiring the reform. Whether this objective will become reality is going to be under scrutiny over next years.

In order to get a size of the great extent of the Package, a study by BCG and Markit (2016) claimed that the business model of financial intermediaries will be strongly impacted by said legislation, along with many other industry fundamentals shifting such as: change in the revenue flow, data management and professional skills, newcomers' entrance with disruptive business models and cost structures.

If we look at macroeconomic trends, those with which the investment industry has to cope are quite stunning, as compared to market conditions of just 10 or 15 years ago: in fact, the cut-off point—from an economic history viewpoint—is the GFC outbreak. The hystéresis in volatility after the 2008 crash has given new life to passive investments, or others pegged to passive ones, especially in the fixed-income segment. This is seemingly the outcome of very low-fee policies: in fact, commissions have been curbed in the fixed-income segment much more significantly than elsewhere. Moreover, the EU suffers from structurally low profitability: very few European funds were able to beat their benchmark, albeit this might actually be interpreted by stating that an investment undertaken within the EU has better prospects vis-à-vis one undertaken overseas, in terms of room for performance improvement. Low-cost funds have benefitted from the GFC, whereas others have suffered heavy divestitures.

Worldwide growth is undeniable in 'asset under management' (AuM) terms; and it is set to continue at least in the short-to-medium term. In this realm, much of growth has to be attributed to the "pioneers" of the sector, which have already reached significant sizes: yet, there might be enough room for newcomers. MiFID II and related legislations have to address this foreseeable reshaping of financial markets, which will likely have a large impact on intermediaries by changing—at the same time or even before—the customers' investment behaviour. 'Specialisation' is the key. It might be centred around the services provided or the products concerned, as well as it might be pursued by outsourcing every activity, or only core ones, or none.

Competition, however, is increasingly global: internationalisation is not only a matter of fact for many investment firms but, also, a viable strategy for many of those which are currently trailing behind. Given the soaring cost-intensity, economies of scale might well be thought as the solution: of course, the Single Market—which somewhat extends itself to non-EU countries endowed with a prosperous financial system, like Switzerland—provides multiple opportunities for the pursuit of internationalisation strategies, given the wide array of activities subject to mutual recognition as well as to the principle—rooted in the free provision of services enshrined in the Treaties—that this can be done with or without the establishment of a branch.

Some other *macro-* trends are worth considering when discussing the likely development of the industry in an environment governed by the Package. For instance, a significant intergenerational transfer of assets is expected to occur over the medium terms (around 15 years), raising many questions about what will come next. In fact, millennials are very hard to describe in terms of their investment profile: other than a vague preference for impact investing (that is, social-oriented, environment-friendly, or similar kinds of undertakings), as they are quite fickle in their decisions. Finally, "direct investments" are growing in segments like real-estate and private equity: while beneficial to larger investment firms, this is an inconvenient to smaller wealth managers, private bankers, and so-called 'family offices'.

Hence, signals are very contrasting one another, and substantially fail to draw up a single picture. Technological progress is neither always, nor everywhere, complemented by changing investors' preferences, which in certain EU countries tend to stick to very traditional, old-fashioned products. Even private equity, which in some large but more fragile EU economies like Italy and Spain is experiencing noteworthy growth, cannot be considered as a "modern" way of allocating financial surpluses. In short, the shape of European markets envisioned by the Package's legislator is dominated by smaller subjects which are customers of large intermediaries, the latter being internally broken down into more numerous divisions, departments, or entities within a group, and each one specialised. Price-making, even by the most powerful players, will likely be more limited than in the past; therefore, competition is expected to face a widespread surge. If the Package will not depart too much from its intentions, this may still be achieved. As we are going to see, however, there are no few obstacles.

8.2 Product Governance and Intervention

Given the wide array of post-GFC reforms passed by the European Union, many of the effects upon intermediaries can be properly understood by looking not just at the provisions encompassed by the single specific EU piece of legislation, but rather at their mutual interactions. This is the case of the principles underpinning the whole wave of financial reforms; namely, according to Di Noia's (2017) classification:

1. product governance;
2. product intervention;
3. relationships between intermediaries and their clients.

In fact, they apply not only to the Package's recipients but, also, to some subjects left out of it, thanks to the interaction between said legislation and UCITS V Directive, AIFMD, EMIR, IDD and other pieces of European legislation.

To understand the mechanism by which the first two abovementioned pillars work—and leaving the third one to be discussed alone, within the broader investor protection framework, we should first underline the Package's distinction between 'manufacturers' and 'distributors', not always ending up charging financial firms with requirements consistent with their actual activity and, thus, potentially representing a first source of market distortion. For a subject to be regarded as a manufacturer, it must play a role in the "concept" of the product, that is:

- assessing which financial purpose to serve;
- designing how it technically works;
- putting in place the operations of a primary issuance;
- advising corporate counterparties on such tasks.

Almost residually, what is beyond primary issuance—regardless of whether it gets carried out directly or, conversely, a different entity is advised on it—is seen as distributor's job, the latter's main task clearly being an involvement into secondary issuances, i.e. the offer or sale to third parties.

From the classification above, therefore, certain activities like underwriting instruments upon their issuance or even prompting institutional investors to join such offering, are still regarded as the 'manufacturer' segment of the process. Hence, the scope of distribution turns out being a relatively narrow one. In light of the burdensome rules envisaged for the latter ones, in addition to those which apply to both, reaching 'end clients'—as prescribed in Recital 71[D]—might become increasingly expensive. However, while distributors face the heaviest provisions in terms of compliance costs, manufacturers are mandated to fulfil one of the most delicate and challenging duties of the entire process: that is, correctly identifying the 'target market for end clients'. Such obligation has been intended by the EU legislator in a dynamic manner, rather than just a static one: therefore, after an initial assessment (which requires much deeper expertise vis-à-vis that needed to administer the suitability and appropriateness tests), the provider of investment services—i.e. the manufacturer—must not only treat the product with a rigorous internal process of internal screening to assess whether it is worth manufacturing but, also, conduct a periodic review by monitoring its absolute performance as well as the target market's reaction and the financial results achieved by investors, which the Package entitles to be advised on their own 'best interest'.

This is reflective of a highly wide-ranging purpose: since the legislator has set forth as an objective to close all the pre-existing regulatory loopholes, with respect to either instruments or venues or transaction reporting. Therefore, the Package tends to spread its effects well beyond the investment industry, and effects themselves are strikingly more coercive than those of MiFID I. In terms of 'product governance', in fact, the role attributed to intermediaries has profoundly changed, such that they now have to carry out much more activities—to address far wider concerns—than those previously envisaged. This is the result of the Package's wording: as compared to its predecessor, while apparently devoting few additional provisions to investor protection, it actually shapes an environment wherein the providers (performers) of investment services (activities) have to openly take care of their clients' financial well-being, though European integration has not already come to the point of creating the same criminal law framework (which has always been a subject strictly left to Member States' autonomy).

As we have already highlighted in Chap. 6, the kind of task that intermediaries are mandated to perform mirrors a cradle-to-grave approach and, most importantly, entails a "dynamic" idea of protection, which must be ensured—by looking at clients' financial condition, investment objectives and horizons, current and future needs, general risk-return profile, and so on—not at a single point in time, but for the whole length of the contract, until it expires. Even before 3 January 2018, legislative changes had already proven—in several countries worldwide—that much damage to mainly retail investors come from a misplaced assessment of underlying risks, for which both manufacturers and distributors have often been held liable. MiFID II has strengthened these obligations: in the meanwhile, in the aftermath of the GFC, several Member States have either hardened criminal sanctions, or taken resources from public accounts to refund aggrieved parties, often deemed not to be guilty of their financial ruin. Moreover, banks have been forced to join the their respective Bank Resolution Funds (BRFs) under BRRD, for a target amount equal to 1% of total banking assets at a national level, with the ultimate goal of setting up an wider Single Resolution Fund (SRF), holding the same proportion of resources as referred to the whole of the countries adhering to the European Banking Union. This raises the question of where a bank's trouble comes from, how it should be addressed (by the intermediary itself, external regulators, or the industry), and which effects has on clients to which it provides investment services.

Just by asking these formally BRRD-related questions, we might have a clue on how far MiFID II provisions tend to go, as well as on the depth of concerns they raise. This should prompt us debating whether, in order to limit the opportunity for regulators to be in the limelight with respect to product governance or intervention, an overhaul of the industry's structure could be advisable. This would require a sort of separation between commercial and investment banking, though for reasons associated not exclusively with investor protection but, also, the defence of taxpayers' money. In fact, the latter is somehow involved in rescuing a troubled bank: the BRRD does not rule out such possibility, which is even possible before resolution tools be employed (see Article 32). This urges us—and should urge the EU legislator as well—to consider that, given the existence of deposit insurance schemes, which Brussels is willing to furtherly implement as a pillar of the European Banking Union (EBU), it is clearly possible that taxpayers' money be used to refund those who have been harmed by the risky investment banking operations carried out by a credit institution. Outside the EBU, bail-out interventions are still allowed and relatively frequent. In light of this, a separation of the two functions should be regarded as an idea worth evaluating: not only to protect depositors or retail investors, which take upon themselves some uncertainty, but mainly to preserve the wealth of taxpayers or the stakeholders of other banks, as they might be called to make systematic contributions to rainy-day funds. Of course, implementing a separation between the two types of institutions would require that regulators take a step backwards, for much of the rationale underlying their role would have been eradicated. The same result could be achieved by repealing any deposit insurance, a fortiori considering that it is widely regarded as the main source of moral hazard by a bank's management (more recently: Anginer et al. 2018). This is because insured depositors would give up exerting due "discipline" and, since the institution would not have to pay anything to harmed customers, even shareholders would leave managers significantly higher freedom than in absence of any guarantee.

Under the present framework, instead, the Package's enactment of product governance and intervention is likely to yield the most burdensome result in the history of European financial legislation. Manufacturers and distributors will have to strengthen their mutual relationship basically in three main areas:

1. collecting data on their operations;
2. undertaking a thorough verification of the information;
3. transmit it to relevant authorities.

Only the latter of these functions could be performed by a single entity alone, which deals with its customers to perform just a single activity; the other two, conversely, would be enhanced by the cooperation with all involved parties. The duty to act "for customers' sake" is so compelling that the manufacturer might not be able to abide by it in case it did not know the distributor's policies, and vice versa. Whenever multiple entities be involved in a service provided or a product exchanged—and, a fortiori, the activity be performed on a cross-border basis—there are additional concerns to be taken into account. In short, from the end client's perspective, risks tend to accrue and, thus, would require stronger protection.

In order to ensure it, relevant coordination duties have been charged upon NCAs, which is to balance the powers they are now endowed with. If intermediaries do not abide by regulatory prescriptions, according to Article 40^R, par. 1, consequences might be highly detrimental: instruments (including structured deposits), as well as financial practices, can be banned from being marketed, distributed, or sold. Since this rule—with the specifications that we are going to detail—is invoked by the legislator as a general principle, even the most plain-vanilla investments might be subject to restrictive measures implemented by supervisors, in case it appeared to hurt those who undertake them. In the aftermath of the GFC, there has been a widespread tilt toward investors' risk-aversion, but the actual riskiness in the financial industry has not narrowed by a comparable size. Coupled with the fact that financial education is not improving everywhere but still stagnates in some EU Member States (e.g., Italy, which is also characterized by one of the most higher level of private savings), that "trust" which constitutes the keystone of financial system might well be endangered even in resepct of plain-vanilla securities and contracts. Because of such threat, very well-established supply chains are ominously forced to change. In addition to this, the EU legislator—in abidance by the principle of subsidiarity, which shapes the *acquis communautaire* as a whole—has envisaged that NCAs, first, have to act in case any systemic danger be detected, ESMA's intervention being residual.

Unfortunately, not all NCAs have in place supervisory practices and regulatory standards consistent with those of the microprudential authority, as long as the goal of a full and effective EU-wide harmonisation is still very far away. Hence, intermediaries in some countries might have to face lower regulatory risk of this kind vis-à-vis their foreign peers. Of course, cross-border institutions would live in much greater uncertainty: while the most general rule is that the intervention carried out in a Member State by the local NCA must be applied in other countries to the same instrument or activity (Article 18^{D}, par. 9), exceptions are still possible under 'exceptional circumstances' (Recital 69^{D}, though not reprised by any Article) which ESMA is called to detail by means of RTSs. Once ascertained that *the proposed action addresses a significant investor protection concern or a threat to the orderly functioning and integrity of financial markets or commodity markets or to the stability of the whole or part of the financial system in the Union* (Article 40^{R}, par. 2), the microprudential authority is entitled to act only if no adequate tool is available under EU jurisdiction and the NCA has failed to address the problem.

8.3 Best Execution

In the survey conducted by BCG and Markit (2016), trading teams were asked about their major concerns related to different asset classes, in turn grouped into a couple main categories: fixed-income versus equity. People in the former group answered by revealing that liquidity, sales, and pricing had substantially the same relevance; conversely, those in the latter highlighted to be more concerned about liquidity provisions, while attributing little importance to pricing. Detailed responses are available in Fig. 8.1.

Looking at the best execution framework, we should notice that we have moved from an 'obligation of means' in MiFID I onto an 'obligation of result' in MiFID II,

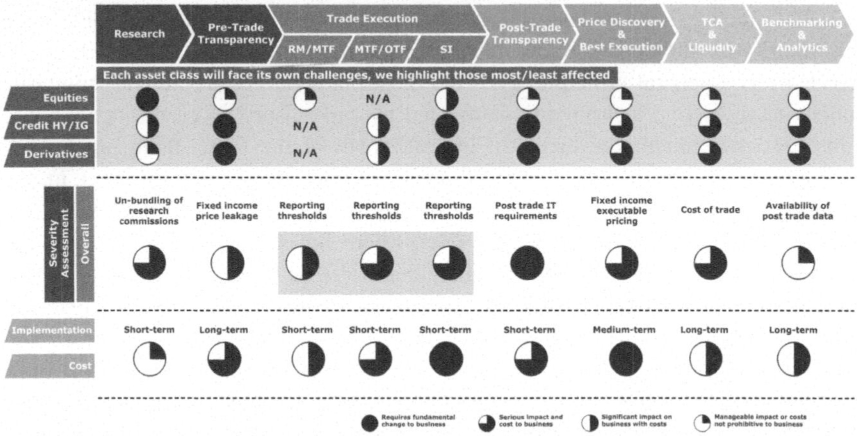

Fig. 8.1 The impact of MiFID II on different parts of the value chain in financial markets and different types of instruments. *Source* BCG and Markit (2016)

as the 'steps' to take, which previously had to be 'reasonable' ones, have now become 'sufficient'. Furthermore, choosing 'sufficient' instead of 'necessary' is a betrayal of the EU legislator's liberal background: nowadays, best execution is required to be absolutely ensured, whatever the cost may be. The provision mandating to measure the 'likelihood of the execution' is among the most salient ones encompassed by the Package: hence, investment firms should analyse all trades submitted by brokers on their behalf (which is a particularly burdensome measure).

Moreover, note BCG and Markit (2016), the material implementation of best execution requirements, as for fixed-income and OTC derivatives, may be quite difficult: in fact, many times there are no specific orders submitted, as *managers are often indifferent between many bonds and trade according to the available merchandise they are offered*. Hence, the dealer-based (i.e. quote-driven) model for exchange platforms is the one which best fits them, rather than the order-driven one. In practice, looking at the application of the best execution principle, this is no assurance that the price finally achieved is the best possible one; therefore, wider availability of information—that is, greater transparency across multiple sources and venues—is the solution to such malpractice, however expensive it might be to get.

Liquidity is another best-execution-related issue which casts several doubts on the Package's provisions being able to deliver on their promises. Bonds are becoming increasingly less fungible: if we look at the thresholds (whose consistency is somewhat disputable) recommended by the EU Commission starting from 2018, only 549 out of potential corporate bonds met the requirements, ESMA assessed. Third-party analyses photographed the same dismal evidence: although refinancing bonds right before their expiration is a good thing for liquidity, the dealers' behaviour has been a blow to it, for they *reduce their inventory in response to higher capital requirements* (BCG and Markit 2016).

If we consider the US market, by regressing the number of days in which a bond is quoted against those in which it is traded, BCG and Markit (2016) obtained quite alarming results which do not allow for any optimism with respect to Europe, where liquidity is even lower: in American bond markets, a hypothetical 1:1 ratio is very far from reality; conversely, most of these securities are traded less than 50 days a year, mainly driven by changes in market sentiment triggered by some particular events. The current trend, as acknowledged by said enquiry, is that bond investors are shifting towards ETFs, as they value the certainty of execution much more than in the past. As highlighted by BCG and Markit (2016), by looking at data on bond issuances in the US, the amount issued but not underwritten has shown huge liquidity gaps between 2003 and 2016, though higher post GFC and almost null during an overhang occurred when the crisis hit, making bonds much more appealing than riskier securities. Conversely, over the same time horizon, the surge in ETFs is empirically undeniable, and even started right upon the GFC outbreak. In the USA, the 2010 Dodd-Frank Act has yielded similar results to that of the Package as for derivatives: in fact, looking at interest rate swaps, the percentage of those centrally cleared has kept growing after the EMIR-related spike in 2013 (73%, compared to 54% the year before), reaching 83% in mid-2016.

Furthermore, changes triggered by the *Securities Financing Transactions Regulation* (SFTR, No. 2365/2015), in force since January 2017 and amending EMIR, have to be taken into account. They encompass a stringent timing for reporting derivatives transactions, still regulating collateral and other relevant features of those contracts, including the collection, organisation, and disclosure of related data. Derivatives trading requires a more detailed insight onto the likely effects of MiFID II, albeit their extent cannot clearly be compared to that of EMIR. First of all, the impact of the likely shift from OTC markets onto trading venues is of great extent: in order to sustain that flow, market participants will be forced to undertake relevant investments; nevertheless, as trading across venues is much more expensive—from the investors' point of view—than doing it OTC, it will be possible that the roles of dealers and brokers get shrunk, as larger players prefer their orders to directly flow through venues.

As regards clearing, margins for uncleared derivatives applied to interest rate and credit derivatives have been significantly lifted. Starting on 1 September 2020, it will be annually reduced, leaving some hopes that the liquidity squeeze is just temporary and will soon be reverted. Moreover, the composition of the industry is somehow changing. For instance, as far as single-name CDSs are concerned, banks are already retreating from the clearing and settlement business conducted OTC, with a resulting decline in exchanged volumes. Conversely, for CDSs as a whole, volumes transacted on 'swaps execution facilities' (SEFs), which are the US alternative to OTC markets for that kind of derivatives, have almost doubled between 2014Q1 and 2016Q1, in contrast to a sharp decline (almost by half) in bilateral markets, driving the comprehensive figure upwards. From this point of view, MiFID II seems to have been not only self-fulfilling before its entry into force, but even in a beneficial manner. However, if we narrow our analysis up to single-name CDSs, we should note that the most liquid bucket in which they can be broken down has suffered a dramatic fall from a score equal to 142 in 2014 to 101 in 2015 and 65 in 2016; the other buckets have improved, but the least liquid one has still plummeted. Taking everything into account, we should acknowledge that the approval of MiFID II has undoubtedly reshaped derivatives markets; yet, we should look at how players have implemented the Package's provisions, rather than just reacting to their passage.

Under the Package, clearing definitely becomes a fundamental part of the infrastructure, not just an ancillary one. Transparency is deemed to be inherent to the well-functioning of markets and the efficiency of trades from a market-wide perspective, rather than just an issue of investor protection with mainly *micro*-aspects to be considered. Technology is currently spreading throughout different kinds of platforms and the Package should not be expected to have any visible effect on such underlying, historical phenomenon. In fact, with reference to a survey conducted by Markit and reported in BCG and Markit (2016), there is also a good degree of compliance between the current 'transaction cost analysis' (TCA) infrastructure and MiFID II provisions (72.1% of answers), though they are used pre-trade much more in equities (47.8%) than elsewhere (39.2% in forex transactions, 30.9% in fixed income, and just 26.7% in derivatives).

In conclusion, strictly "regulatory" adaptation is going to be far more expensive than merely "technological" one, as long as the Package has crystallised some ongoing trends in the industry. As noted in BCG and Markit (2016), making an informed decision when trading in derivatives is not an easy task: especially if seeking a thorough analysis ranging across various products and asset classes, *in many firms, this is unchartered territory*. But the drive for front-office efficiency and alpha generation [Jensen's 'alpha' denoting the idiosyncratic profitability of an asset] will make it increasingly common.

8.4 Advisory

It is no doubt that advisory is one of the investment industry's areas that are going to be hit the most by the Package's rules. Similar to the activities involving a large role for research (that we shall discuss later on), the change ahead is not merely on the operations carried out on a day-by-day basis, nor it only deals with compliance costs and the regulatory risk to be managed: conversely, it will entail an overhaul of the business model. In fact, advisory will rely increasingly less on that intuitus personae which has characterised the advisor-client relationship hitherto, and increasingly more on blue-ocean strategies which entail battling with competitors on an international arena.

As we have seen, the ban of the manufacturer rebating monetary inducements to the distributor—though limited to non-independent advisors—is one of the major innovations carried out by means of the Package. Although some domestic jurisdictions have tried to mitigate MiFID II provisions on this subject, their reversal would have openly betrayed the European legislation's esprit. As a result, such an unlevel playing field between EU Member States would have been created such that the final outcome would have inevitably been a formal infringement procedure by the EU Commission, also in light of how salient this rule is for investor protection purposes. Hence, it must be taken as carved in stone, though one might still be unconvinced that benefits exceed negative spill-overs. Like for research-related provisions, consequences are not so easy to envisage, given the paradigm shift involved.

In light of the new framework, and considering together the rules on both research and advisory, one logical outcome would be that advisory stricto sensu, intended as research on possible investment opportunities conducted on behalf of a customer, is expected to increase its relevance over time. Rather than encompassing research within the proper execution of the service, investment firms—as well as other financial intermediaries involved in advisory services—will have to perform it as a separate, stand-alone activity. Therefore, it has to receive ad hoc monetary valorisation, i.e. a specific price paid in exchange for the intermediary's business of acquiring knowledge on market trends, technical analysis, design of a set of investment opportunities, or choices regarding already-ongoing investments, just to be prospected to the customer, with or without an ultimate recommendation on the decision to make. If research and advisory per se get unbundled both formally (in terms of payment) and substantially (in terms of operations), the latter option—whether or not prompting the customer to make a choice—will likely lose part of its relevance. In fact, without the mandatory establishment of 'research payment accounts' (RPAs) envisaged by Delegated Directive No. 2017/565, the presence (absence) of a specific recommendation, as well as the degree of detail on market insights provided by the intermediary, would have marked the difference between 'investment advice', which is an investment service (activity) pursuant to MiFID II, vis-à-vis 'general advice', which is just ancillary. If research is compensated per se, this will likely give an incentive to the parties for arranging research-only agreements, leaving advice alone. Of course, the latter's content—'investment' versus 'general'—will determine, at least in "big picture" terms, the structure of the output delivered to the customer.

MiFID II itself helps clarifying the content of the two types of advice, though by plainly restating what MiFID I had already envisaged. The 'general' one is specified in the Directive itself (Article 4[D], par. 1, no. 4), along with other definitions. It entails *the provision of personal recommendations to a client, either upon its request or at the initiative of the investment firm, in respect of one or more transactions relating to financial instruments*. Hence, one major characteristic is highlighted: first, a very strong intuitus personae, for such a service cannot be envisaged without a 'recommendation', nor without having a single customer as the recipient rather than, potentially, the general public. If the latter were the case, the analysis conducted would be unspecific and offer an insight on publicly-available information, rather than on the customer's practices covered by industrial secrecy or some other kind of protection against dissemination. In other terms, 'general' advice would be about how a generic firm would have to behave in case it faced a given situation, with no regard for the customer's conditions: otherwise, it would be consistent with an investor-protective framework which requires—inter alia—to perform the suitability and appropriateness tests. Therefore, the intuitus personae envisaged by such MiFID II definition would be better intended extensively: i.e. as referred not merely to the subject demanding advice but, also, to the potentially concerned operations (intuitus actionis, we might say). Who takes the initiative is of no importance, however relevant it may be for transparency and investor-protective purposes; nor is the object of the service, which can be either a single investment (the intermediary may give a suggestion on every aspect of the decision to be taken: either an, quomodo, or quando) or a choice within a set of multiple investment opportunities.

Instead, 'general advice' is defined in Annex I[D], Section B, as encompassing two distinct yet very similar activities:

> an advice to undertakings on capital structure, industrial strategy and related matters and advice and services relating to mergers and the purchase of undertakings; or, alternatively, investment research and financial analysis or other forms of general recommendation relating to transactions in financial instruments.

This is a much deeper specification than that of investment advice, for it describes the concerned activities. Yet, it is crystal-clear that the same exact business, wherever performed with the above-referred intuitus, would automatically be regarded as MiFID-compliant investment service or activity. Of course, the extent of Package's rules that do apply to ancillary services is much narrower, such that intermediaries have a clear incentive to keep their advice as general as possible. Since there has been no deviation from MiFID I, it is quite unlikely that financial firms experience a significant change vis-à-vis the past, but the overhaul in the research industry is a "black swan" potentially able to trigger a definite shift from 'investment' to 'general' advice.

In fact, the two substantially diverge in terms of pricing: at least theoretically, the latter is cheaper not only due to the less extensive technicality entailed but, also, because of the significantly lower compliance costs associated (as a result of a lighter regulatory burden). Thus, as long as advisors are mandated to clearly denote the costs of research, providing the 'general' version would likely enhance their competitiveness and appeal to customers. In addition to this, we should consider that, since this kind of advice is more standardised, different intermediaries, on behalf of different customers, would produce similar reports if asked to analyse the same industry's trends. Therefore, a subject able to deliver a better product would increasingly create its own niche in the market, to be duly exploited in terms of revenues: from a very theoretical standpoint, the structure of the general advice industry might be seen as a monopolistic competition, whereas investment advice has always been concentrated in the hands of a few big players. Given the unbundling of research from execution per se, concentration in the research segment is expected to decrease along with MiFID II rules being enacted.

In other words, advisory is set to face something like a "flight to quality", differentiating research not only along with industry's segments, client categorisation, or the type of investment concerned, but—in particular—providing a tailor-made service to each customer, regardless of the required degree of detail and the aim of the advice. Such trend would be even stronger in case of advisory provided 'on an independent basis', whose characteristics strikingly reduce the distance between advisors and their customers. In fact, since the former are not bound to any 'issuer or provider' of investment products, as well as in light of the ban on inducements (descending from the former), they would have a clear incentive to pursue more "aggressive" marketing policies vis-à-vis those that tied agents tend to carry out on behalf of their employers, which might be frightened by reputational risk rapidly spreading onto other clients. In fact, the two categories of advisors are going to give rise to a couple distinct business models and operating criteria, subject to sharply different regulatory regimes. Also, the two models are going to diverge as far as human resources are concerned: if we look at distributors (mainly banks), regardless of whether they coincide with manufacturers, independent advice will likely be provided by a larger amount of back-office employees than front-office ones, whereas non-independent ones will display higher commercial "boldness" toward customers and, thus, prefer front-office resources.

Moreover, it is reasonable to expect that the former category, once deprived of inducement income, will charge higher fees on those which they advise, and there still is great uncertainty on the market-wide effect of prices being shifted upwards. Notwithstanding the current expansion in the investment industry as a whole (something with clear systemic, macroeconomic roots, rather than idiosyncratic to that sector), a decline—whose magnitude is actually hard to determine—should not be ruled out for years to come. To mitigate risks, and for an investor-protective purposes, the EU legislator has tried to arrange some measures aimed at preventing such "aggressive" pricing or marketing policies to be implemented by investment firms when providing advice. Hence, in MiFID II is indiscriminately envisaged that every party must serve the clients' best interest, as said above. We cannot say a priori whether this might suffice or, conversely, represent a fig leaf unable to avoid the betrayal of the Directive's rationale, once applied to reality. Observing the industry over future years will tell us whether tied agents have been used as a scapegoat (such that the outcome is even worse), or the relationship between advisors and their clients is actually improved.

The EU Commission is currently proposing rules to harmonise the tool of class action, which is now encompassed by several jurisdictions and is often deemed to be applicable to the financial sector. Though comparisons will not be possible for each country (but, clearly, only for those already admitting such legal procedure), the dynamics of class actions against the providers of investment advice will give us an idea about the success of MiFID II provisions. Of course, establishing direct causal relationships between the latter ones and the path of lawsuits filed for by customers against agents would present the utmost difficulty, as many other variables should be taken into account. For instance, further analysis is due as for the advantages related to the effort undertaken to act in the client's 'best interest'. In fact, large advisors have higher downside risk than small ones, for they basically have more at stake; conversely, the latter have higher upside one, as they might show their expertise by getting increasing marginal benefits (at least, up to a certain level), whereas large advisors are often very well known, their expertise is widely known and, therefore, they would benefit a little from providing a better service.

The business model in the industry is largely expected to change, especially with respect to advisory provided on an independent basis. In fact, having the client's interest as almost the first objective to be pursued—even before fee maximisation for the advisor's own sake—yields relevant consequences in practical terms. The overall effect would be that said service be ultimately aligned with a broad array of MiFID II requirements: above all, assessing the client's suitability to that kind of investment, first, and then the appropriateness of taking that specific financial decision in that specific moment. There is no way of escaping them apart from explicit waivers encompassed by the Directive itself. The result would be a compensation structure modelled by services, rather than products, which is somewhat the financial industry equivalent of the overall economic trend of the tertiary sector growing at the expense of the secondary one. In fact, the regulatory burden is substantially getting transferred from manufacturers onto distributors: just by reading its provisions, MiFID II will partly appease that spontaneous recent trend, partly enhance it. As a result, of course, it will likely keep mounting.

Yet, there is no industry consensus regarding the future of advisory, either independent or not. In fact, notwithstanding the clear orientation provided by the Package's rules, there also are some constraints—arising from the contrast between law and the underlying reality—which could eventually impair the change which one might reasonably envision. The supreme warning deals with the cost and the timing of implementation. The Package as a whole has not had an easy life when coming to its transposition into Member States' domestic jurisdictions; and the debate over advisory has been particularly harsh in many countries, due to the potentially extremely wide-ranging consequences of the new rules. First of all, the severe limits imposed to inducements have made revenue forecast to fall, something which the industry is particularly concerned about. Moreover, the likely extension of products and services to be provided—strongly advocated by the Package, as we have already highlighted—hardens the contrast between two "groups" within the investment industry: on the one hand, dimensionally smaller yet more numerous entities, wherein manufacturers and distributors tend to coincide; on the other, larger institutions increasingly moving toward specialisation on either issuance or marketing of them. Both groups may well encompass any kind of advisory. In the former, tied agents hired by "universal" investment firms will likely compete with independent subjects willing to skim the best opportunities to be prospected to customers. In the latter, a sharp divide is likely to arise: while manufacturers will strive to convince independent agents to recommend the securities they issue, distributors will keep needing to recruit tied agents in order to enhance their business, with the remarkable disadvantage that—due to the squeeze in inducement-related income—they will have less cash-on-hand vis-à-vis the past to cover such expenses.

From an organisational point of view, the separation between independent and non-independent advisory is not an easy task. In particular, other than the ban on inducements (Article 24^D, par. 7, letter *b*), another feature of 'independence' might be extremely burdensome to face: namely, the obligation that investment firms providing advice obey the following principle:

> assess a sufficient range of financial instruments available on the market which must be sufficiently diverse with regard to their type and issuers or product providers to ensure that the client's investment objectives can be suitably met (Article 24^D, par. 7, letter *a*);

without being limited to commercially related parties, intended as those to which the firm is bound by 'legal or economic relationships'. If an entity, though promoting its activity as 'provided on an independent basis', had actually been used to issue recommendations by giving preference to certain investments over different ones because of an established partnership with the manufacturer, it might have to struggle in order to meet the abovementioned MiFID II definition and, thus, be able to keep the likely competitive advantage associated with the 'independent' label (a fortiori, considering that even non-independent advisors will be bound to the pursuit of clients' interests).

Finally, a very concerning flaw of the new advisory discipline is not different from that affecting the Package as a whole. In fact, the EU legislator tends to envision investors in a dichotomic manner: either they know everything thanks to their expertise, or they know nothing because of their limited practice with the financial industry. Yet, the latter ones are often regarded as able to understand each piece of information if only provided with it: unfortunately, this is a clearly pretentious assumption with no match in reality. Hence, the industry is legitimately worried that, once advisory starts being explicitly designated as 'independent', investors will be well aware of the actual difference, correctly weighing pros and cons and ultimately deciding which kind of advisor to follow in its recommendations. This would occur in a frictionless world, where legislations would always achieve what they are intended for. Instead, we should doubt this to be the outcome: investors will probably attribute to independence either lower importance than it should have or, conversely, might even overstate its role and drop profitable investments just because a tied agent, rather than an independent one, had proposed them. This would start as a *micro-* flaw, but nothing theoretically prevents it from resulting in a *macro-* misallocation of resources with systemic consequences on financial markets.

Sabatini (2015) summarises the content of MiFID II in respect of different aspects of the advisory business: as an overarching separation, we can investigate (i) compensation and (ii) requisites. The former encompasses both fees directly paid in exchange for advisory itself and monetary inducements; the latter can be broken down into the array of products, the organisational separation, the 'suitability model' (product vs. portfolio), the quality of the service provided, and non-monetary inducements coupled with disclosure requirements. Salient points are displayed in Table 8.1.

Of course, so-called 'baseline free advisors', the advice being provided on a non-independent basis (BFA-NIs), do not receive from customers any lump amounts, disentangled from the outcome of the potentially undertaken investment;

Table 8.1 New scenarios on advisory models for banks

		Baseline free advice (non-independent)	Baseline onerous advice (non-independent)	Onerous independent advice	
Compensation	Advisory fee	✗	✓	✓	
	Monetary inducements	Allowed upon a previous **assessment** of their legitimacy	Allowed upon legitimacy test: the qualification of the service must justify a direct fee on the service and rebates on products	✗	
Requirements	Range of products	It is a **choice instrumental** to justifying the increase in the quality of the service to legitimise possible inducements	Faculty/obligation in case of remuneration from fees and inducements, to be determined based upon the level of the service to the client	**Obligation** to [advise on] a wide and sufficiently diversified range of products	
	Organisational separation	✗	✗	✓	[Separation must be] contractual, [regarding] information to clients, the personnel, the process of selecting products, etc. … **Separate legal entity** [needed]?
	Suitability model (product vs. portfolio)	Possibility of an approach either by **product** or by **portfolio**	The approach by product threatens the sustainability of compensation, however not formally prohibited	Approach by **portfolio**	

(continued)

Table 8.1 (continued)

		Baseline free advice (non-independent)	Baseline onerous advice (non-independent)	Onerous independent advice
	Level of service	Additional functions of the service (e.g., periodic assessment of the portfolio) are **optional**, instrumental to supporting inducements[a]	Additional functions of the service are not mandatory, yet implicitly recalled for supporting the compensation scheme	Additional functions are a **business choice** for supporting the compensation explicitly asked to the client
	Non-monetary inducements and disclosure	Allowed only if they lift the quality of the service, do not cope with the duty to pursue the best interest of the client, and are disclosed to clients		In addition to the requirements regarding baseline advice, they must be *minor*
		Obligation to periodically report on all the monetary inducements on a customised basis (including the punctual value of inducements). As for non-monetary ones, a descriptive account of salient ones is envisaged		

[a]In MiFID II, the discipline of allowed inducements envisages that, if advisory gets used to show the enhancement of the quality of the service provided, it be based upon either the width and the diversification of the range of products or the level of the service (e.g., by means of a periodical assessment of the portfolio, including legal and real-estate aspects, etc.)
Source Sabatini (2015)

yet, it relies on possible monetary inducements (as long as they have been permitted, upon the assessment of their legitimacy). The other side of non-independent advisors, which are those providing an 'onerous' service (BOA-NI), will charge a fee but, also, will have to pass a more engaging 'test' in order to be allowed to receive inducements from the originator of the product or service. In particular, the EU legislator has consented to them in case they are *designed to enhance the quality of the relevant service to the client* and do not contrast with different, overarching compliance duties (Article 24^{D}, par. 9). Clearly, 'onerous independent advisory' (OIA) has no other source of income than by directly charging fees upon its customers.

The different structures of compensation yield different outcomes in terms of the operations carried out. The degree of diversification is mandatorily high for independent advisors, whereas non-independent ones have higher degrees of freedom. The rationale underlying the choice about how diversified investments to recommend is mainly seen as the counterpart of inducements: in absence of them, the advisor will more easily manage to orient its customers toward a given originator, whereas the rebate of monetary benefits from customers to originators will have to be "justified" by proposing a sufficiently diverse range of products. As for the organisational separation, it must be ensured by independent advisors, whereas the others will not be forced to put in place arrangements designed to clearly write down independence in contractual terms, duly inform clients, subject products to a thorough "vetting process", and so on. Whether this would require the establishment of a separate entity will be left to the autonomous valuation by advisors, in light of the fact that any explicit obligation set forth by NCAs—or, more in general, at a domestic level—might potentially represent a form of gold-plating.

As for the suitability model—i.e. the approach to be followed when assessing the 'suitability' of a product (or an asset class) of an investor with a given (general) profile, in abidance by the *know your merchandise* rule—, BOA-NIs and OIAs express different attitudes toward the same issue: since fees have to be collected individually from customer to customer, whereas inducements may be globally rebated by originators, a product-based approach is sustainable only for BFA-NIs, whereas BOA-NIs will have no incentive to choose such model and would spontaneously prefer a portfolio one, clearly mandated to independent advisors.

As for the 'level of the service', BFA-NIs and BOA-NIs need to put in place something able to legitimise the inducements they can charge, as the Directive allows them exclusively in case an improvement in the quality of the service be effectively shown. Therefore, BFA-NIs might devote themselves to periodically review the portfolios (or even single products) they use for providing advice, thus allowing originators to rebate some monetary amounts to them. The situation is strikingly different as regards OIAs, for the ban on inducements and the almost-exclusive reliance upon fees calls for sustaining a high level of quality—mostly intended in terms of "customer care"—throughout the duration of the service being provided, making some "benefits" rendered to clients as a clear business decision: in fact, given the compensation structure, clients are much more likely to rapidly flee in case they are not satisfied, considering that they may face a relatively high upfront expenditure.

As for non-monetary inducements and disclosure requirements, the main divide is still between non-independent and independent. While the first kind of advisors may get such incentives only in case they enhance the quality of the service and make no harm to customers (instead, pursue their best interest), and are fully disclosed to them. Unsurprisingly, BOA-NI have to face higher constraints: even non-monetary inducements are banned in general, though admitted only if they are "minor" ones. Anyway, each kind of advice requires the investment firm to act with the utmost transparency, making clients aware of the contractual value of monetary inducements and providing a thorough descriptive account of non-monetary ones.

More in general, however, MiFID II has been found to strengthen the advisory model based upon networks (Colafrancesco 2017), in the sense that it rules out the idea that passing the suitability and appropriateness tests is enough to ensure the client's best interest. This would implicitly strengthen the concept that the price of a service is related less to its characteristics and more to the way in which it is provided, i.e. to its quality. However, there is a close counterpart in costs: the higher the level of quality desired, the larger the costs to be faced and, thus, the higher the final price charged upon customers. In fact, it is strikingly difficult to provide high-quality investment services without facing adequate expenditure: this is a fortiori true in the new framework modelled by MiFID II, where research must be clearly disentangled from the other components.

This, argues Colafrancesco (2017), has also led to greater concentration in the industry. In a sense, this follows a mechanism which, as long as the Package is enforced, could be thought as the 'structure-conduct-performance' (SCP) paradigm working backwards: given the new rules on inducements and the higher compliance costs to be faced, in order to achieve a desired performance is required adopting a certain conduct, resulting from the overhaul of pre-existing business models; in turn, this is likely to yield a more concentrated market structure. As observed in said article, the whole meaning of advisory has radically changed over the last few years, when the model of universal banks has started being adopted throughout Europe, ending the restrictive era followed to the recession of the Thirties. In fact, financial, insurance, and pension needs are increasingly difficult to satisfy; besides, the classification is not always straightforward, as the intersections are full of complex products which the legislator fails to address individually, having no choice other than exerting a generalised tightening upon them. As we have seen, the Package's legislator is so concerned about being too lax that the default classification is that of complex products, whereas non-complex ones can be recognised as such only if they show certain characteristics.

The intertwining between very different kinds of products urges the legislator to consider the interest of the client not under a single perspective, but rather with a full-range view. Direct knowledge of the counterparty is the best means to address an investment firm's policy toward sustainable profitability: this entails shifting from a product-based rationale to a service-based one, continuing on the trail blazed by MiFID I. Therefore, establishing a 'human relationship' with the client (*rectius*, with the natural persons which are customers themselves, or represent a customer entity) becomes inevitably consequent to the adoption of the Package (Colafrancesco 2017). Networks of financial advisors, at least in those countries where private banking and retail asset management are either well-established sectors or growing ones (e.g., Italy, Spain, partly France). This model can thrive only under a thorough regulation of off-premises offerings, as most of the financial contracts signed under the provision of investment advice are shaped in that way.

8.5 Research

The basic idea upheld by the EU legislator is that the relationship between brokers and their clients should be based upon the 'best execution' principle. Therefore, the practice of charging customers with costs that do not directly refer to the service has been seen as a violation of said principle, which therefore is worth limiting or at least subjecting to higher transparency. Two main solutions have been envisaged: either investment firms pay research by themselves (the so-called 'profit and losses' method, or P&L) or they charge it upon customers by setting up 'research payment accounts' (RPAs). It is no doubt that the latter will be widely preferred, as it formally allows investment firms not to drop a relevant source of income. Of course, expected inflows are much lower than before.

RPAs can be managed in a twofold manner: either by an *accounting method* approach, requiring the customer to pay an annual amount out of which payments for specific pieces of research are drawn whenever they get provided; or a *transactional method*, in which the exchange occurs each time, even by having research costs still bundled with other ones, though further unbundling is required (and research-related costs must be credited on an RPA). According to KPMG (2017), the choice between these alternatives will be driven by the size of the investment firm. While larger ones will have no problem to directly face research costs, presenting this choice to customers as a benefit and to distributors—which have to be informed about what they are going to recommend—as a non-monetary inducement; therefore, the major players in investment banking might well prefer the P&L method. Conversely, smaller entities, whose financials are more deeply impacted by research, would not be able to withstand losing a similar source of revenue and, thus, would rather opt for setting up RPAs.

Nevertheless, implementing the more detailed best execution principle has its own consequences. First of all, a much wider array of products is nowadays included: in particular, non-equity asset classes like derivatives, fixed-income securities like bonds, warrants or contracts for difference, including the relevant category of those instruments whose transaction costs are netted rather than periodically disbursed (e.g., futures). In addition to this, the obligation to publish information on executed transactions should also been accounted when assessing the degree of regulatory burden charged upon investment firms (e.g., top five execution venues to be disclosed quarterly, the annual report on the quality of execution, and so on). The industry has reasonably cast many doubts on the firms' chances of remaining profitable after the wave of compliance costs they have to face. ESMA itself acknowledged this in its Q&A on the Package, admitting that a firm is not expected to obtain the best possible result in every occasion.

On market infrastructure (this phrase not being circumscribed to *pre-* and post-trade transparency but extended to exchange platforms), the surge in requirements charged upon investment firms is a remarkable one. Moreover, AT and HFT have been dramatically hit, and are expected to show the most concerning effect, fortunately mitigated—and probably offset—by the continued surge in their use throughout markets. In general, however, all trading venues are going to be substantially overhauled from an organisational standpoint. An EY (2015) report (Fig. 8.2) attempted to envisage the degree of the impact of various kinds of intermediation. The most severely hit are investment banks. Of course, given their involvement in trading, changes to market structure (regarding venues and SIs, as well as dark pools et similia) will likely be quite invasive, whereas 'main access' (i.e. the provision of DEA) has often been granted to them, given their size, reliability, and cross-border extent of operations (though much less ensured to smaller institutions); finally, even obligations related to derivatives trading, though significantly reshaped by EMIR, is another element to be taken very seriously.

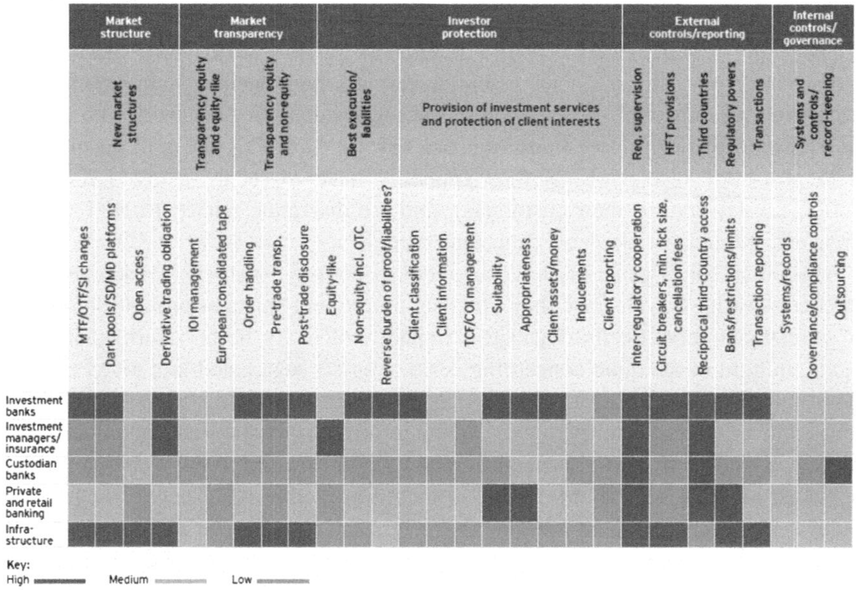

Fig. 8.2 Preliminary heat map of MiFID II impacts. *Source* EY (2015)

As regards transparency, investment banks will suffer little impact with respect to management; yet, a significantly higher impact should be envisaged as far as the handling of orders, along with pre- and post-trade transparency, is concerned. Best execution is a very burdensome framework for investment banks, except when related to equity-like instruments. Related to the provision of investment services, just a few functions (e.g., informing clients) have a little impact due to their baseline meaning, whereas *know your merchandise* and the suitability and appropriateness tests will require heavy disbursements. Reporting to clients will have a lower impact, but communication addressed to authorities will be extremely burdensome instead, whatever their object (rules on HFT, cross-border activity in extra-EU countries, and so on). Finally, relevant checks and balances had already been put in place in a number of investment banks, mainly because of their size (along with the fact that they are listed) had already pushed either regulators to envision stricter requirements or intermediaries to self-regulate themselves, to defend both internal efficiency and external regulation.

The Package's rules are deemed to be lighter the more focused is an entity's business; hence, while investment banks are particularly hit because of the degree of diversification of the activities they undertake, insurance companies and investment managers will benefit from a sort of "hedge" given by the fact that their business is not directly addressed by MiFID II or MiFIR, but by different pieces of EU legislation instead (Solvency II and IDD for the former, UCITS V and AIFMD for the latter, are the most recent ones). They are highly impacted not only by rules on derivatives trading, best execution on equity-like instruments (which are the main types of securities in which they are generally invested, unlike investment banks), the cooperation between regulators and third-country access (as cross-border operations are an essential part of their business). In many other segments, the impact of the Package is just intermediate: for instance, with respect to exchange platforms, pre-trade transparency (in fact, they are quite acquainted with post-trade disclosure, as they generally have to secure a given return or periodical payment to their customers), and the discipline related to HFT (circuit breakers, minimum tick sizes, cancellation fees).

Custodian banks generally have an ancillary activity—namely, safekeeping—as their core business; yet, since they often are investment banks or provide some kind of investment services, the Package's impact will likely be an intermediate one: again, in light of the quite concerning issue of assets segregated in a given country on behalf of an investment firm (generally a financial company, in charge of a CIS) located in a different country, the discipline informing cross-border operations is the most potentially impacting. Instead, some of the information-related obligations are expected to show some light effects: in fact, the peculiar bond between custodian banks and their clients (that is, the underwriters and managers of a CIS) has already forced the former ones to a careful disclosure. Furtherly narrowing the scope of operations, private and retail banking should be envisaged to suffer mainly from the group of rules referred to external controls and reporting, as well as the requirements that will be applied mainly to retail clients, such as the suitability and appropriateness tests.

The last layer encompassed in EY (2015), which is the infrastructure, is probably the one expected to be harmed the most as a proportion to the extent of its business, which is a very limited one. Of course, the operators of RMs and MTFs (those of these latter ones, which are investment firms, are now able to ask for establishing OTFs under MiFID II) will be hit by the provisions on that matter (including product intervention), as well as by the whole transparency framework, the constraints on HFT, transaction reporting, and—again—novelties related to the cooperation between regulators and reciprocal third-country access, which may well be regarded as the area most disruptively addressed by the Package.

Changes in research-related provisions are likely to make a twofold model of that activity to emerge within markets where investment services are provided. On the one hand, we are likely to have what might be labelled *low-touch research*, which entails a low degree of contact between research providers and their clients, whereby the majority of information is gathered automatically or semi-automatically, as opposed to the *high-touch* one, whereby the personal commitment is higher and gets balanced by more complex pricing criteria, based upon RPAs. These two models suit to extremely different categories of investors: the former is more apt to "passive" ones, which mainly care about having a second periodic return, whereas the latter is ideal for "active" ones, tendentially more sophisticated (which means that, regardless of their official MiFID categorisation, they are more interested in detecting which asset classes are more likely to yield better results.

8.6 Transparency

MIFID II is deemed to have the potential of transforming the financial markets of Europe, especially if we account for indirect effects. In the abovementioned BCG and Markit (2016) enquiry, these latter ones are found in growing automation accompanying enhanced transparency. The Package is expected to change the whole economics of securities trading, as for trade execution as well as investor protection, reporting, settlement.

The reshaping of transparency obligations has been a deep one. Under Article 26[R], record keeping, and trade reporting requirements are extended to at least 65 reporting fields, pursuant to ESMA RTS 22. Out of the 23 original reporting fields, only 13 are kept in place; even equities are overhauled. The *onus* is overly evident: in fact, investment firms do not seem to be able to withstand the data tracking and broader data management charged upon them by MiFIR. In order to abide by such prescriptions, massive investments would be necessary. A study by BCG and Markit (2016) summarises the likely impact of the Package on various parts of the value chain and various asset classes. Research will have an impact mostly on one of the simplest asset classes like equities; nevertheless, the unbundling will also have a serious effect and charge relevant new costs, mainly in the short term. Conversely, pre-trade transparency will likely spare equities, but have a major effect on the FICC segment, including commodities, though mainly subject to a long-term implementation. When we come to trade execution, the impact is quite concerning, but much more significantly on SIs than trading venues, and will be mainly implemented over the short term.

What follows along the value chain is the most frightening part of the Package: post-trade transparency, along with price discovery and best execution, will likely overhaul the exchange of non-equity instruments, whereas equities will be only minorly affected (over the short and the medium term respectively). The furthest parts of the chain—namely, TCA and liquidity, on the one hand, coupled with benchmarking and analytics, on the other—will be touched in a lighter way, still with equities bearing the softest burden. In relation to this, the cost of trade will actually be the most concerning issue, though only from a long-term perspective.

In general, as we may spot from Fig. 8.1 (BCG and Markit 2016), FICC will have to face the strongest reshaping in their business. This is mainly due to the fact that they have been widely exchanged in an automated manner on OTC platforms, in fact representing what the Package's legislator tends to look in a suspicious light. Considering the buy side, the new rules do not carry only advantages: while more information will be available, this would entail greater responsibility in taking decisions about trading. More granular post-trade data require that investment decisions be taken with a relevant human interaction, not being totally left to algorithms.

The enactment of the new transparency regime has come along with the envisagement of severe sanction. Notwithstanding the complex set of waivers and deferrals (mostly dictated by reasonable assumptions), the actual enforcement of such punishments would be particularly disruptive, even for market infrastructure as a whole in case the failure to comply came from large investment firms. Therefore, we may reasonably to think that the industry will face fundamental change over the next few years to become much more resilient and well-functioning in spite of the heavier regulatory burden. The seeds of that evolution are already in place: in percentage terms, stock exchanges are increasingly shifting their business toward information and, conversely, trading-related revenues are shrinking. The logical follow-up would be the integration between venues, on the one hand, and data and analytics providers, on the other; not only in terms of exchange of information (which will be clearly enhanced by making internal systems even more compatible), but by directly undertaking M&A operations aimed at consolidating the whole scope of market infrastructure into fewer players, able to comply with various Package-related obligations, thanks to functions being concentrated upon that single entity.

Alternatively, greater abidance by the Package's discipline might be ensured by re-orienting trades toward benchmarks, as this would clearly yield a simplification in pre- and post-trade data to be collected. Moreover, even the content of trading—in terms of asset classes—will have to be revised, as long as very different transparency obligations are charged upon different types of instruments: that choice pertains to market participants as well as execution venues (*rectius*, the subjects operating them). Moreover, it can be easily foreseen that *best execution and TCA will be vital in liquidity and price discovery* (BCG and Markit 2016). The overall result is that the price of the operations carried out post-trade, including price and liquidity discovery, will likely soar, in line with an increase of the value added.

8.7 The Interactions Between MiFID II, PRIIPs, and IDD

To carefully evaluate the Package's effect, we could not consider it as disentangled from some other pieces of EU legislation which, though mainly addressed to insurance companies, widely deal with investment products: in particular, the PRIIPs Regulation, enforced starting from 1 January 2018, and the *Insurance Distribution Directive* (IDD, No. 2016/97), which very closely mirrors the Package's investor-protective principles and entered into force on 23 February 2018. In a PwC (2017) report, 15 areas have been detected in which the joint effect of those legislations will bring the most relevant changes. The first, major novelty is the significantly increased closeness between the intermediary and its clients. Managing the range of products is, thus, expected to become increasingly difficult, due to the informational burden associated with it, and might eventually affect prices: therefore, a revision of the whole of the offer is deemed to be necessary, in order to select the products able of pursuing value-generation for both the firm and the customer.

Much more relevant to highlight is that investment firms will need endeavouring to have an 'integrated view' of their clientele and the markets, taking care of the possible gap between the customers' expectation and the investment's state of the art, especially for the sake of increased efficiency and reduced costs. This entails having relevant skills related to products and processes, to be used in dealing with customers as well as suppliers in a rapidly-changing environment. Another salient novelty attains to the management of forex forward contracts. In certain cases, they are classified as financial instruments and, thus, subjected to the Package: alternatively, they would be paralleled to spot contracts and, thus, regarded as means of payment, which implies their exclusion from the latter's scope. The concerning difference vis-à-vis the past is that MiFID I did not encompass forex contracts: the impact on this asset class is therefore expected to be one of the heaviest in the whole of financial markets, with major consequences on operating costs and business models.

Insurance-based investment products are clearly impacted by the PRIIPs Regulation (No. 1286/2014), which is mainly referred to 'packaged' ones (i.e. assembled in advance). One of the main novelties is that the Key Information Document (KID) will have to be administered to investors purchasing a wide range of products: from CIS units to financially-based insurance plans, up to a wide category of derivatives. The KID has to be organised with a standardised layout and a uniform content; however, it must be "tailored" in accordance with the 'target market of end clients' to which it is addressed, categorising risks pursuant to a standard classification, prospecting performance scenarios, and—most importantly—all the costs, either direct or indirect, charged upon clients. Assessing the KID's consistency, as well as the impact on business and update over time, are among the most burdensome processes which now distributors have to comply with. Moreover, warns PwC, the new MiFID II and IDD rules on personnel's qualifications should not be underestimated: they are potentially able to determine a surge in operating costs and, still, on wages paid to more skilled professionals holding various positions within a bank or an investment firm. Some requisites must be shown not only with respect to the provision of investment services but, also, for ancillary ones. This has been intended as a push toward greater professionalism in distribution networks and, thus, better relationships between intermediaries and their clientele; anyway, an organisational restructuring will be needed.

Still within the investor protection framework, MiFID II introduces the mandatory recording of telephone or electronic communications, especially in case of proprietary trading, or order-receptions, or execution-only services. Even face-to-face meetings with clients must be properly traced, as they can potentially lead to an order being submitted, though clearly subject to proper internal screening. Relationships with clients are, also, expected to undergo a massive reshape due to the surge in robo-advisory. The approach from which the industry is moving away is that of the so-called 'teller-to-client', whereby individuals speak directly to their customers, due to increasing digitalisation. Mobile technology is projected to play a pivotal role in such transformation: in particular, smartphones and tablets will help clients to "self-make" their investment decisions, though properly guided and monitored by intermediaries.

The underlying phenomenon, however, is much wider and more significant than just technological disruption: in fact, it reflects the generalised trend toward disintermediation, such that customers are expected to increasingly take their decisions autonomously (once become more financially literate or, more likely, with the assistance of automated systems). In a context like this, in which banks are going to foreclose several physical branches, the intrinsic value of human relationships between advisors and customers should be expected to soar, given the higher "marginal utility" rendered by such interaction. This is not a recent trend, however, nor one triggered by some specific piece of EU legislation. In fact, although robo-advisory has been made possible only under current technology, the idea of strengthening customer care in advisory by means of disintermediation is not new: some large players—e.g., the Italian bank Mediolanum—have been able to expand their business mainly by following such business model, starting from mid-Nineties or even before. Nowadays, however, the trend is much broader, and mimetic pushes to follow the example of first-movers are undoubtedly increasing.

References

Anginer, D., Demirgüç-Kunt, A., Huizinga, H., & Ma, K. (2018). Corporate governance of banks and financial stability. *Journal of Financial Intermediation, 130*(2), 327–346.

BCG, & Markit. (2016, June). *White Paper MiFID II: Preparation Without Delay*. In R. Flatley, M. Aldridge, P. Garside, R. Khasawneh, W. L'Heveder.

Colafrancesco, M. (2017). La consulenza: innovazione, educazione e valore tra modelli normativi e modelli di business. *Rivista Bancaria. Minerva Bancaria, 73*(4–5), 123–131.

Di Noia, C. (2017, June 15). *Hearing at the finance committee of the Italian House of Deputies*. Rome.

EY. (2015). *The world of financial instruments is more complex. Time to implement change. Capital markets reform: MiFID II.*

KPMG. (2017). *The time to act is now.*

PwC. (2017). *MiFID II, PRIIPs e IDD: final rush.*

Sabatini, D. (2015, November 25). *Impatti della direttiva MiFID 2 sulle banche italiane*, in Ascosim, *La Direttiva Mifid2 e la consulenza finanziaria* Conference, Milan.

Chapter 9
Conclusions

Abstract In this book, we analysed the Package's long journey, from its roots until the implementation in the leading EU economies. We stressed many times that the GFC paved the way to a new wave of regulation, including the revision of the MiFID I which, at the time of the outbreak of the crisis, had come into force less than one year before. Accordingly, we can come to our first conclusion, which is far more an open question: despite MiFID I being revised to take into account the issues brought by the GFC, might have the crisis been prevented, or the effect been smoother, had MiFID I come into force some time before? More reasonably, we can claim that the GFC can be interpreted as a really severe, but unfortunately realistic, stress test for the new-born MiFID I, very quickly become olden.

Having already underlined the continuity between the two Directives, we also pointed out the different emphasis given to the objective of the level playing field: in fact, MiFID II seems less effective in pursuing such important aspect for the Capital Markets Union. This initial lax enforcement of the principle, in the opinion of the authors, have had some consequences in the implementation phase, whereby many Members have been called back to transpose the MiFID II more in line with the required standard. Conversely, it would have been important to facilitate the elimination of barriers between countries to unleash market forces. By doing so, competitive pressure can trigger virtuous mechanisms and contribute greatly to eliminating inefficiencies, which then reverberate to the detriment of retail investors. The extant residual areas of non-competition allow for the survival of inefficient intermediaries, which take advantage of the competitive force towards smaller operators. Smoothing dominant positions in the investment industry is another salient objective, theoretically pursued by the Package, which actually delivered unsatisfactory results.

MiFID II was received by the industry with much less enthusiasm and much more scepticism than MiFID I, whereas the latter had been welcomed as a liberalising novelty in financial markets. In fact, it had been due more to the "technical" need to discipline unregulated areas than by the intent of reshaping markets. It actually came in a very crucial moment for banks and other financial institutions,

M. Comana et al., *The MiFID II Framework*,
https://doi.org/10.1007/978-3-030-12504-2_9

struggling with several—and continuously changing—reforms, to be put in place along with a deep review of the business model.

Indeed, we must acknowledge that some complex products (e.g., certain derivatives) may have contributed to the GFC, but MiFID II—following EMIR—carries out a sort of "regulatory retaliation". Needless to say, the latter cannot be the best way to fix a broken market. If we aim at reinstating the stability and efficiency of financial markets, we have to move towards a cleaner and fair system, putting in place a friendly regulatory setting, and trying to establish a favourable environment for operators and investors. Instead, the "pendulum theory" is reaffirmed: after a period of loose rules, or deemed to be such, a phase of very strict rules follows. In fact, neither a too lax nor a too strict legislation may be regarded as optimal. Paradoxically, overwhelming constraints on certain products and transactions endanger the same market stability which they are intended to preserve. We need the "right" level of both control and freedom, lest intermediaries are in a position to take advantage of less expert investors (usually retail clients), or they might not be able to exert their activity and their stabilization function which is fundamental to market efficiency.

All the main areas of the Package witness the struggle between an olden interventionist view and a modern, "liberal" one. The former seems to have prevailed, without financial markets apparently functioning in a better way than before. In particular, will OTFs be able to capture trades away from OTC markets? When talking about the GFC, many overlap, or even switch, causes and effects: the surge in OTC transactions actually followed the crisis, rather than preceding it, as it had a much deeper impact on trading venues than unofficial, unregulated platforms.

By envisaging a "bridge" (namely, OTFs) between trading venues and unregulated platforms, the EU legislator seems to have made its "best effort" against market fragmentation. Now it should commit itself to efficiency, whose pursuit has been seemingly abandoned following landmark Directive No. 1989/646/EEC, whose pillars were mutual recognition and home-country control in banking, though some appreciable elements can be found in BRRD.

The whole of the market infrastructure discipline is quite convoluted, probably redundant, and charges heavy compliance costs upon many intermediaries. Nevertheless, it would have been difficult to envisage something else, given the compelling need to strengthen transparency.

As far as the intermediary-client relations are concerned, we noted that some customers might even become less aware than before MiFID II, due to information overload. Other than with suitability and appropriateness tests, investment firms might in fact burden clients with additional documents and requests in order to identify a 'target market of end clients' pursuant to the *know your merchandise* rule. Since correctly retrieving financial needs and behaviours is much more difficult than material goods and non-financial services (also, because of lacking financial literacy), said rule is no assurance of resources being efficiently allocated.

Actually, some provisions are in fact difficult to understand and implement. Some others are the result of wrong hypotheses (e.g., some stocks might be riskier than the most "plain-vanilla" of complex products), or they mandate intermediaries to behave illogically (e.g., tied agents must anyway act 'in the best interest of the client'!). In fact, they can be paralleled with consumerism in non-financial sectors. The provision on the mandatory establishment of research payment accounts (RPAs) is profoundly disruptive and has the potential to overhaul investment banking: once known which price has been charged for doing research rather than providing the service itself, firms (e.g., those willing to go public) will likely be more reluctant to undertake operations. Anyway, investment banks' income will be hit. Another potentially disruptive novelty is that subjects providing advisory on an independent basis are banned from receiving inducements (other than 'minor non-monetary benefits'), with the result that the two categories (independent vs. not) will be sharply divided in organisational and business-model terms. The former, having to drop inducement-related income, will have to charge higher fees to their direct customers.

MiFID II, compared to MiFID I, reshapes the concept of transparency: not only it charges financial intermediaries with more obligations and higher costs compared to MiFID I but, also, places a certain burden on clients who: in line with the principle of *you must be aware of what you are buying*, it requires them to be more transparent by providing data and information on their needs, their patterns of purchase, their consumption and use of financial products, their life goals. This should make the relationship between supply and demand for financial services more efficient and effective (thus, adequate). Yet, the paradigm seems to have shifted, for the new legislation entails a reversal of the approach to the savings management by placing the clients' financial education of at the centre of the process by prompting them to disclose their personal financial habits. In fact, if this did not occur, the intermediary-client relationship would remain flawed by information asymmetries.

In addition to this, is worth mentioning that the entry into force of MiFID II is likely to undermine the old-fashioned way of establishing trust between the contracting parties, whereby it was the result of the excessive confidence placed by the customer upon its financial advisors, and often stirred by poor financial literacy. MiFID II tries to address this issue by imposing a standardised behaviour in approaching clients. Such ex ante "trust" mechanism is interrupted by the greater disclosure obligations for financial intermediaries, that must clearly declare on whose behalf they operate and make the costs public along the entire production chain, thus increasing the transparency and comparability of both the position of the person to whom customers entrust the savings and the intrinsic characteristics of financial products. The clients, on the other hand, must favour the process of financial education, allowing the consultant to correctly profile their financial needs and, thus, build an investment portfolio that is appropriate to the type of client, consistent with their financial behaviour and suitable to their risk-return profile. Therefore, trust becomes the result of an ex post structured process. It is clear that, in this type of context, the role of consultancy becomes fundamental and a true element of differentiation and enhancement of the offer.

Among the triggers of the reform, some concerns regarding systemic stability were also raised by looking at the impact of technological transformation. AT and

HFT had sometimes led to ‘flash crashes’ (e.g., 6 May 2010, 6 October 2016); hence, they are strongly regulated by the Package. We are trying to control progress by legislative means: shall we succeed? Or development is unstoppable and, thus, a too restrictive approach should be expected to be worse? In our opinion, a certain level of risk is unavoidable and, thus, must be accepted. We have to look for a more balanced approach, leaving market forces work for the development of new tools, new practices, and procedures, as well as—at the same time—keeping risk under control. The way in which markets “improve” include a relevant part of experience, as they proceed by trial and error. Financial authorities should be smart enough to identify the onset of any problem or critical situation and ready to fix it as quickly as possible. We do not deem MIFID II to be a clear example of speediness in reacting to market crisis. And should we need a demonstration, just look at the very long time it took from its original construction to the final delivery. This is not the timing which markets are used to work with.

At the end of our analysis, we conclude that MiFID II deserves a thorough revision, to be undertaken right after an unprejudiced assessment of its effects. Regulation comes at waves: restrictive ones have already hit the markets more than they should have. It is time to stop considering investors as either omniscient or completely ignorant. In the latter case, the MiFID II legislator seems to think that, if each piece of information currently denied were actually provided, every friction would magically disappear. This is really naïve.

Among the triggers of the reform, some concerns regarding systemic stability were also raised by looking at the impact of technological transformation. AT and HFT had sometimes led to ‘flash crashes’ (e.g., 6 May 2010, 6–7 October 2016); hence, they are now strongly regulated by the Package. We are trying to control progress by legislative means: shall we succeed? Or development is unstoppable and, thus, a too restrictive approach should be expected to be worse? In our opinion, a certain level of risk is unavoidable and, thus, must be accepted. We have to look for a more balanced approach, leaving market forces to work for the development of new tools, practices, and procedures; as well as, at the same time, keeping risk under control.

Another crucial question is the following: is the MiFID II/MiFIR package “out of scope”? Should it have created a different (more powerful) design of incentives to allow some regulation of shadow banking, similar to the commendable effort to make trading migrate from dark pools and OTC markets onto trading venues? As one can imagine, our answer is a positive one. Yet, in order to give a more complete explanation of our point of view, the existing legislation should be more deeply investigated. In this book, we have limited our analysis to a couple of pieces of EU law, so that the room for further enquiries is remarkably large.

The manufacturer's authorised representative in the EU is Springer Nature Customer Service Centre GmbH, Europaplatz 3, 69115 Heidelberg, Germany. If you have any concerns regarding our products, please contact ProductSafety@springernature.com

Printed and bound by CPI Group (UK) Ltd, Croydon, CR0 4YY
05/10/2026
02228137-0001